Using

For Continuous Improvement in Educator Preparation

"A value-add read! This one-of-a-kind volume centers data use and quality management in educator preparation. This volume shares a caravan of provocative cases, all focused on leading and understanding continuous improvement in educator preparation programming. While the conditions of professional accreditation serve as a central backdrop, the authors collectively elevate the importance of cause, context, and culture. They clarify the purposes, organizational opportunities and constraints, and environmental changes resulting from data use to inform course, programmatic, and even state-level continuous improvement. Implications for practice, scholarly inquiry, and policy can be readily derived for the reader."

Jacob Easley II, PhD, PMP
Xcelerated Excellence Consulting, CEO

"With a focus on continuous improvement, this book highlights innovative ways of using data to inform education preparation programs. The chapters show how privileging research within the accreditation process leads to programmatic changes based on student outcomes such as certification exams, program assessment, and dispositions. The authors also explore the critical roles of collaboration among faculty, administrators, students and/or key stakeholders within a Quality Assurance System."

Virginia Goatley, PhD,
Dean of the School of Education
University at Albany
State University of New York

"The breadth and sophistication of this volume is a welcome tonic in this era of decisions driven by impressions and opinions. As educators training educators, we must strive to strike the balance between creative, unique methodologies and empirical findings. They can, they must, go hand in hand as we find new and improved paths for learning. *Using Data for Continuous Improvement in Educator Preparation* explores the science and provides guidance for ALL educators looking to substantiate their programs' story."

Dr. Rebecca Pelton
President of the Montessori Accreditation Council
for Teacher Education (MACTE)

"It is difficult to find a resource on using data that speaks directly to and in the language of educator preparation programs. Thankfully, this book has 'cracked the code' and is a testament to what happens when you craft a text that involves those of us who are deeply committed to put quality educators in every classroom and every school building in its design and delivery. Setting the table for continuous improvement by linking course and program-level learning outcomes that align with state educator standards is both refreshing and incredibly useful. In addition, providing for program assessment to be structured in the form of action research questions allows faculty to immediately view their research course differently. The chapter on continuous improvement to enhance student advising and support is helpful, as is the use of data to monitor and support candidate dispositions. The book is seamless in its application to the AAQEP standards and should be read and discussed by any EPP that is considering national accreditation."

Tam Jones, Ed.D.
Assistant Dean/Associate Professor
Department of Educational Leadership
College of Education and Human Development
Texas A&M University Central

"McKee, Read, and Rickey have curated an innovative anthology, *Using Data for Continuous Improvement in Educator Preparation*, that presents a compelling narrative of progress and transformation in educational practices. Each chapter embarks on a profound exploration of data's pivotal role in shaping the future of teacher preparation. From the strategic utilization of improvement science to the implementation of action research methodologies, this book offers a comprehensive roadmap for fostering excellence in the field of educator preparation. It is a must-read for educators, administrators, and policymakers committed to cultivating a culture of continuous improvement and innovation in educator preparation programs."

Dr. J. Aaron Popham
President & CEO
Popham Innovations, Inc.

Using Data

THE ASSOCIATION FOR ADVANCING QUALITY IN EDUCATOR PREPARATION PROGRAM EVALUATION IN EDUCATION

AAQEP-Mark LaCelle-Peterson – Series Editor

BOOKS IN THE SERIES

Using Data for Continuous Improvement in Educator Preparation
edited by Linda McKee, Sylvia Read, and Debbie Rickey (2024)

Locating Quality in the New Educator Preparation Landscape:
Multiple Paths, Consistent Quality
edited by Christine DeGregory, Mark LaCelle-Peterson,
Karen Lowenstein, and Stephanie Schneider (2024)

Using Data

For Continuous Improvement in Educator Preparation

EDITED BY Linda McKee,
Sylvia Read, and Debbie Rickey

Myers
Education
Press

Gorham, Maine

Published by Myers Education Press, LLC
P.O. Box 424
Gorham, ME 04038

Myers Education Press is an academic publisher specializing in books, e-books, and digital content in the field of education. All of our books are subjected to a rigorous peer review process and produced in compliance with the standards of the Council on Library and Information Resources.

Library of Congress Cataloging-in-Publication Data available from Library of Congress.

13-digit ISBN 978-1-9755-0590-5 (paperback)
13-digit ISBN 978-1-9755-0591-2 (library networkable e-edition)
13-digit ISBN 978-1-9755-0592-9 (consumer e-edition)

Printed in the United States of America.

All first editions printed on acid-free paper that meets the American National Standards Institute Z39-48 standard.

Books published by Myers Education Press may be purchased at special quantity discount rates for groups, workshops, training organizations, and classroom usage. Please call our customer service department at 1-800-232-0223 for details.

Cover design by Teresa Legrange.

Visit us on the web at **www.myersedpress.com** to browse our complete list of titles.

CONTENTS

PREFACE

For decades, educator preparation professionals have dedicated time and effort to studying the outcomes of programs that prepare teachers, school leaders, and other professional educators. The self-study reports produced as part of the accreditation process for the various accreditors that have served the field have been exhaustive and extensive. They have documented the learning and performance of tens of thousands of new educators—the samples, both locally and collectively, have been comprehensive! Evidence has been gathered from course assessments, licensure tests, performance evaluation, surveys, interviews, and observation—no data collection source has been left unplumbed. Unfortunately, the results of these extensive studies have generally gone nowhere.

As a result, the extensive data collection, analysis, and reporting that have been part of accreditation self-studies over the decades have made negligible contributions to the knowledge base in the field of educator preparation. With the exception of a relatively small number of conference presentations at the annual meetings of the American Educational Research Association (AERA), the American Association of Colleges for Teacher Education (AACTE), and more recently, the Association for Advancing Quality in Educator Preparation (AAQEP), the benefits of the lessons learned through accreditation have reached no further than the local campus and the small number of professional colleagues who participated as peer reviewers in the accreditation site visit. AAQEP seeks, through this book series, to widen the circle of learning from accreditation, to foster broad dissemination of findings and insights from quality assurance work, and to put the knowledge generated through the accreditation process into circulation so that others may benefit from those who have gone before.

Each volume in the series will feature empirical work by those engaged in educator preparation and in the evaluation of educator preparation programs. The aim of the series is to ensure that, beginning a few years hence, there will be a robust set of answers to the question "What has the field learned collectively from the time and effort we invest in self-study for quality assurance?"

INTRODUCTION

This book has set the stage for a transformative journey into the world of using data for continuous improvement in educator preparation programs. As we move through the chapters, we will delve deeper into the role of data to shape the future of education, explore the innovative methods of data collection and analysis, and discover how these insights can empower educators to better serve the needs of our PK-20 field. The road ahead is paved with challenges and opportunities, but through the dedicated commitment of educators, administrators, and policymakers, we can chart a path toward an educational landscape in which data-driven improvement becomes the norm, not the exception. With each chapter, we will unravel new layers of this critical conversation and work together to enhance the foundation upon which future generations of educators will stand.

As we work with educator preparation programs, through their practice of continuous improvement, we have seen some trends and themes of that work that we find both interesting and encouraging.

Some programs are engaging in program assessment as a form of research. For example, in this volume Duerr and Wise describe and discuss how data can be more effective when structure is applied in the form of research questions, especially questions formed by the faculty rather than the administration. Faculty-developed questions might be more targeted to a particular program or subset of students or address whether or not changes that have been made to programs have had the desired or intended effect. For example, a question like "Does the proposed change in our Math for Elementary Teachers class improve candidate performance on the math section of the state licensing exam?" might be more meaningful to math education faculty than a more general question such as "How do candidates perform on the state licensing exam?"

Garcia and Estrada describe how they used improvement science as a theoretical framework to collect, analyze, and act upon data to investigate a persistent problem, e.g., the pass rate of teacher candidates on the content licensure exam. They provide a rich description of the process of forming a networked improvement community

(NIC) that included faculty from three departments. This group decided which problem to investigate and then engaged in a series of processes built around tools (fishbone diagram and driver diagram) that then led to a series of small actions using the Plan-Do-Study-Act model.

Kalnin, Hon, Flora, Merk, and Ralston, in their chapter, describe how they used an action research approach to identify focus areas for continuous improvement and targeted change efforts. Their Clinical Practice and Partnerships Committee triangulated data across various performance assessments. Although the assessments were designed and assessed using different scales and for different purposes, comparing the data allowed them to focus on a specific programmatic focus on "research into practice." Engaging the faculty in the interpretation of the findings led to improvement proposals, which in turn led to changes at the course level and to program processes. Framing their work as action research gave this EPP a way to productively structure and scaffold their continuous improvement efforts.

Three chapters specifically dive deeper into course-level revisions that occurred as the result of analyzing data and identifying ways to improve candidate performance. Mecham's chapter describes numerous changes that she made to a course on assessment and differentiation in response to elementary education teacher candidates' performance on the Praxis Performance Assessment for Teachers. Course changes began by assessing the existing course goals and learning outcomes and updating them to align more closely both with state policy and practice and with the expectations of a state-mandated performance assessment. Some aspects of the course were eliminated, others were expanded, and still others were added. Although the data are showing signs of improvement, the program is continuing to examine and analyze the data to determine if the course changes are having an impact.

Tochelli-Ward, in her chapter, specifically discusses how an EPP used New York State's Educating All Students (EAS) exam scores to provide evidence for AAQEP standards 1c and 2d. Based upon the evidence, Tochelli-Ward developed a course project on diverse books. The students' performance on the project was measured using a rubric that included a criterion matched to 2d that evaluated teacher candidates' ability to analyze books in terms of bias or stereotypes. This is emblematic of how programs can use existing data, even state-mandated assessment data, to be a catalyst for program improvement through course-level revisions.

Bower's chapter also describes course revisions, specifically for classroom and behavior management courses in her institution's educator preparation programs. She describes the entire data cycle and details the key revisions they made. The results so far are promising. All three of these course-level revisions are prime examples of how educator preparation programs may not necessarily need wholesale program changes to engage in meaningful and impactful continuous improvement.

Continuous improvement is an approach also used to help make changes and uncover better processes and procedures to be used in gathering data. The following chapters have both used the process of continuous improvement to assist in looking at their approaches and processes around candidates and dispositions in order to understand their data and to look at their processes in a more holistic way.

The first chapter by Castro and Lee uses continuous improvement to help focus on the question of how to develop and improve their student advising and support system. Questions had arisen about the overall progression of their candidates and through the improvement process, they were able to focus on the application process and developed an instrument to help assess candidates' dispositions. This new self-assessment instrument, along with the coordinating tools and input from faculty, brought forth rich data about their candidates. With these data they were able to redirect support and guidance for those that showed deficits or challenges. This new instrument, along with the changes in their approach with candidates from the application time, has shown promise and has increased faculty agency and more opportunity for student reflection.

The following chapter by Genereo also utilized the same components of continuous improvement to help assess and evaluate a new process for teaching and evaluating dispositions. This refined 5-Layer Dispositional Assessment System, as it was called, was the foundation of the process. The resulting data from the 5-Layer system was found to be helpful with candidate monitoring and remediation with dispositional issues. They were able to find those more quickly and provide support. But perhaps more significant than that, the process also encouraged more data sharing among faculty. Using the data obtained, more evidence-based discussions and opportunities for sharing among faculty occurred, which led to improvements for candidates and also to ideas for improvements in their programs and processes overall.

Using a continuous improvement model for larger-scale program improvements has also been used in various ways by our AAQEP members. The following chapters help illustrate this use through the development and use of the continuous improvement model to structure data gathering and feedback in the area of candidate and completer feedback.

The first chapter by Haughey, Strickland, Dimmitt, Singleton, Wall, McBride, and Wall showcases a Quality Assurance Team approach to implementing a student teacher feedback survey and process to assist in gathering data on the candidate experience. A process just over 4 years in use has yielded not only deeper and more specific results from candidates gathering written and oral feedback, but the further process has also proved to be meaningful and valuable for faculty. Summaries prepared by the Quality Assurance Team of the candidate feedback have provided a foundation for rich discussion and analysis by faculty with results being used to improve programs.

The following chapter by Rush, MonDragon, Bahr, Plumeau, Boe, Hon, Sauve, and Darwich provides another lens of continuous improvement on a broader scale of candidate/completer feedback by using a model at a state level to gather information around a new state initiative of social and emotional learning (SEL). The process developed at the state level was a survey of new teachers (recent completers) and the state educator preparation providers in order to develop aspirational standards for SEL in a holistic and more authentic way. The state knew they wanted information and feedback that they could incorporate into realistic SEL standards that would promote and support the needs of their K-12 students in the area of SEL. This large-scale approach to gathering information using an improvement model provides a framework for collaboration with state entities and their stakeholders in order to make improvements and provide opportunities for feedback in developing a process.

The continuous improvement process cannot be implemented without the active input from relevant stakeholders, especially faculty who will be using the data to review their courses and programs. The following chapters give some ideas of how faculty can become an integral part of the improvement process.

In the chapter by Atchley and Ross, we delve into the critical importance of implementing a systematic approach to continuous improvement in principal preparation programs. The chapter focuses on a case study that employs the Bambrick-Santoyo conceptual framework, which is designed to promote continuous improvement through an iterative process of improvement, emphasizing data-driven decision-making, intentional practice, and targeted feedback. This chapter will provide an in-depth analysis of how this framework serves as a blueprint for shifting gears in principal preparation programs, fostering the culture of sustained improvement. One central aspect presented involves data meetings that are thoughtfully designed to examine results from previous assessments and to transform the culture and outcome of the programs by focusing on the highest-leverage actions and strategies that can yield different and improved results. Throughout this chapter, readers will gain insight into the transformative power of a systematic approach to continuous improvement in principal preparation programs, ultimately contributing to the enhancement of principal education and the success of future school leaders.

In Driskill's chapter, we delve into the transformative journey of a small, private institution facing resource constraints yet driven by the imperative need to establish a quality assurance system. This system, aimed at documenting continuous improvement, has been a pivotal component in enhancing the institution's educational offerings. The chapter details how the institution embarked on this journey, highlighting the crucial steps taken toward a shift towards a culture centered on data-driven decision-making. Central to this transformation was the adoption of the Data-Driven Dialogue Protocol, developed by Brambick-Santoyo. The chapter explores the major climate shift throughout the program that was essential to adopting the new protocol. Collaboration and cooperation became components guiding this change, fostering a sense of shared responsibility for the program's overall improvement. In summary, this chapter encapsulates the program's journey towards a data-driven culture and demonstrates a commitment to continuous improvement, coupled with the adoption of a proven protocol for making more objective, informed decisions, ultimately benefiting the institution and its students.

In the chapter by Howerton-Fox and Kessler, the reader is taken through a journey marked by a transformative approach to continuous improvement. This chapter explores the pivotal role of data retreats in reshaping the programs' perspective and introducing the Plan-Do-Study-Act (PDSA) Model that has revolutionized methods in articulating questions, planned improvements, and anticipated outcomes. The narrative unfolds with a realization that earning accreditation is no longer a matter of producing data to appease external bodies, yet has transformed through a profound shift towards effectively collecting, analyzing, and employing data to address internal questions. The PDSA process is presented as a path for transitioning the faculty from merely data-informed programmatic decisions to a community authentically committed to disciplined inquiry. The pages of this chapter unravel the dynamic process, harnessed through the PDSA, to establish a true culture of evidence. As you journey through these pages, you will witness the profound impact of data retreats and the PDSA cycle in the ongoing quest to create a more vibrant, responsive, and student-centered educational landscape.

In the chapter by Kozimor, we investigate the significance of inter-departmental collaboration and explore how the utilization of student performance data analysis, collaboration with curriculum developers, and the establish of a virtual faculty community have played a pivotal role in elevating the success of the Early Childhood Education (ECE) program. The chapter illustrates key strategies, including the implementation of a centralized curriculum, the promotion of instructional autonomy, and adoption of the

Plan-Do-Study-Act (PDSA) Improvement Model. The chapter highlights the transformative potential of data-driven decision-making and underscores the profound impact that collaboration can have in the field of higher education. It showcases how the PDSA Model operates with an improvement paradigm, encouraging the faculty members to meticulously analyze student outcomes and make informed decisions aimed at enhancing the program's overall effectiveness. This case study serves as a testament to the critical importance of communication, collaboration, and the cultivation of continuous improvement within the realm of higher education. It exemplifies how cross-departmental teamwork and data-driven decision-making can be harnessed to not only identify areas for improvement but to drive holistic and sustainable enhancements in educational programs.

In this transformative chapter by Wahleithner, a shift from the traditional notion of educational accountability to a dynamic focus on continuous improvement is detailed. It begins with providing the programs with invaluable scaffolds to guide their work into the realm of data collection and analysis, specifically tailored to address the multifaceted aspects of an accreditation process. The chapter discusses the pathways that serve as foundation for the intricate steps of selecting and analyzing data as the faculty is encouraged to embark on the next step in their data practice: identifying specific actions that the faculty will undertake to address the findings derived from the data analysis and the rationale behind them, accompanied by an implementation timeline. As presented in the chapter, this scaffolded continuous improvement process in the service of accreditation is the development of data literacy among the faculty members. The accreditation journey is portrayed as a transformative experience, leading faculty across programs towards deeper insights into improving their practices for nurturing new educators. Moreover, it extends beyond mere accreditation, revealing the vital role of data in fostering meaningful and continuous learning within educational institutions.

Before there is continuous improvement based on data, there must be a process for selecting and presenting the data to stakeholders. This chapter takes us full circle by sharing very practical ideas on how to build the foundation of an assessment system and then use its data with a focus towards relevance in the improvement process.

In this enlightening and informative chapter by Duerr, readers investigate the critical aspects of data management with advice on selecting and effectively presenting data to a variety of audiences. Furthermore, the chapter provides guidance on structuring the thought process of education preparation programs for enhanced data reporting. By identifying the various types of data and acknowledging the potential limitations, programs are empowered to more accurately and compellingly represent their data. The chapter investigates the significance of data to the program, emphasizing that understanding what the data mean is a fundamental component in building an assessment system that aligns with the programs' needs. This chapter and its author emphasizes the value of building an assessment system geared towards continuous improvement. It proposed that if your assessment data work for you, are grounded in fairness, reliability, and drive data-informed decisions, accreditation becomes a natural consequence. In essence, the chapter stresses that your data should not only serve as a tool for improvement but also as a means to effectively narrate your program's story.

Thank you for embarking on this enlightening journey with us. The chapters that follow will illuminate the possibilities and practicalities of using data for continuous improvement. Through shared knowledge and a commitment to progress, we aim to create an educational ecosystem that equips educators with the tools they need to excel, enabling students to thrive and reach their full potential. So, let us turn the page and march forward, armed with data, determination, and the shared goal of nurturing the next generation of lifelong learners and visionary educators.

CHAPTER ONE

Adding Structure to Existing Assessment Practices with Research Questions

SUNNY DUERR AND NICOLE WISE

Drilling into data to answer questions leading to program improvement or accreditation standards is not always straightforward. As administrators, we must maintain a global view of available data sources, the reliability and validity of the data, and how we can use the data to foster a culture of continuous improvement. The sheer volume of available data can overwhelm faculty and contribute to frustration in approaching program improvement efforts. In this chapter, we provide examples of how two institutions have approached working with faculty to enhance existing practices, creating a system with reliable and valid data for continuous improvement efforts at the program level while facilitating external reporting at the institution level.

By enacting such procedures and beginning with a research question, relevant data can be identified and analyzed, conclusions can be drawn, and the implementation of data-driven improvements can be identified and documented. Embedding a system by which data are reviewed based on questions and embedding these practices into existing annual data review and reporting activities can lead to a more efficient process for tracking changes over time.

General Conceptual Overview

One of the barriers that an assessment system needs to overcome to be useful is the sense of value to the faculty and the program. If the faculty do not value the assessment data, or view the assessment data as flawed, they will not feel invested in the associated assessment processes. Many institutions have addressed this issue by having regular "Data Days"—a designated day once a year or once per semester set aside for reviewing the program's assessment data, discussing it as a unit, and drawing some conclusions. While a great practice, we feel it can be improved by providing additional structure. Including a research question in assessment data conversations and processes can provide a degree of focus to the data analysis; if the research question is administratively determined, an institution can ensure that all programs are investigating common concepts or constructs, while research questions that the program faculty determine can create an additional level of faculty engagement.

The form of the research question can vary considerably and will depend on the available data and which approach the institution is taking (e.g., administrative or faculty determined). For example, an administratively determined research question might be, "To what degree does the assessment data support the claim that program candidates possess the necessary pedagogical knowledge and skills to enter the profession?" In this example, all programs in the unit might look to their adopted assessment of pedagogical practice, their student teaching evaluation forms, or their state-mandated teacher performance assessment to answer the question. This approach is advantageous when the institution uses the resulting report to satisfy a campus-level reporting expectation or as evidence for an accreditation report.

Faculty-driven research questions will often be more specific to each program. For example, a childhood education program might ask, "Does the proposed change in our Math for Elementary Teachers class improve candidate performance on the math section of the state licensing exam?" In contrast, an adolescence social studies program might ask, "To what extent do candidates in the program understand international and global perspectives, and are they able to demonstrate this through effective lesson planning and teaching?" Obviously, the data sources for each of these programs' research questions will be different. However, the faculty for the program will likely be more engaged in the resulting data and the answer to their question. Once the research question has been defined, the process becomes relatively straightforward: identify the data sources that will be used to answer the question, analyze the data, draw conclusions from the analysis, and act based on those conclusions. Figure 1.1 below shows the entire process as a cycle of program improvement.

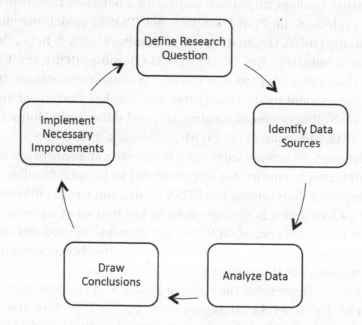

Figure 1.1. Cycle of improvement using data-informed research questions.

Figure 1.1 shows that the second step in this process is identifying the data sources necessary to answer the research question. The degree to which this will be challenging depends upon the research question's purpose and whether the data are already available. The purpose behind the research question is contextually vital for each program. If, for example, an institution has a campus-level expectation for reporting on assessment data in a very structured way, the research question would ideally align with this data-reporting need, and the data sources for answering the research question would be the program's assessment data. However, if there is no structured campus-level expectation, the research questions could rely on data sources beyond the program's assessments, such as enrollment trends before and after a significant program revision. The important consideration here is that 1) the data either need to exist already or 2) the program must identify a way to capture the data to answer their question (e.g., through a student satisfaction survey or a survey of mentor teachers).

Astute readers might see similarities between this improvement cycle and the Plan-Do-Study-Act (PDSA) model introduced by Deming (1986). Originating out of Deming's work to help rebuild Japanese industry after World War II (Deming, 1986), the PDSA model has been adopted as a change management and continuous improvement model throughout the world in a variety of industries, including business, healthcare, and education (Donnelly & Kirk, 2015; Shakman et al., 2020; Stensaasen, 1995).

Although we acknowledge such similarities and encourage readers interested in continuous improvement to become familiar with the literature surrounding the PDSA model, some slight differences make us feel that it is disingenuous to say that what we have outlined is necessarily *based on* PDSA. For example, assessment activities in higher education often rely on actions already occurring in the environment. For this reason, our cycle has "Identify Data Sources" rather than "Implement the Change Practice," a common interpretation of "Do" in PDSA (Shakman et al., 2020). Therefore, the "Do" step of PDSA would qualify as a less intentionally identified intervention within our context than what might be expected if PDSA were implemented with complete fidelity.

Program Improvement

The system aims to provide insight into program effectiveness, leading to program improvement. In starting a study with a research question, faculty can focus on a topic they are particularly interested in investigating, or establish meeting a requirement such as a standard (e.g., accreditation, professional standard). With thoughtful design, the system can provide the ability to track changes over time through reoccurring themed questions.

The research questions can be created to gauge the general effectiveness of a program, such as the example highlighted above, "To what degree does the assessment data support the claim that program candidates possess the necessary pedagogical knowledge and skills to enter the profession?" A more directed research question such as "What does our enrollment data tell us about our cohorts?" may result in data that answers the initial question but leads to further investigation, such as "Are there disparities between different groups such as first-generation or underrepresented minorities?" One method to ensure the research question remains relevant is to embed it within the structure of other assessment reporting requirements. We have approached this by including it in our annual campus-level continuous improvement goal and progress reporting. Program improvements are not always clear and straightforward, and they often take time to identify, implement change, and track the results.

Developing a thoughtful research question that allows data to be identified, refined, and tracked over time is especially beneficial when the question can be linked to accreditation standards, other compliance reporting, or both. For example, institutions with education preparation programs are required by law to complete an annual report that satisfies federal Title II regulations. In this report, institutions submit a list of candidates enrolled or who have completed preparation programs leading to certification. The list of submitted candidates is compared to state testing records to ensure the unit meets the minimum certification/licensure pass rate. A second component of Title II reporting is constructed written responses related to program assurances, goal setting, the use of technology, and teacher training related to students with disabilities. Within those constructed written responses, an opportunity presents itself for programs to align continuous improvement practices embedding into an existing required annual reporting mechanism.

While some reporting requirements change over time, careful consideration should be given to remaining nimble. For example, contextual factors must be considered for reporting mechanisms spaced further apart, such as a holistic program review occurring every five to seven years. Research questions may be related to identifying if a difference in GPA for face-to-face or online classes exists. A 5- or 10-year trend may yield results that need careful interpretation based on context; an example would be the effects of the COVID-19 pandemic and increased technology for online courses. Further, considering that research question, faculty may wish to drill deeper into the data to determine if GPA discrepancies exist for underrepresented minorities. Using the system to study a long-term trend may be helpful; however, the research question may be adapted or expanded where new or additional data sources are identified, resulting in a better understanding.

Extended Uses

As the designated "data nerds" for our institutions, we feel that the system we have outlined in this chapter speaks for itself in terms of usefulness. Without any other description or extrapolation, including research questions in existing assessment processes can help guide programs toward continuous improvement. However, the real impact that this type of approach can have is in the number of different situations to which it can be applied beyond the primary purpose of program assessment and improvement. To demonstrate this utility, consider the following example.

The large institutional accreditation agencies (previously called regional accreditation agencies) grant accreditation holistically to institutions after reviewing the institution's policies, procedures, and alignment with their standards; in our case, in New York State, the Middle States Commission on Higher Education (MSCHE) has its set of accreditation standards, many of which include assessment-related substandards or aspects. Among other things, MSCHE is looking for evidence that an institution's programs have defined program learning outcomes, are assessing those program learning outcomes, and are making decisions informed by that assessment data.

In addition to institutional accreditation, education preparation providers seek accreditation through the education accreditation agencies, which also want to see evidence of assessment and data-informed decisions; for the Association for Advancing Quality in Educator Preparation (AAQEP), this manifests in Standards 1 and

2 in terms of the direct application of assessment data, but also in Standard 3 (aspects C, D, and E) when the institution makes the argument for its internal quality control practices.

As an added layer for consideration, the SUNY Board of Trustees has identified two mandatory constructs, called core competencies, that must be embedded within every program's learning outcomes in the SUNY system. These core competencies are Critical Thinking & Reasoning and Information Literacy. A byproduct of this requirement is that all programs must assess the two constructs regularly and report on the assessment data.

Assume an institution has implemented a system similar to what we have outlined in this chapter, a system in which programs identify a research question at the beginning of each year, use their assessment data to investigate the research question, and submit a brief (one-page) report on the results at either the end of the year or the beginning of the following year. In order to satisfy the Middle States requirement that each program learning outcome is assessed regularly, the institution can set up an assessment plan for each program that diagrams when each program learning outcome will be the focus; note that the SUNY Board of Trustees competencies are included in the assessment plan. Figure 1.2 shows an example of such an assessment plan.

Construct	Year 1	Year 2	Year 3	Year 4	Year 5	Year 6
Content Knowledge						
Planning						
Assessment						
Pedagogy						
Dispositions						
Critical Thinking						
Information Literacy						

Figure 1.2. Six-year program assessment plan.

Following the assessment plan, programs know that their research questions for each year will need to focus on specific constructs that are measured by their assessments. In this example, a program might have three research questions, one focusing on content knowledge,

one focusing on candidate lesson planning, and one focusing on critical thinking skills. Alternatively, a program might design a single
research question incorporating the assessment data from all three
constructs.

No matter how the program decides to proceed with their research questions, they would spend that academic year reviewing
that specific assessment data and answering those research questions, and at the end of the year or beginning of the following year,
they would submit a report with their findings, conclusions based
on the data, and any improvement plans they can identify based on
their research conclusions.

At the end of each cycle, the institution will have a report from
each program based on the program's learning outcomes that will
include how it uses the program's assessment data and identified
plans for continuous improvement. In addition to the intended purpose for the entire process—program improvement—this report
becomes documentation that can be used as evidence supporting
AAQEP and Middle States accreditation activities and also satisfies local assessment requirements for the SUNY-mandated core
competencies.

This process can be taken a step further. Accreditation is a cyclical process with a regular timetable; institutions know when their
next accreditation self-study report will be expected and when the
next site visit will happen, and all of the things that need to fall into
place before those activities can occur. This purposeful investigation of program assessment data can be adapted to help inform the
accreditation process by engaging in a more extensive program-level
review before the institution-level report writing begins. Such an
activity could be considered an Individual Program Review (IPR)
with the following four sections:

1. Context
   a. Candidate selection criteria and milestones, program of
      study, alignment between courses and standards, descrip-
      tion of how key assignments within courses align with stan-
      dards

    b. Curriculum and assessment maps with alignment with standards

    c. Description of clinical experiences

    d. Description of enrollment trends for the past three years

    e. Summary of faculty information and qualifications

2. Assessments

    a. Table of Program Learning Outcomes and their affiliated assessments

    b. Table demonstrating alignment between assessments and program standards

3. Data-Driven Program Improvement

    a. Two examples of how data have been used for program improvement *(these examples are drawn directly from the annual process we have outlined in this chapter)*

4. Research Questions

    a. One common research question set by the administration: *(e.g., To what degree do program candidates meet the established learning outcomes of the program, and to what degree does the program meet its disciplinary standards?)*

    b. One common research question set by the assessment council: *(e.g., How do the current assessment measures sufficiently capture valuable information necessary for quality assurance and continued improvement? What gaps can be identified, and what are some possible solutions to close those gaps?)*

    c. One research question defined by the program: *(e.g., How satisfied are new transfer students entering the program? Does the seamless transition process work, and how could it be improved?)*

The first two sections of the IPR are relatively static, meaning once the program has completed these, they will only need to be modified or updated when the program changes or the assessments change. Section 3 and 4 of the IPR are more relevant to the current conversation. Section 3 specifically utilizes the reports that the program has generated through the cyclical system that this chapter has discussed, and Section 4 expands upon the concept of including research questions within assessment practices by embedding three research questions within the accreditation report.

Thus, the IPR serves multiple purposes. It provides a structured process for programs to self-reflect on their assessment data and activities over time, directs specific investigations into the quality assurance system, provides evidence that programs use assessment data regularly, and demonstrates how assessment data have been used to inform continuous improvement. The IPR and the annual reports can then be included as evidence for education and institutional accreditation efforts.

References

Deming, W. E. (1986). *Out of the crisis*. Massachusetts Institute of Technology Center for Advanced Engineering Study.

Donnelly, P., & Kirk, P. (2015). Use the PDSA model for effective change management. *Education for Primary Care, 26*(4), 279–281. https://doi.org/10.1080/14739879.2 015.11494356

Shakman, K., Wogan, D., Rodriguez, S., Boyce, J., & Shaver, D. (2020). *Continuous improvement in education: A toolkit for schools and districts*. National Center for Education Evaluation and Regional Assistance at IES, United States Department of Education.

Stensaasen, S. (1995). The application of Deming's theory of total quality management to achieve continuous improvements in education. *Total Quality Management, 6*(5), 579–592. https://doi.org/10.1080/09544129550035233

CHAPTER TWO

Using an Improvement Science Approach for Creating a Learning Culture at a Hispanic-Serving Teacher Preparation Program

CRISELDA G. GARCIA AND VERONICA L. ESTRADA

Teacher educators commonly engage in improvement work in their efforts to innovate and strengthen the quality of their teacher candidates' (TCs) overall experiences during their teacher preparation. As educational disparities continue to persist in the post-pandemic era, teacher preparation programs (TPPs) face additional pressures to explicitly adopt data and equity-driven reform efforts. Although most teacher educators would agree that continuous program improvements are important and necessary, a common challenge that many TPP leaders face is finding ways to motivate faculty members to participate in authentic, meaningful improvement work. Most often, efforts toward improvement are driven in response to compliance standards set by state and national accreditation entities, which generates lackluster engagement from faculty members. Education has historically utilized the research and development (R&D) model for improvement in education, and it has not always produced exceptionally reliable results (LeMahieu et al., 2015). This model relies solely on research to produce best practices for improvement. As LeMahieu et al. (2015) contend, the R&D model for improvement does not consider the importance of context in getting improvement ideas into practice. We agree with their assertion that "attributional research helps us to know that some practice can produce some effect; [however] it does little to show us how to produce those effects—over and over and across people and places (p. 446).

We contend that data sources, by themselves, provide us with snapshots of a program as they cannot capture the full story, particularly when the story is about minoritized students. Too often, TPPs over-rely on standardized summative performance measures, such as exit test scores, which, when examined in isolation, fail to provide significant information for creating changes that lead to improvement. We believe there is need to "humanize" the data to fully appreciate the student learning experiences in search of answering critical questions such as, "Why do certain problems continue to persist? Examining data with an approach that presents the full story requires the full context of "what works, for whom and under what conditions?" (LeMahieu et al., 2015).

In this chapter, we use a case study approach to describe how a university-based TPP at a Hispanic-serving institution (HSI) in South Texas in a bilingual Hispanic/Latino community used an improvement science framework to create a culture of teacher educator learners. We present a story of how faculty members representing three departments operated as a quasi-networked improvement community (NIC) of teacher educators in a TPP who worked together to identify a persistent problem of practice toward continuous improvement centered on the experiences of TCs, heretofore referred to as "users." We will provide examples of how the group engaged in data-informed improvements to create small but significant changes to improve the teacher candidates' experiences in the TPP.

Context

The context of this work is significant and unique. Ninety-six percent of the K-12 student population is identified as Hispanic/Latino (Texas Education Agency, 2022) and 85% is identified as economically disadvantaged. The TPP is a top producer of Hispanic teachers in the state (Texas Education Agency, 2023). Ninety percent of the teacher candidates enrolled at the university are Hispanic/Latino, and most originate from the area where the TPP is located. The TPP admits an average of 450 to 500 teacher candidates per academic year. The program includes practice-based coursework, performance-based key assessments, and field/clinical experiences.

The teaching vision of the TPP is centered on a social justice perspective that promotes culturally and linguistically sustaining pedagogies as a staple in the program. The bilingual/bicultural local context presents distinctive challenges and opportunities to design teacher preparation to be culturally and linguistically responsive. Three specialization programs, including bilingual education, special education, and early childhood, are offered, with one department offering the professional pedagogy sequence coursework. The TPP's bilingual specialization consistently has the highest enrollments as compared to the other specializations. The bilingual specialization coursework is offered in English and in Spanish.

An Improvement Science Theoretical Framework

Improvement science was originally founded to understand and address the root causes of systemic inequities in education (Bryk et al., 2015; Gallagher et al., 2019; Hough et al., 2017).

An improvement science approach maintains that to fully understand a problem, we must consider the views and lived experiences of the "users" who are experiencing the problem. Beginning in 2020–2021, we used the improvement science approach as a framework, design, and methodology in our attempts to operationalize our social justice teaching vision by launching a new teacher educator committee created to tackle persistent problems in the program. We decided to use an improvement science approach for collecting, analyzing, and using data to improve the learning experiences of our teacher candidates in efforts to strengthen our program.

Improvement science is a problem-specific and user-centered approach (Bryk et al., 2015) that relies heavily on a clear comprehensive view of a "system." In our case, the system that we are examining is the TPP that is nested within larger systems, such as the university and the state accountability systems, inclusive of the capacities and conditions that are producing a persistent problem in need of improvement. By delving into the root causes of systemic inequities, an improvement science approach has shown to support equity-focused initiatives.

Purpose and Objectives

The overarching purpose of the chapter is to offer an example of how one teacher preparation program utilized an improvement science approach to undertake a persistent problem of practice. The objectives of this chapter are: 1) to describe the creation of the organizational learning structure resembling a networked-improvement community; 2) to describe the process of confronting a persistent problem using improvement science tools; and 3) to share the challenges of using the approach. Inspired by case study methodology, we conducted participant observations, wrote field notes, and analyzed documents and other relevant artifacts in our effort to record the experiences of the teacher educators who chose to participate in the improvement science process (Birk et al., 2015). Two questions guided our inquiry: How can the use of an improvement science approach build organizational learning capacity among TPP leaders? How can we operationalize our social justice teaching vision when engaging in improvement efforts?

Impetus for Shifting the Paradigm

Participants and Setting

To engage in continuous improvement and curriculum alignment, TPP core faculty engage in curriculum alignment activities, annual data summits with school district partners, and other activities designed to address accreditation standards. During one of these meetings held in the spring semester of 2020, TPP faculty members voiced concerns about the ineffectiveness of our established routines with the traditional curriculum mapping process. There was a need to increase interdepartmental communication and collaboration between teacher educators who teach in the elementary teacher certification program, an interdisciplinary degree program.

Based on this discussion, a college level standing committee was formed. The purpose of this committee was to function much like a NIC collectively problem-solving using improvement science. The committee was formed with stable membership of TPP academic leaders with the intent of inviting guests such as teacher educators, other university TPP faculty, school districts, and teacher candidates to join periodically to create a network of educators for extending learning capacity. The overarching goal of the NIC was to create a learning culture that consistently focuses on using an equity lens for tackling and improving student learning experiences.

Methodology

To explore the utility of an improvement science approach toward addressing some aspects of continuous improvement, we describe the formation of a teacher preparation committee in a university-based program using a case study methodological approach. Consequently, we chose to frame our analysis of data as a bricolage by integrating components of improvement science and case study methodology to depict our TPP's experiences in innovating and improving through disciplined data and equity-driven continuous improvements efforts. The data sources supported a holistic convergence of the data including the use of participant observation and reflection in the sensemaking process. The chapter builds on self-analysis by the authors who are experienced members of the improvement science framework. We tell our story of how we organized a university teacher preparation program committee and introduced improvement science as a new user-centered approach toward continuous improvement. Sources of data to guide the self-analysis are the artifacts resulting from the committee work, notes, and reflection.

Introducing NIC Principles to Create a Learning Culture of Teacher Education Faculty Members

Dissatisfied with the traditional curriculum alignment approach, college leaders expressed a need for change to design vision-focused collective improvement efforts across the departments to strengthen the quality of the TPP. Collectively, the TPP team decided to reframe a new collaborative space for improvement efforts, aside from the traditional curriculum mapping, alignment, and reporting tasks, as part of continuous improvement. The result was the formation of the Teacher Preparation Standing Committee, which operates as a NIC insofar as members are TPP faculty members who invite guests/stakeholders as participants.

Introducing Improvement Science and Tools

To introduce the concept and language of improvement science, TPP faculty members received a copy of the book, *Learning to Improve* (Bryk et al., 2015). We, along with two other faculty members who are also members of the state-level NIC, facilitated conversations and understandings about the new approach. To operate as a NIC-like committee, we aligned to several essential features of a conventional networked improvement community. These features include focusing on a common aim, guided by a deep understanding of the problem and the system that produces it; striving to be disciplined with a commitment to follow the improvement science approach; and networking to accelerate learning by using data-driven measures such as iterative testing cycles (Bryk et al., 2015).

In our first monthly meeting, we provided the background as to how and why the new committee was formed, announcing that we would apply an improvement science approach to learn more about our persistent problem since we had agreed collectively that the TPP's greatest challenge was increasing the pass rates of our teacher candidates on the content licensure exam. We agree with Sandoval and van Es (2021) that the experience of constructing an aim is complex in implementation. However, within our context, because it has been a longstanding problem, faculty members swiftly constructed an aim having reached a strong consensus on resolving this specific issue.

Causal System Analysis

As facilitators, we introduced various improvement science tools to begin the process of understanding the full context of the problem. To launch a casual system analysis, we guided faculty members in brainstorming the reasons for consistently having low pass rates on the first attempt of the content licensure exam in the elementary education program. Next, we engaged them in filling out a *fishbone diagram,* a cause–effect brainstorming activity to generate reasons or causes. Although rarely are causes of complex problems attributed to the "people" in the system, during this activity, a vast number of reasons seemed to be related to students. It is not uncommon that at the onset of this type of analysis, there is a tendency to blame those immediately connected to the problem.

Significantly, Bryk et al. (2015) point out that causes usually involve how we organize the work that we ask people to carry out (p. 61), while a very small percentage of causes relate directly to people in the system. Usually, the root cause is more likely to be related to processes in a system, and so the intention is that through this deep dive into root causes, the design of better processes for carrying out the work results (2015). As facilitators, we continually asked "why" to guide committee members to fully examine the context and exhaust all possibilities. As we mapped out causes, heavy emphasis was placed on interrogating the complexity of the system to better understand who's doing what, how, and when. Through this process, as opposed to examining a dataset, we engaged in conversations about our teacher candidates exploring possible obstacles they may encounter from the time they are freshmen through admission into the teacher preparation program (a 2-year period). Initially, only a few faculty members participated in the first iteration of the fishbone diagram, but we revisited the diagram at the next meeting to ensure more members provided their ideas; thus, another version was created. Since we met monthly, this slowed the pace of the work since this phase was necessary before continuing to the next. We reminded the group that the activity is not fully exhaustive but rather continues to change as we gain additional perspectives and learn more. Quite inadvertently, this type of activity engaged faculty members in significant conversations about our own teaching and learning. (See Figure 2.1: Example of Visual Graphic Organizer Used for this Activity.)

During this process, some faculty members became frustrated, wanting to move the discussion from a "problem space" to solutions. While we emphasized the importance of learning together, several faculty members believed that we needed to initiate changes right away instead of talking about the problem. Having designed a set of "community agreements" as norms for working together, we reminded the

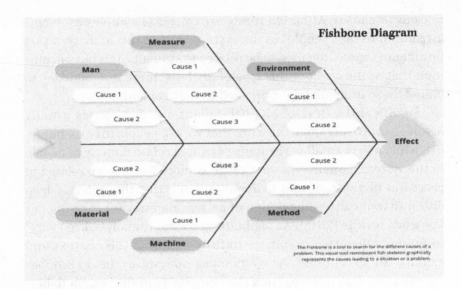

Figure 2.1. Fishbone Diagram.

group of one agreement that we made to avoid "solutionitis"—the inclination to suggest a "quick fix" or solution. The problem that the committee chose to tackle was a persistent problem in the program; therefore, it was quickly determined that what we had done prior was not working, and we needed a different approach.

From Fishbone Diagram to Driver Diagram

After the brainstorming activity, we moved the discussion to the next phase by introducing an analytic tool, the *system improvement map*, to dissect the subsystems that comprise the entire system. In most education systems, these are instructional, a human resource system, information infrastructure, student support services and institutional governance that includes budgetary support, policies, and external systems (Bryk et al., 2015). We used the analytic tool to talk about processes, policies, and context that may contribute to the problem. By understanding "where" this occurred, we were able to determine if the problem was within the direct purview of the TPP or whether it occurred in a subsystem that we had no direct influence over such as those in external systems (e.g., state governing policies). Through this exercise, we focused on subsystems that we could change to improve immediately. During these conversations, facilitators strategically posed questions that focused on how our students experience this system. Faculty members recognized that the system required them to navigate institutional, college, and departmental offices with varying policies, processes, and procedures.

Additionally, we posed questions that made us think about how we operationalize our own social justice-oriented teaching vision. Discourse shifted to possible systemic disparities that may hinder access to information, support, and resources for our students. As facilitators, it was important to reinforce the principles of the approach in understanding that the tools merely guide initial discoveries, but we continue to refine as we learn more and include multiple perspectives. This shift in paradigm was difficult for faculty members because heretofore the tendency was to offer perceived solutions and focus on anticipated results, and not to think deeply about systems or processes. Using improvement science as a type of organizational learning supports building learning capacity at the program level. The thinking is that substantive improvement is more likely to result from sustained inquiry from examining how the program produces its results. As Dolle et al. (2018) contend, an "[o]rganizational learning approach focuses on identifying when, where, and how to make changes to achieve a specific outcome" (p. 2). Ideally, through these efforts, committee members recognized the value of learning together through the improvement process.

After exploring the system improvement map, the conversation turned to designing a working theory by identifying the aim as a measurable goal—that is, what does the committee want to accomplish and by when? The answers to these questions are illustrated in a driver diagram. Collectively, the committee decided on the system they wanted to focus on and could control with the intent of resolving the problem and thereby developing a working theory. The working theory can be tested empirically, and it represents a set of theories and ideas that can support improvement to the problem. "In a practical context, this knowledge is best articulated as a testable prediction of activities and infrastructure necessary to achieve a desired outcome" (Bennett & Provost, 2015, p. 38). The driver diagram serves to organize the improvement efforts since it illustrates structures, processes, and norms that require change in the system for improvement (Bennett & Provost, 2015). Learning from brainstorming and analytic tools facilitates the development of a plan in the form of a diagram that focuses on a set of small hypotheses about key "levers" for producing positive outcomes (Bryk et al., 2015, p.73).

As we continued to facilitate the design of the driver diagram, we introduced a driver diagram protocol to guide this phase. At this time, some faculty members expressed frustration that they were learning "another new tool." They struggled with keeping up with the new language affiliated with the approach. At times, the improvement science vernacular posed issues since many faculty members were not familiar with the framework. To our advantage, it was helpful to have a small team of faculty members in this committee who were also participants in the state-level NIC to support the process. During a virtual meeting, subgroups were organized to work in breakout rooms. We intentionally placed one of the knowledgeable faculty members in each subgroup to lead in participating in the driver diagram design. Key faculty followed this driver diagram protocol to guide discussion with prompts to designate primary drivers that directly support and/or achieve the desired outcome, known as a key set of hypotheses with secondary drivers to describe "where" in the system these exist (such as structures or processes). Then, subgroups shared their work with the larger group for feedback and discussion. This process resulted in the first version of the driver diagram's primary and secondary drivers.

Disciplined inquiry is a core principle of improvement work where data, research, and best practices improve processes and affect outcomes. As the group created the driver diagram, they were reminded that the intent is not to develop "change ideas" (concrete examples of specific solutions) for each "driver," but to work within areas that are considered "small scale changes" that do not require investment in too much time and resources. These set of drivers are general, but with continued prompting and thinking, develop into a few change ideas, which are detailed initiatives in the form of introducing new work processes, changing existing processes, or introducing new tools to produce positive change (Bryk et al., 2015).

The committee's goal was to create small-scale testable changes to learn quickly to improve outcomes for the users (teacher candidates) without making drastic large-scale systemic changes. Through iterative tests, also known as learning cycles, the theory was refined. Because TPP leaders had some ideas of how to tackle the problem, and there were some efforts in place already, we plugged these in to the driver diagram as starting points for beginning to test these change ideas.

For example, for our aim, the committee identified one primary driver as test preparation with a secondary driver as support offered for students in the form of a testing protocol or roadmap. The change idea detailed the adoption of a new testing protocol as policy for students to follow to receive testing support prior to test approvals. Additionally, they were offered support such as individual tutoring (see Figure 2.2: Sample Driver Diagram).

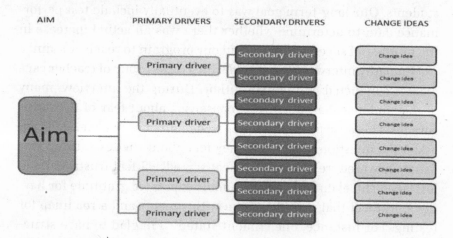

Figure 2.2. Driver Diagram.

Data-Driven Measures for Testing Changes

Another way that the group operationalized a social justice teaching vision was by using data to inform an equity-focused improvement process. We introduced a Plan-Do-Study-Act (PDSA) cycle to test our change ideas. The PDSA cycle is an improvement tool that is used to apply the scientific method in operational space (Bennett & Provost, 2015). Through PDSA cycles, immediate small rapid tests take place to support better understanding regarding the improvement.

A Plan-Do-Study-Act cycle (Figure 3) was launched to learn more about the new testing protocol's impact since this was quite different from what had been in place. Previously, the TPP had a testing protocol that offered recommendations to teacher candidates for preparing and completing state licensure exams. Historically, program completer data revealed that many students disregarded program recommendations for testing that delayed the state certification/licensure process well beyond graduation.

As part of our first PDSA cycle, we included empathy interviews and surveys to learn about the teacher candidates' perceptions and experiences with the new protocol. With these data sources, we would learn immediately if anything needed change along with learning about the protocol's components that were working for students. Our long-term goal was to eventually include test performance data to determine whether there was an actual increase in the number of successful testers in our program to reach our aim.

Empathy interviews were held with a focus group of teacher candidates conducted by the first author. During the interview, many of the students shared a strong consensus about fear of the licensure tests because they felt unprepared or anxious in general. When asked the question about how they feel about the tests, three students answered, respectively: "I feel scared"; "I feel frustrated and lost"; and "I feel dumb." Some students expressed gratitude for having a protocol that provided them with support and a roadmap for testing. For instance, one student stated, "I'm glad to have structured support for our test preparation." A few students expressed concern over the complication of the testing protocol and the number of steps to reach eligibility to take the actual tests. For the initial PDSA cycle, survey data were collected and analyzed. Survey data confirmed some of the information shared in the empathy interviews. Three broad themes emerged from analysis of empathy interview transcripts and the survey including the following:

- The protocol/roadmap lacks clarity in the instructions.
- The protocol/roadmap fails to consider timeline (e.g., time

investment to reach test readiness status, program-level approval processing time, and state-testing schedule).
- Orientations to support student understanding of new testing protocol/roadmap will be helpful.

After the first PDSA cycle, the data were shared with the committee. After a deep dive and discussion of the findings, along with other feedback that program chairs and coordinators had received, revisiting the protocol and communication made sense. Making small changes allows for the use of low-cost improvements that don't require additional human capital or resources. As such, commitments toward ongoing communication campaigns to benefit both students and faculty were launched, such as presenting the protocol at multiple faculty meetings, visiting classrooms to explain the new protocol directly to students, and providing teacher candidate additional support in the college through the test preparation lab. Also, TPP leaders revisited the protocol to remove any unnecessary steps and improve communication. Through refinements of the protocol and increase of communication, these problems have been minimized. The learning cycle ends when a change idea is refined and adopted; however, the committee continues to review and analyze data collected from other reform efforts for the purpose of assessing if our aim has been reached (see Figure 2.3: Sample PDSA Form)

Emerging Themes: Challenges and Positive Outcomes

Adding a new approach to continuous improvement presented various challenges, but some positive outcomes. We, as facilitators, reflected on the process, based on participant observations, meeting notes, and artifacts such as the fishbone diagram versions, system improvement map tool, driver diagram versions, and data from PDSA cycles. Our process for examining and reflecting on this journey produced various themes affiliated with challenges and positive outcomes. To converge the data into themes, we developed this table (see Table 2.1: Key Themes, Description, and Data Support).

PDSA FORM

Test Title			Date		
Tester			Cycle #		Driver
What change idea is being tested?					
What is the overall goal of the test?					
		*Identify your overall goal: To make something work better? Learn how an innovation works? Learn how to test in a new context? Learn how to spread or implement?			

1) PLAN			3) STUDY
Questions: Questions you have about what will happen. What do you want to learn?	Predictions: Make a prediction for each question. Not optional.	Data: Data you'll collect to test predictions.	What were the results? Comment on your predictions in the rows below. Were they correct? Record any data summaries as well.
Questions: •	Predictions: •	• (10-question survey) • (Observation Notes)	
Details: Describe the who/what/when/where of the test. Include your data collection plan.			What did you learn?
2) DO Briefly describe what happened during the test, surprises, difficulty getting data, obstacles, successes, etc.			**4) ACT** Describe modifications and/or decisions for the next cycle; what will you do next?

Figure 2.3. PDSA Form.

Table 2.1. Key Themes, Description, and Data Support

Key Themes	Description	Data Support
Challenges		
Approach warranted a paradigm shift.	The new approach seemed to be in opposition to a traditional solution-oriented quick action mindset. The pacing appeared slow with too much time spent in the "problem space," with some faculty not understanding the purpose since they wanted to focus on sharing their ideas about how to solve the problem.	Reflection of meeting notes Participant observations

Key Themes	Description	Data Support
Challenges		
Learning of new language and tools.	At times, the faculty struggled with the vernacular of the approach and the number of tools introduced.	Reflection of meeting notes Participant observations
Time investment.	Throughout the process, concern over the slow pace was expressed by multiple members. Learning the new approach requires time.	Reflection of meeting notes Participant observations
Unstable membership.	Members of the group did not consistently meet each month. Buy-in for all key TPP leaders was essential yet some were absent from some of the meetings. Some members may have become dissatisfied with the process.	Reflection of meeting notes Participant observations
Positive Outcomes		
Remaining user-centered supported staying equity-focused.	During the phases of introducing tools such as the fishbone diagram and the system improvement map, discourse surrounding equity-issues surfaced. This gave us the opportunity to examine how our practices and more importantly our actions supported our teaching vision in concrete ways.	Fishbone Diagram System Improvement Map Empathy interviews Student surveys Student emails Focus group interviews
Engage in multiple methods to improve the TPP.	With the new committee, TPP leaders committed toward using improvement science to supplement continuous improvement efforts with the overarching goal of creating an organizational learning culture.	Reflection of meeting notes Participant observations
Elevated student voice in our continuous improvement process.	Data collected to learn more about improvements, included students' perspectives. This process altered our traditional discourse around data.	Reflection of meeting notes Participant observations Empathy interviews Focus group interviews Student surveys

Conclusion and Directions for the Future

Using data sources for continuous improvement, without capturing the full student experience as context, fails to provide significant information that can offer opportunities to accelerate learning and refinements to reform efforts. The TPP committee engaged in honest difficult conversations in a slow-moving problem space that challenged our traditional approach. Like the work of Sandoval and van Es (2021), we discovered the significance of the facilitator's role in this process. As facilitators, we delicately balance a critical role of consolidating new learnings while navigating new aims in our improvement science work. As facilitators, we recognized that this approach would disrupt silos and elicit critical conversations to force us to make explicit connections between our program's stated vision with action in the form of our procedures and policies.

We continue to facilitate this work. In the last year, our committee has identified a new aim as we continue to collect data on our original aim. We have invited other university-based TPP leaders into our learning space to offer their perspective and insight with similar problems of practice. As authors and facilitators of this improvement project, we have made strides toward building organizational learning capacity among our TPP leaders, but we have more to do.

As we reflect on our experiences as facilitators, we find value in examining our TPP from a systems perspective, allowing us to view our program more holistically. The use of improvement science tools elicited new understandings about our students' experiences while equity-focused data (such as empathy interviews) served to refine our working theory. Through our process, we remained focused on our aim despite the slow-moving process and sometimes perplexing vernacular. The critical discourse that we engaged in regarding equity issues forced us to explore if, how, and when we operationalize our social justice vision in TPP policies and practices.

References

Bennett, B., & Provost, L. (2015). What's your theory? *Quality Progress*, 37–43.
Bryk, A., Gomez, L. M., Grunow, A., & LeMahieu, P. (2015). *Learning to improve: How American's schools can get better at getting better*. Harvard Education Press.

Dolle, J., White, M. E., Evans-Santiago, B., Flushman, T., Guise, M., Hegg, S., Myhre, O., Ramirez, E., & Won, N. (2018, October). *Improvement science in teacher preparation at California State University: How teacher preparation partnerships are building capacity to learn to improve.* SRI International and WestEd.

Gallagher, H. A., Gong, A., Hough, H. J., Kennedy, K., Albright, T., & Daramola, E. J. (2019). *Engaging district and school leaders in continuous improvement: Lessons from the second year of implementing the CORE Improvement Community.* Policy Analysis for California Education. https://edpolicyinca.org/publications/engaging-district-school-and-teacher-leaders-improvement

Hough, H. J., Willis, J., Grunow, A., Krausen, K., Kwon, S., Steen Mulfinger, L., & Park, S. (2017). *Continuous improvement in practice.* Policy Analysis for California Education. https://edpolicyinca.org/publications/continuous-improvement-practice

LeMahieu, P. G., Edwards, A. R., & Gomez, L. M. (2015). At the nexus of improvement science and teaching: Introduction to a special section of the Journal of Teacher Education. *Journal of Teacher Education, 66*(5), 446–449.

Sandoval, C., & van Es, E. (2021). Examining the practices of generating an aim statement in a teacher preparation networked improvement community. *Teachers College Record, 123*(060306), 1–31.

Texas Education Agency (2022, Fall). *Public Education Information Management System.* Retrieved from https://www.escl.net/cms/lib/TZ21000366/Centricity/Domain/17/FALL%20Region%201%20Dashboard%2022-23.pdf

Texas Education Agency. (2023). *2021-22 Educator Preparation Program Commendations.* Retrieved from https://tea.texas.gov/texas-educators/preparation-and-continuing-education/program-provider-resources/2021-22-educator-preparation-program-epp-commendations

Triangulating Data Through Action Research to Set Priorities, Connect to Partners, and Design Program Improvements

JULIE KALNIN, DEIRDRE HON, JOAN FLORA,
HILLARY MERK, AND NICOLE RALSTON

As the University of Portland School of Education began to transition away from CAEP accreditation in the spring of 2021, our faculty continued its focus on using data for continuous improvement while embracing the possibilities for responsive program innovation afforded by AAQEP. This case demonstrates how our Clinical Practice and Partnerships Committee (CPPC) triangulated data across candidate performance assessments to identify focus areas for change and describes how we engaged with faculty, partners, and university supervisors to implement new practices in coursework and clinical experiences. The case proves important both in what we have learned through our action research process and in the ways the steps we took offer a model for ongoing program development.

Context

Recognized by *US News & World Report* in 2022 as the top regional university in the Western region, the University of Portland is a Catholic, undergraduate-focused university serving about 4000 students in Portland, Oregon. University faculty pride themselves on the liberal arts core and Holy Cross charisms that are infused throughout the undergraduate experience, whether students major within the College of Arts and Sciences or in one of the four professional schools (Business, Education, Engineering, and Nursing). The School of Education (SOE) is the smallest unit on campus, with 13 tenure track faculty supported by excellent adjunct instructors and clinical faculty (university supervisors). In its initial teacher preparation programs—undergraduate, MAT, and Catholic residency—the SOE graduates about 100 new teachers each year.

School of Education faculty have long been engaged in accreditation efforts through NCATE and CAEP; the unit received Frank Murray Leadership recognition for its most recent accreditation review in 2020. While we had been successful within the CAEP framework, our desire to be more agile in responding to what we were learning from our data and our partners served as the catalyst for our shift to AAQEP.

SOE accomplishes accreditation/program improvement through its committee structure (see Figure 3.1). All faculty participate on at least two of these committees. This ensures first that expertise is aligned to each committee's goal and second, that cross-committee awareness is fostered. To enhance program-wide communication and coordination, committee chairs report monthly to Committee 5: Continuous Improvement. When the work of two committees overlaps, as it necessarily does, additional processes are in place for cross-committee review. For example, when clinical assessments are developed within the CPPC (Committee 2), these must be reviewed by the program assessment group (Committee 4) before being presented to the faculty as a whole. While this case is focused on initiatives facilitated by the Clinical Practices and Partnerships Committee, the SOE committee structure supported the involvement of multiple faculty groups.

Action Research Phase: Reconnaissance

Our process incorporated an action research approach (Elliott, 1991) based in a change model that identifies "unfreezing" as a first step

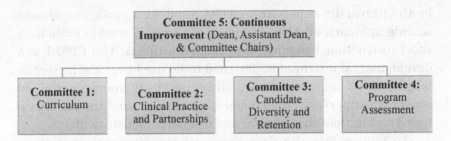

Figure 3.1. UP School of Education Committee Structure.

toward change (Schein, 1996). This choice was essential in our situation because we had years of data about our candidates' performance on three major program assessments: a) the Candidate Preservice Assessment of Student Teaching (CPAST), developed by VARI-EPP, a consortium of universities led by the Ohio State University; b) edTPA, developed by the Stanford Center for Assessment, Learning and Equity (SCALE) and managed by Pearson; and c) a Unit Plan internally developed by our own committee and refined over multiple cohorts.

The fact that we knew quite a bit at the outset about our candidates' performance meant that we needed intentionally to pose questions of the data that we could not yet answer. In the Spring of 2022, we began with an initial query: "What if, rather than interpreting candidate performance by individual assessments, we devised an approach to compare performance across those assessments?"

Our reconnaissance began, then, with identifying potential points of comparison. Committee members referenced matrices—published or previously developed internally—that identified how the tasks and the associated indicators (rubric items) of our three major performance assessments aligned with InTASC standards (CCSSO, 2013). This step confirmed that a comparative approach was potentially workable.

At the same time, we knew that evidence, scoring assumptions, and scoring procedures are vastly different, and perhaps incompatible, across the three assessments. The UP Unit Plan—a five to seven lesson unit with reflections on lesson plans, materials, and assessments, uses a four-point scale on 21 rubric indicators, and is scored by the university supervisor. edTPA employs a proficiency-based scoring approach on 14 to 18 indicators; trained scorers evaluate a short instructional segment and related artifacts. The CPAST is a developmental instrument, designed to be used over a semester or longer; the 26 indicators are scored by consensus among the trained university supervisor, the cooperating teacher, and the candidate based on multiple observations and diverse candidate artifacts.

To triangulate the data across these disparate, but standards-aligned assessments, we opted for a straightforward process that ranked the mean score on each rubric indicator for each assessment from high to low, first for all students, and then disaggregated by program type (i.e., undergraduate, MAT) and level (i.e., elementary, secondary). What we found surprised us. In spite of our oft-touted programmatic focus on "research into practice" and a comparably valued emphasis on instructional reflection, the lowest ranked rubric score(s) on all three assessments—with between 14% to 30% of our candidates scoring below proficient ratings—were related to our candidates' ability to connect their instruction to research and theory (CPAST Item M: Connections to Research and Theory, edTPA Rubrics 3 and 10, Unit Plan Planning iii d, and Instruction i c). Taken together, these rubrics touch on the full scope of a candidate's abilities to draw upon research and theory: appropriately discussing connections between teaching and research/theory (CPAST Item M), providing rationale for instructional decisions (edTPA Rubric 3, Unit Plan Planning iii d), interpreting instructional effectiveness (edTPA Rubric 10), and analyzing formative assessment (Unit Plan, Instruction i c). Learning that across assessments and types of tasks a group of our candidates were consistently not able to draw meaningful links between research and theory and their teaching practices was sobering.

Action Research Phase: Planning

After identifying this pattern, the two questions our committee was faced with answering were, "So what?" and "Now what?" We articulated and acted on these questions in two settings: with our faculty peers and with clinical partners through our Unit Advisory Consortium.

Faculty Interpretation and Improvement Proposals

First, at a faculty meeting, faculty were given a summary of the triangulation from the CPPC analysis and asked to interpret those data. Notes from that meeting showed a variety of responses: dismissing the data as not being significant enough to warrant a response, suggesting the data might not be a reliable indicator of our candidates' "true" abilities, or questioning the assessment scoring processes. Our committee noted this feedback for further discussion. We then reminded our colleagues that they had seen each of these data points previously in isolation. When seen one assessment result at a time, we wondered aloud, might it have been too easy to explain the results away? In the fall unit plan, candidates hadn't really gotten their feet under them. They would do better with edTPA. With CPAST, without access to course assignments or other assessments, cooperating teachers might not have enough evidence to contribute to the consensus score accurately. It would be better in the spring, after edTPA. With edTPA, students were too anxious and weren't doing their best work. Now that we had seen that those suppositions were faulty because these indicators were the lowest across the three measures at different time periods and with several types of data, we asked the faculty to consider "Why do we care?" and "What can we do?" After a rich discussion of why individuals saw it as essential that all our candidates be able to demonstrate their ability to draw on research and theory to inform their teaching, the faculty went to work in small groups to address the following prompts:

- What strategies are currently being used in coursework to build students' understanding of how research and theory are integrated in their practice?
- What could we adjust in the course assignments, clinical support, or in the Unit Plan assessment?
- What other ideas do you have, based on the data?

From the notes developed by small groups, two action items emerged. The first was for course instructors to design a tool that students could use to record information about research findings and theories and apply these concepts to instructional practice within and across courses and into their student teaching. The second was to alter our lesson planning template to require candidates to link their instructional decisions explicitly to research and theory.

Unit Advisory Consortium Interpretation and Improvement Proposals

Our next step was to engage our clinical partners in a similar process of data interpretation, problem-posing, and solution generation. The School of Education has a Unit Advisory Consortium (UAC) made up of principals, cooperating teachers, and UP SOE alumni. As faculty had, UAC members reviewed the data summary in small groups at their spring meeting; they were asked to note any observations about the scores and to identify factors that might contribute to them. The conversation highlighted an issue mentioned in the faculty meeting. Cooperating teachers in the group described they had no information about research or theory that was being taught in courses. Building on this identified problem, UAC members were given an outline of the two proposals from faculty: to develop a tool for recording research and theory and to add research and theory to the lesson plan template. In small groups by role (former student teachers, CTs, principals), they were then asked to provide written feedback to the following question:

- How might we support candidates, cooperating teachers, and university supervisors to ensure candidates are applying research and theory to improve student learning? Consider how we can connect coursework to student teachings and integrate school/district priorities into student teaching.

In the discussion that followed, it was suggested that the School of Education faculty should provide CTs and university supervisors with a summary of courses and key research findings/theories taught in each one. As the discussion proceeded, this suggestion was reexamined. "Shouldn't the student teacher be the one communicating this?" one cooperating teacher asked. The group quickly affirmed this idea. Knowing that a student teacher would have a tool developed through their coursework, cooperating teachers and university supervisors described how they could ask the student to refer to their notes to inform lesson planning and to reflect upon during observational debriefs. UAC members also agreed that the proposed change to the lesson plan should be tried. CTs in the group took this idea one step further and asked that an item emphasizing research and theory be added to UP's lesson observation instrument, a formative tool aligned to the CPAST. Principals made one final and important suggestion—to develop a way for CTs to communicate research-based initiatives that were strategic priorities for the district or school so that the emphasis on research/theory would be reciprocal, not coming only from the university.

Action Research Phase: First Step Action

From the input from faculty and the expansion on that input from clinical partners, the CPPC had a clear plan of action. We needed to develop a course-based tool that could improve our students' documentation and application of research and theory across their coursework. Once that was in place, we needed to inform CTs and university supervisors that this tool existed, and they could request it from their teacher candidates as a resource. We also needed to change three clinical documents: our lesson plan template, the lesson observation form, and our initial conference form.

Course-Based Change

Three CPPC members agreed to develop and pilot a new tool for supporting students with documenting and applying research and theory. This tool was named the Theory and Research in Education or TReE log. Although initially just a descriptive acronym, the TReE name led to a discussion of how the metaphor of a tree could illustrate important relationships among theories, empirical research, and instructional practice. Theories might be the roots of our understandings that feed the trunk and branches—research studies that help us verify those theories; the leaves that emerge are our instructional practices. The TReE log is quite simple in design (see Figure 3.2), though in practice we also lean into adding clip art of trees and roots.

Theory and/or theorist and/or research	APA citation Summary including key terms & ideas	Example of an educator putting this theory/research into practice at a specific grade level
Student entry	*Student entry*	*Student entry*
Student entry	*Student entry*	*Student entry*

Figure 3.2. Initial Theory and Research in Education (TReE) Log Format.

Two CPPC members and authors (Hon and Kalnin) first initiated the use of the TReE log in a summer MAT course focused on human development and cognition. Each of us used the process slightly differently. With the secondary MATs, Hon established a Google Doc that students completed collaboratively as a review when course instruction on a specific theorist was complete. With the elementary MATs, Kalnin asked students to complete an entry individually after assigned readings and then to work with others to refine and revise their ideas. In reviewing our students' work and reflecting together, we found that the TReE log format helped students focus on key ideas, and we noted that asking students to provide a specific and contextualized example (grade level, subject area) helped students identify a logical enactment of the theory that made sense in their own practice. We noticed, however, that the collaborative review process implemented by Hon resulted in students focusing on "big ideas" as well as theorist names (see Figure 3.3); this did not happen in Kalnin's class, where students reported only the "theory or theorist name" as indicated in the TReE log header. Based on this difference, Kalnin plans to implement the TReE log process in summer 2023 in the same manner as Hon did in 2022.

In the fall, both instructors continued to implement the TReE log in consecutive MAT courses and to introduce undergraduate education majors to the process. In the first undergraduate education course of the program (Human Development and Cognition), Hon adapted the TReE log by providing more structure; she identified a theorist name and citation for each of the required entries (see Figure 3.4).

Theory and/or theorist and/or research	APA citation Summary including key terms & ideas	Example of an educator putting this theory/research into practice at a specific grade level
Adolescents are primed to learn	Davidow, J. Y., Foerde, K., Galván, A., & Shohamy, D. (2016). An upside to reward sensitivity: The hippocampus supports enhanced reinforcement learning in adolescence. *Neuron, 92*(1), 93–99. https://doi.org/10.1016/j.neuron.2016.08.031 -Increased sensitivity of rewards makes learning more efficient for adolescents	Teachers should offer students opportunities to learn new things in a way that stimulates their reward center, thus strengthening the connection between learning and rewards in their brains.
Abraham Maslow/ Hierarchy of Needs	Maslow, A. H. (1954). *Motivation and personality* ([1st ed.].). Harper. -Illustrated as a pyramid, the needs from the bottom to the top are: physiological, safety, love and belonging, esteem, and self-actualization	Teachers must recognize that effective learning can only occur once physiological, safety, and belonging needs have been met. Teachers can build community to help foster a sense of safety and belonging.

Figure 3.3. Collaborative TReE Log Entries.

Kalnin, teaching an assessment course for seniors, drew on Hon's summer model and developed a collaborative activity so that students could look back at all of their education coursework and gather resources to use in their student-teaching year. For this use of the TReE log, the instructor created a Google document and listed each of the course names. Students were assigned to each course in groups. Figure 3.5 shows a sample entry from the class-wide retrospective completion of the log. In each of these iterations, Hon and Kalnin reflected on the process and observed that the TReE log routine was an effective support for students generating accurate summaries with clear links to applied practices.

Theory and/or theorist and/or research	APA citation Summary including key terms & ideas	Example of an educator putting this theory/research into practice at a specific grade level
Sociocultural Theory on Cognitive Development *Lev Vygotsky* Vygotsky, L. S. (1978). *Mind in society: The development of higher psychological processes.* Harvard University Press.		

Figure 3.4. Undergraduate Course TReE Log Adaptation.

ED 250/251 theory and/or theorist	APA citation Summary including key terms & ideas	Example of an educator putting this theory/research into practice
Schema theory Jean Piaget	Wadsworth. (1996). *Piaget's theory of cognitive and affective development: foundations of constructivism* (5th ed.). Longman Publishers. Schema: Mental frameworks that help interpret information Forms throughout one's life and builds foundations Has to do with how one organizes knowledge and connects new information to what is already known • Building Schema: Adaptation - Building schema through direct interaction with the environment	• Sensorimotor experiences can be used to help build (the first) schema • Providing tools and manipulatives such as blocks, puzzles, and props • Making lessons relevant and relatable by drawing on students' background knowledge and experiences and using those to introduce, work with, and solidify new concepts • Making anchor charts, concept maps, graphs, or picture dictionaries • Developing and encouraging real-world associations and applications

Figure 3.5. All Course Retrospective Collaborative TReE Log.

Clinical Changes

The first change that the CPPC prepared for fall 2022 implementation was a revision to our lesson planning template. As with the TReE log, the change was simple. If we wanted students to incorporate research and theory in their planning process, one faculty member had told us, asking them to do so explicitly might be a reasonable starting place. Accordingly, we added a column (in gray) to the original three column task outline that had previously been included on our lesson plan template.

Time Frame	What is the teacher doing?	What are the students doing?	Research/theory connection

Figure 3.6. Addition of Research/Theory to the UP Lesson Plan Template.

As our partners had requested, we also added an item to our formative lesson observation tool, which is used by both cooperating teachers and university supervisors to provide feedback to candidates. This instrument, developed by the CPPC committee and used during our last accreditation cycle, would not have been eligible for revision under the previous accreditation framework. Our ability to make this change in a timely way that is responsive to our partners reflects the value we find in AAQEP's approach to continuous improvement. The research-focused item (highlighted in light gray) was added to our Planning for Instruction section of the instrument (see Figure 3.7).

+	**Planning for Instruction and Assessment** Potential evidence for this section: Lesson plan and pre- and/or post observation discussion.	?
	Objectives, goals, and standards are **aligned** (CPAST A) and are **appropriate** for the learners. (CPAST E)	
	Goals/**objectives** are **measurable**. (CPAST C)	

+	**Planning for Instruction and Assessment** Potential evidence for this section: Lesson plan and pre- and/or post observation discussion.	?
	Tasks provide opportunities for students to **practice and monitor their progress toward objectives.** (CPAST A)	
	Materials selected are aligned with goals/objectives and knowledge of student interests/assets/needs. (CPAST B)	
	Selected **materials** improve **content relevance**, provide **accurate** information, and encourage **individualization.** (CPAST B)	
	The lesson was designed to make connections to **students' prior knowledge** and **incorporate their interests and cultural assets.** (CPAST D)	
	The lesson activities are **sequenced** thoughtfully. (CPAST E)	
	The lesson design incorporates **differentiated approaches** to increase the comprehensibility of content and its relevance to learners. (CPAST D)	
	The lesson plan includes intentional checks of student understanding. (CPAST L)	
	The lesson explicitly identifies how the design of learning tasks has been informed by research-based practices and/or learning theories. (CPAST M)	
Observations/Comments:		

Figure 3.7. Addition of Research and Theory Indicator to Lesson Observation Form.

Finally, we added a discussion prompt to our Initial Conference Record (see Figure 3.8). This document is required by Oregon's Teachers' Standards and Practices (TSPC) to ensure that the university supervisor, cooperating teacher, and student teacher have had an opportunity to review important guidelines and establish common expectations. For this reason, the initial conference form was an appropriate vehicle for us to use to ensure that cooperating teachers could identify research-based initiatives that were being emphasized within the school or district. Sharing this information at the beginning of the placement was important in orienting the supervisor and the student teacher to research-based practices valued in that instructional context. Knowing these priorities, we hoped, would motivate the student teacher to develop their understanding of the theoretical and empirical bases for practices they would be responsible for enacting.

Conference Topics
1. Candidate expectations/responsibilities
2. Cooperating Teacher expectations/responsibilities
School and/or district initiatives that are in place or upcoming:
3. University Supervisor expectations/responsibilities
4. Mentoring & Coaching
• Co-Teaching vs. traditional model
5. General clinical observation cycle
• Submit lesson plan prior to observation/preconference
• Observation
• Post conference
6. Fall Part-Time: Unit Plan
Winter/Spring Full-Time: edTPA Portfolio
7. UP handbook, timelines, due dates, procedures for paperwork collection

Figure 3.8. Addition of School/District Priority Topic to Initial Conference Form.

Before asking cooperating teachers and supervisors to implement these changes in the fall of 2022, Joan Flora, author and Clinical Placement Director, brought drafts of these documents to principals and cooperating teachers in partner schools where groups of our student teachers are placed. She also asked for feedback from university supervisors. At the fall university supervisor meeting, the supervisors discussed in small groups how they could best draw on the changes that had been made to support candidates and cooperating teachers in articulating how research/theory informed instructional practice. These steps were significant in highlighting how these slightly changed tools could only be used purposefully if cooperating teachers and university felt comfortable emphasizing the new elements.

In their winter meeting, university supervisors described the change to the lesson plan and to the lesson observation as successful in building candidates' integration of research and theory. They did recommend, however, that the structure of the lesson plan be amended slightly. Rather than linking research and theory to every step in the task outline, they suggested that research and theory connections should be described once at the bottom of the tasks.

This recommendation will be put into place for fall 2023 (see Figure 3.9). With the feedback from and support of participating cooperating teachers and university supervisors, these changes to our clinical forms were implemented easily and were perceived to have accomplished their purposes.

Time Frame	What is the teacher doing?	What are the students doing?
Research/theory connections:		

Figure 3.9. Revision of Lesson Plan Template to Reposition Research and Theory Connection.

Action Research Cycle: Reflect/Evaluate

To understand whether the changes we implemented have had any impact, we will repeat the triangulation process that we used previously. To date, we have analyzed our Fall Unit Plan data. We found that although the mean score for the two rubrics focused on research and theory had improved, the change was not statistically significant. The rankings remain among the five lowest scores. The first cycle of action research will come to a close when we reflect on recently received edTPA scores and CPAST final evaluations.

Even though our data analysis is not yet complete, we have identified at least two focus areas for our next cycle in the action research process. First, the changes that we made have increased, rather than minimized, university supervisor and cooperating teacher requests for more information about the integration of research and theory in students' coursework. Supervisors have specifically requested information about and examples of how to draw on the TReE log in clinical conversations. They particularly want to facilitate conversations about the role of research and theory in improving student learning. Further efforts to strengthen the bridge between coursework and clinical experiences are clearly necessary. Second, the two course instructors who have found success with the TReE log know that this tool will have the most impact if all course instructors use it. Hon made an appeal at our end of the year faculty meeting for other instructors to take up the practice so that we can be assured that all students have access to this tool throughout their program. The effort to broaden instructor use of the TReE log will be integrated in our second cycle of implementation.

Reflecting on the Case

Implementing an action research approach to continuous improvement within the AAQEP framework proved valuable to our committee for multiple reasons. First, it provided us with a systematic structure that guided the steps of our inquiry. Focusing on a provocative question pushed us to examine established data sources in new ways. Data triangulation, in our case as simple as comparing rankings, helped us "unfreeze" by illuminating a pattern that had been right in front of us, but which we had not seen as urgent until the comparisons across datasets irrefutably demonstrated that we faced a gap in our candidates' preparation.

Action research is useful in describing what is, but the process also engages us collectively in identifying what should be. Our data analysis led to meaningful conversations among our faculty about our convictions that a solid base of research and theory supported our candidates in improving PK-12 students' learning. In affirming the importance of these relationships, we have turned with renewed attention to examining the standards upon which this belief is based, how we can cultivate our candidates' knowledge and competence, and how we can engage more thoughtfully with our partners and clinical faculty. The terms "research" and "theory," we have found, are not stated in the InTASC standards on which our program and the performance assessments we have chosen to use are based. Instead, forms of knowledge, practice, and disposition are threaded throughout, from the focus on learner development and learner difference (Standards 1 and 2) into the instructional and content-focused applications of Standards 4 through 7 (CCSSO, 2013). Our change effort has fostered a more intentional focus on knowledge and skills that have impact on student learning that we believe will continue to shape our conversations about effective teacher preparation.

Finally, this case demonstrates that through bringing data purposefully into interaction with our programmatic aims, conversations among campus-based teacher educators and our field-based partners can yield creative and actionable innovation. Focused, data-based conversations with individuals from various perspectives informed what might be considered quite simple changes. Designing these simple and doable changes has meaningfully strengthened our relationships and enhanced our shared work through heightening clarity of purpose. Our action research is still in progress—we have data to interpret that may show us that our efforts have yielded the improvements that we sought. These data may, on the other hand, suggest that we haven't yet moved the needle. Perhaps we will learn that we are not even asking the right questions. Whatever the outcome, documenting our efforts to serve candidate and PK-12 student learning through systematic inquiry creates the conditions for reconnaissance—to know again, to see anew. Disciplining ourselves to stick with the process of questioning, examining evidence, designing, acting, analyzing, and reflecting, is both our continuous challenge and our only way forward. AAQEP's recognition of the importance of these processes has given us renewed focus and energy to learn with our partners to make purposeful change.

References

CCSSO (Council of Chief State School Officers). (2013, April). *Interstate teacher assessment and support consortium InTASC model core teaching standards and learning progressions for teachers 1.0: A resource for ongoing teacher development.* Washington, DC: CCSSO. https://ccsso.org/sites/default/files/2017-12/2013_INTASC_Learning_Progressions_for_Teachers.pdf

Elliot, J. (1991). *Action research for educational change.* Open University Press.

Schein, E. H. (1996). Kurt Lewin's change theory in the field and in the classroom: Notes toward a model of managed learning. *Systems Practice, 9*(1), 27–47.

CHAPTER FOUR

Practicing What We Preach: Using Data from the PRAXIS Performance Assessment for Teachers to Guide Instruction

EMMA L. MECHAM

Each semester when I introduce my elementary education undergraduate students to the concept of assessment, I emphasize that while assessment can and sometimes is used as a tool for shaming, blaming, excusing, and attaching value to students, teachers, and schools, that isn't what it is most useful for. The point, I tell them, of assessing students is to gather information that helps you make better instructional decisions (Will et al., 2019). My colleagues and I know this, but when our students' initial round of scores on the Praxis Performance Assessment for Teachers (PPAT) came back lower than we would have hoped, I heard and thought a little of all of those reactions.

The Utah State Board of Education, responding to an ever-changing matrix of factors, recently made the decision to change its requirements for professional licensure. Previously, preservice and novice teachers qualified for an initial license by securing a passing score on the PRAXIS 2, Elementary Education Multiple Subjects exam, a test that assessed their content knowledge of Reading and Language Arts, Mathematics, Social Studies, and Science. Then, in their first three years of teaching, novice teachers needed to pass the Principles of Learning and Teaching (PLT) exam to receive a professional license. The PLT sought to assess novice teachers' pedagogical knowledge and skill set. In January 2020 (USBE rule R4277-303), USBE replaced PRAXIS with PPAT. Then, on June 30, 2020, they discontinued the use of PLT and eliminated levels of licensing. (Each of these assessments is a product sold by Educational Testing Services.)

Conversations regarding the impact of these changes to the teacher licensing process in the state began infiltrating our faculty meetings in November 2018, when our Associate Dean informed us of an informational meeting about PPAT to be held at a public university 2-1/2 hours away. To be frank, I paid this issue only passing attention at the time. I did not attend the meeting and did not invest myself in learning about the proposed changes. Our program excellently prepares teachers to be successful in the classroom. It's a program I am proud to be a part of for the quality of work that my colleagues and I do. Surely, I imagined, we simply needed to continue to do our work well, and whatever the new assessment, it would capture that.

The rollout semester for our pilot of PPAT was in spring semester of 2020. When the COVID-19 pandemic hit our area in March, everything shut down. Student teachers were no longer in classrooms. The chaos of getting online school up and running in our local school partners meant that supervising teachers had no bandwidth and very few skills for mentoring university students about how to teach in circumstances and use technology with which they were unfamiliar. While we tried again to pilot the PPAT with students in the fall semester of 2020, there were so many disruptions with illness, quarantines, and school shutdowns, once again the results were sporadic and uninformative. In winter of 2020, the Utah State Board of Education responded to concerns from public universities across the state and maintained the pilot status of the PPAT until fall of 2023. Spring semester of 2021 faced many of the previous semesters' challenges, although the disruptions had begun to lessen. By fall semester of 2021, it felt reasonable to assume that the data were representative.

Baseline Data

In the fall of 2021, elementary education students in our program scored an average of 38.55, but in spring of 2022, the average dropped to 34.6 (see figure 4.1). The cut score for passing the test is 36. As a faculty, we were concerned—for our students' success, for our program's reputation, and, of course, as the end point of everything we do, for the learning of the elementary students our students would serve in their careers. In faculty meeting, a variety of explanations were put forward.

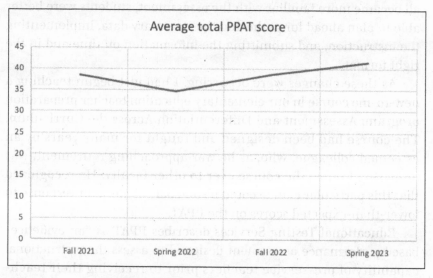

Figure 4.1. Average Total PPAT Score.

Were our less-than-expected scores representing a lack of student buy-in? The assessment was still in pilot phase with our students and they knew this. While we earnestly tried to motivate them to care about the assessment, they were less committed than they could have been. Were the assessment or the scoring of the assessment unreliable or invalid? Did our students not know how to represent their knowledge or skills in the language of the test? Could our students not be as well prepared as we believed they were? As the discussion continued, our Associate Dean, while acknowledging these possibilities, reminded us that "the data are the data" and required a response from us in order to improve student success. Working together across several semesters, we did respond.

It would be faulty to identify any one factor as the singular reason for steady growth in the average score of our graduates over the next two semesters, as shown in Figure 1. Certainly, the end of the pilot and the beginning of clear consequences impacted student motivation and thus, performance. The continuing recession of COVID impacts on classrooms and most students' personal lives undoubtedly had positive impacts. Then too, so did faculty, staff, mentor teacher, and student awareness of the assessment. As we all became more familiar with the assessment, students were better able to plan ahead for gathering the necessary data, implementing the instruction, and submitting the information on time and in the right format.

As these changes were occurring, I had just begun teaching a new-to-me course in our elementary education teacher preparation program: Assessment and Differentiation Across the Curriculum. The course had been designed and taught for many years by an esteemed colleague, who, as he was approaching retirement, was preparing to turn the course over to other faculty. He recognized that this particular course could be one part of our joint response to lower-than-expected scores on the PPAT.

Educational Testing Services describes PPAT as "an evidence-based performance assessment designed to assess the instructional capability of pre-service teachers prior to receiving their teaching license" (PPAT Assessment Candidate and Educator Handbook, 2022). The test is divided into four tasks. The first task focuses on teacher candidates demonstrating an understanding of the context in which they teach and their students learn. In addition to broader community and school context, the task calls for teacher candidates to demonstrate an understanding of students' broad pre-existing knowledge and skills. Each of the following tasks even more explicitly addresses teacher candidate knowledge of and skill in gathering and interpreting evidence of student understanding, designing differentiated instruction based on that evidence, and then assessing the impact of that instruction. Each of those skills are taught and practiced throughout our teacher education program, but most specifically these are the very skills the Assessment and Differentiation Across the Curriculum course was designed to teach students.

Working together, my colleague and I made a broad assessment of how the course could be redesigned to better prepare teacher candidates to learn and demonstrate the skills most significant to success on the PPAT. Both total assessment average and task-specific data from the PPAT informed our decision-making, but so did information from the wide array of assessment data (Wherfel et al., 2022) we gathered in teaching the course. Over the course of the last three semesters, I've worked, most especially with the Undergraduate Teaching Fellow hired to support the course, to reimagine and refine the course. I've worked to do with my own teaching precisely what I am trying to prepare teacher candidates to do: look at relevant data to identify baseline understanding, use it to make instructional decisions, differentiate my teaching, and assess for instructional impact before beginning the whole process again in one recursive round. The process is far from complete, and while, if history is any predictor, the PPAT will likely be rolled back or replaced before I'm done teaching the course, the experience has sharpened my ability to apply these essential skills.

Instructional Changes

Over the ensuing semesters, we made a variety of changes to the course (as seen in Table 1), responding not only to changes in PPAT scores but also to other sources of data, including typical errors on course assignments and exams, feedback from students and colleagues, observations of student affect in class, and student questions—what is sometimes called professional noticing (Amador et al., 2020). While the kickstart to the revisions was addressing PPAT data, the refinements have made positive impacts beyond what is measured in that singular way.

Introducing the PPAT Earlier

One of the changes that we made throughout our elementary education teacher preparation program was to simply inform students earlier in their education that they were going to be taking the PPAT.

Following the adage of our retired Associate Dean, we communicated with teacher candidates "early and often." Anecdotally, this
appears to have reduced some anxiety for students. Rather than
feeling taken by surprise about the expectations they face in their
final semester of teacher education, teacher candidates now have a
much longer time to ramp up their understanding of the assessment
and their social learning from others in the program about how best
to succeed.

The form this change took in the Assessment and Differentiation
Across the Curriculum course is both formal and informal.
Informally, we simply point to the overlap between what the PPAT
asks for and what we are discussing as it comes. Formally, in the final
week of the course, we now devote time to introducing the teacher
candidates to some of the tasks that the PPAT includes and talking
through the ways they can use the skills and knowledge they've
gained in the class to successfully approach those tasks both on the
assessment and in their future classrooms. One of the things we've
come to realize is that a weakness many students bring with them
to their teacher education is an inability to transfer knowledge and
skills from one context to another. So, while we know that teacher
candidates have successfully demonstrated the skill of planning for
inclusion while teaching math, they are sometimes unable to transfer that skill set to inclusion on the playground or while teaching
science. The PPAT asks students to demonstrate those skills in particular contexts with particular parameters, and sometimes it is the
transfer of those skills from one context to another that stymies students, not the actual skill set. Deliberately articulating for students
that a particular task is calling for evidence of a particular skill set
gives them both the confidence and the metacognition to make use
of their full range of abilities. For example, in an August 2020 faculty meeting, we examined data that showed that the section on the
PPAT students were having the most trouble with was for task three,
steps two, three, and four. Step two asks teacher candidates to provide differentiation for two focus students they have identified. It
wasn't that teacher candidates weren't able to do that, but that they
were not selecting focus students who allowed them to show the
breadth of their skill sets. Now when I have an assignment in which

teacher candidates select focus students from the case class study, I specifically charge them with the task of making that selection on the basis of identifying students who will allow them to maximally demonstrate what they know.

Eliminating Content

Among the first revisions we made to the course was eliminating content that distracted students from the essential knowledge and skills. Two things were at work here: the first is that education is a constantly changing and evolving field. Some content that teacher candidates made use of when the course was designed is no longer central to their ability to carry out the skill set necessary to teaching in the state today. In the previous course design, significant time was spent on learning the difference between norm-referenced assessments and criterion-referenced assessments, using case study data for students' test scores on the Iowa Test of Basic Skills (ITBS). While conceptually an understanding between the two types of tests is valuable for understanding assessment, students in Utah haven't taken the ITBS since 2010 (Utah State House Bill 166). Most often, our students encounter no standardized norm-reference tests in their teacher education or in their career as an elementary teacher in the state of Utah today. Philosophically, the Utah State Board of Education has made efforts to move teachers further toward criterion-referenced assessments, including a push toward competency-based training (Utah State Board of Education, 2021a) and standards-based grading (Utah State Board of Education, 2021b). While the concept of norm-referenced assessment still makes an appearance in the course instruction, we devote little time to the concept and no time to students learning to parse and use data from ITBS. This frees up course time to focus on the skills teachers do use in Utah classrooms today. We retained the successful use of a case class study, which gives teacher candidates the benefits of working with authentic data (Burstein et al., 2017), but replaced the ITBS data with sample Acadience data—a test that Utah students do take.

One of the strengths of the course in its previous design was the inclusion of a lot of elements of student choice. This allows students to see and experience the value of differentiation guided by student preference. However, one of the difficulties we identified as we read student work was that sometimes those choices led to confusion for students. This manifested particularly with regard to student choice of grade level standards to use as they demonstrated the skills of inclusion, differentiation, and assessment. The importance of deep content knowledge for skillful teaching is well documented (Brobst et al., 2017; Brownell et al., 2010; Depaepe et al., 2018; Watt et al., 2021). One of the joys and difficulties of being an elementary school teacher is being a content generalist—teaching all the subjects all the time, ideally integrating them together. This requires teachers to develop depth of content knowledge for grade-specific standards each time they teach a new grade. Asking teacher candidates to create a plan for differentiating instruction based on student readiness requires that they have a fair amount of content expertise. Student feedback suggested that while students valued the choice given to them to choose a grade level and a core objective for assignments like this, they often made choices that required them to either newly develop depth of content knowledge on a particular subject area objective in order to do the assignment, or they failed to develop that depth and their differentiation plan showed their lack of expertise. In the redesign of the course, we eliminated these choices (while preserving others) so as to reduce the obscuring of differentiation skills by content unfamiliarity. Instead, we used only third-grade standards and chose objectives that we could provide easily accessible materials for refreshing or developing their content knowledge as they worked with those objectives. In the end, teacher candidates knew a lot about honeybee adaptation, and we could see more clearly what they did and did not know about how to differentiate instruction.

Emphasizing PPAT Terminology and Models

One of the earliest realizations we had about student success on the PPAT had to do with terminology. The PPAT repeatedly asks students to use baseline data. It wasn't that our students hadn't been asked to identify and make use of data from pre-assessments throughout their teacher education; it was simply that, as a program, we didn't define or consistently use the term "baseline data." When students encountered directions to gather, use, or chart baseline data on the PPAT, they weren't sure what all that included. This was an easy data point to respond to. Together with the course Undergraduate Teaching Fellow, I identified all the places in course materials where we could use the term baseline data and used it. Then, as we encountered those course materials throughout the semester, I defined the term and reminded students what it was and how they were already using it.

This points to a broader adjustment in the course. The PPAT assessment calls for teacher candidates to not only demonstrate their knowledge and skills as a teacher, but to articulate the metacognition behind it. It's a sort of "show your work" model. This is perhaps where the greatest disjuncture was between what our graduates knew and could do and what the PPAT was capturing. They had skills that they thought through and demonstrated in practice that they were novices at articulating; they could do the work, but struggled to explain how they knew how to do the work. We thus incorporated a lot of practice into the assessments for the course that required students to articulate the reasons they made the choices they did—not just "here's how I differentiated my instruction" but "here's how I differentiated my instruction in response to these factors based on this understanding of learning."

Another change was incorporating the PPAT lesson plan template. Across our teacher education program, teacher candidates gain familiarity with different templates of lesson plans. Some are preferred by certain content experts; some reflect different points on the trajectory of student learning. The instructions for submitting a lesson plan on the PPAT do not require that teacher candidates use the PPAT-specific lesson plan. However, we've seen that PPAT submitters who do are more likely to do well on that task. In order to familiarize teacher candidates with the template, in our course we adapted all of the lesson plan materials that students access and use in this course (largely from the Utah Education Network repository of lesson plans) to the template format preferred by PPAT. While the substance of the content remains unchanged, we hope that familiarity with the formatting will be one less obstacle to demonstrating their knowledge and skills.

Added (Presumed) Prerequisite Knowledge

Early semester assessments of teacher candidates revealed another weakness in the course design. Students were beginning the class with less mastery of two key pieces of prerequisite knowledge than we thought they would have. The first of these had to do with breaking down standards into manageable pieces. In order for students to differentiate or assess, they first need a solid understanding of the objective. While teacher candidates had a global understanding of what core standards were, and in the case of some standards, particularly in math, could identify the scope, sequence, and prerequisite knowledge for learning those standards, in other cases, they could not clearly identify what they were looking for, or how to recognize, teach, assess, and report on it. On three of the four tasks in the PPAT, teacher candidates must identify what standard their task is related to and have a thorough understanding of how to interpret and teach that specific standard. In order to better prepare students, we added a module to the beginning of the course in which we focus on unpacking standards. After implementing this change, teacher candidates demonstrated more objective-aligned work in the class. However, it's too early to say if it will impact PPAT scores, as the majority of students who experienced the change have not yet submitted their PPAT assessments. The module remains in need of refinement, as fewer students demonstrated mastery of this objective than any other in last semester's course.

Additionally, because of PPAT data, we became aware that teacher candidates did not have the skills to build strong rubrics—a skill we had presumed they had already developed before enrolling in this class. In our program's PPAT data, there is a pattern of teacher candidates receiving poor scores because they have created rubrics that are too broad, without sufficient descriptions of what makes the difference between a 15 and a 20 on an assignment or without clear descriptors of the work they are looking for. As a result, we introduced a module to the course that focuses on developing clear rubrics. In the module, students get practice both at looking at and analyzing many rubrics and also at developing rubrics that articulate for their future students precisely what they are looking for in the assessment.

Built-in Redundancy

Finally, throughout the full course we built in additional redundancy. Rather than having teacher candidates demonstrate singular skills for each unit, we worked to create assignments and assessments that explicitly built on beginning objectives by asking students to "show their work" from one step to the next. Rather than just asking students to identify how they might assess student understanding, we ask them to begin with breaking down the standard, and then preceding step by step through finding and analyzing baseline data, identifying differentiated, inclusive instruction that is responsive to the needs they identify in that baseline data for readying students to master new content, developing and implementing formative and summative assessment, and using data from those assessments to do it all again. In each case we ask students to articulate all the thinking that goes into the decisions they make, and to do it in specific language that mirrors the language the PPAT uses in directions and rubrics. This practice helps students master not only the teaching skills, but the description skills that will help them be successful on the PPAT. It also helps students to move to a less siloed understanding of the course content. Like others (Janice et al., 2021), we recognize the difficulty for teacher candidates in applying what they know in new contexts. In this way, they get to practice applying it using different student case files and on different subject objectives. See Table 4.1 for a summary of all course changes.

Table 4.1. Course Changes

Types of Instructional Changes	Course-Specific Examples
Introducing the PPAT Earlier	1. Concrete discussion of PPAT in the course
Eliminating Content	1. Iowa Basic Skills Test 2. Multiple grade level/subject content knowledge
Emphasizing PPAT Terminology and Models	1. Emphasizing "baseline data" 2. Model using the language of the tasks in answers 3. Incorporating PPAT lesson plan template

Types of Instructional Changes	Course-Specific Examples
Added (Presumed) Prerequisite Knowledge	1. Unpacking standards 2. Rubric design
Built in Redundancy	1. Completing tasks from beginning to end 2. Changing conditions of skill performance

The Work Continues

At each turn, we were introspective about "teaching to the test." This is the assessment right now; it matters for our students and for us as a program that they demonstrate their knowledge successfully. However, we did not choose this assessment, and while we can see positives in it, we're also aware of the questions and critiques circulating about PPAT, and about teacher performance assessments in general (Sawchuck, 2014). An awareness of the limits of the assessment tool itself is an important part of making data-based decisions (Will et al., 2019). We have watched our students' student teaching experiences become dominated by PPAT, rather than by the hundred other learning necessities of their final practicum experience. Rather than hearing teacher candidates focusing on their classroom management challenges, our student teaching director reports that they are focused on uploading artifacts, meeting deadlines, and articulating skills rather than practicing them. It is not clear that success on teacher performance assessments, like the PPAT, has predictive value for quality teaching (Peck et al., 2021). Some teacher candidates have done very well on the PPAT, while not being able to build rapport with students or provide clear, engaging instruction.

While we want to help teacher candidates be successful on the PPAT, our broader and more important concern is that they can apply this knowledge in their classrooms as teachers. Constant reflection about managing to prepare teacher candidates for both necessities at the same time has meant more than a little second-guessing of revisions and of the time dedicated to preparing students to demonstrate their knowledge in this particular format. As Holly Thornton (2020) has argued in her analysis of the impact of Educative Teacher

Performance Assessment or EdTPA (another end of teacher performance assessment used for licensing), our job as professionals is to "define the language and focus of the edTPA assessment tool for ourselves. We can focus on relationships, responsiveness, and professionally grounded decision-making, instead of the rote procedures of didactic teaching, or the technical steps of 'doing' the edTPA" (p. 29). Making those professional choices is not easy.

Despite the changes, 11% of our most recent elementary education cohort didn't pass the PPAT. Assuming they continue down this career path, they have 3 years to pass the PPAT in order to qualify for licensing. We want every teacher candidate to be successful at demonstrating their knowledge and skills on the PPAT, and while we can influence only one small part of the matrix of ever-increasing attrition from the teaching ranks, excellent preparation is the space for teacher education programs to move that needle. There are, therefore, more changes to be made to the course, adjusting for areas of weakness in design and instruction, making better use of our limited time, and building on what all our pieces of data—from PPAT scores to the looks on students' faces—tell us about how to improve. Rather than fearing that data, I'm excited for what it can teach me.

References

Amador, J. M., Glassmeyer, D., & Brackoniecki, A. (2020). Noticing before responding. *Mathematics Teacher: Learning & Teaching PK-12, 113*(04), 310–316.

Brobst, J., Markworth, K., Tasker, T., & Ohana, C. (2017). Comparing the preparedness, content knowledge, and instructional quality of elementary science specialists and self-containedteachers. *Journal of Research in Science Teaching, 54*(10), 1302–1321. https://doi.org.dist.lib.usu.edu/10.1002/tea.21406.

Brownell, M. T., Sindelar, P. T., Kiely, M. T., & Danielson, L. C. (2010). Special education teacher quality and preparation: Exposing foundations, constructing a new model. *Exceptional Children, 76*(3), 357–377. https://doi.org.dist.lib.usu.edu/10.1177/001440291007600307

Burstein, K., Casbergue, R., & Zamudio, I. (2017). Equity for all learners through formative assessment: Rapid recognition of instructional needs. Paper presented at the 2017 annual meeting of The American Educational Research Association. San Antonio, 2017. AERA Online Paper Repository. https://doi.org/10.3102/1187153

Depaepe, F., Van Roy, P., Torbeyns, J., Van Dooren, W., Verschaffel, L., & Kleickmann, T. (2018). Stimulating pre-service teachers' content and pedagogical content knowledge on rational numbers. *Educational Studies in Mathematics, 99*(2), 197–216. https://doi-org.dist.lib.usu.edu/10.1007/s10649-018-9822-7

Janice, S., Schmeichel, M., McAnulty, J., Grace, C., & Wegrzyn, K. (2021). Assessing teacher candidates' pedagogical judgment: An analysis of clinically-based instructional assignments. *Journal of Educational Supervision 4*(3), 1–16.

Peck, C. A., Young, M. G., & Zhang, W. (2021). Using teaching performance assessments for program evaluation and improvement in teacher education: Evaluating and improving teacher preparation programs. National Academy of Education Committee on Evaluating and Improving Teacher Preparation Programs. National Academy of Education. https://doi-org.dist.lib.usu.edu/10.31094.2021-3-3

PPAT Assessment Candidate and Educator Handbook. (2022). Retrieved May 15, 2023 from https://www.ets.org/pdfs/ppat/ppat-candidate-educator-handbook.pdf

Rule 303: Educator Preparation Programs, R277-303. (2023). https://adminrules.utah.gov/public/rule/R277-303/Current%20Rules?

Sawchuck, S. (2014). ETS wades into market for teacher performance exams. *Education Week 33*(22), 6.

Thornton, H. (2020). We don't teach to the edTPA: Maintaining authenticity and attaining high edTPA scores. *Current Issues in Middle Level Education, 25,* 26–29.

Utah State Board of Education (2021a). *Competency Based Endorsements.* Utah State Board of Education.

Utah State Board of Education (2021b). *Utah's Personalized Competency Based Learning Framework.* Utah State Board of Education.

Utah State House Bill 166: Reductions to Education Mandates. (2010). https://le.utah.gov/~2010/bills/static/HB0166.html

Watt, S., Conoyer, S., Ford, J. W., Foegen, A., & Luckey, G. (2021). Raising the power of curriculum-based measurement tools in preservice training. *Teacher Education and Special Education, 44*(1), 78–92. https://doi-org.dist.lib.usu.edu/10.1177/0888406420916829

Wherfel, Q. M., Monda-Amaya, L., & Shriner, J. G. (2022). General education teacher practices: Assessment, decision-making and the influence of co-teaching. *Preventing School Failure, 66*(1), 42–51.

Will, K. K., McConnell, S. R., Elmquist, M., Lease, E. M., & Wackerle-Hollman, A. (2019). Meeting in the middle: Future directions for researchers to support educators' assessment literacy and data-based decision making. *Grantee Submission, 4,* 1–8.

CHAPTER FIVE

Bringing Global Texts into the Classroom: Challenging Preservice Teachers to Engage with Diverse Books

ANDREA TOCHELLI-WARD

Introduction

This chapter will describe my efforts at continuous improvement in developing a course project to meet AAQEP standards over the last three years working with elementary preservice teachers. In our Quality Assurance Report, submitted in 2021, we used our students' scores on New York State's Educating All Students (EAS) exam as support for success for several of AAQEP's standards including 1C (culturally responsive practices) and 2D (global and international perspectives). In Table 5.1 are the results for the completer cohorts from 2018 to 2020. The scaled scores on the EAS range from 400 to 600 with a passing score of 520 without using the Safety Net, which allows for passing scores between 500 and 519. The sub-competency scores range from 1 to 4. Our areas of concern are the darker gray boxes, indicating that our mean scores overall were below our threshold. There are several areas of concern noted across the completers in our program for this exam. With the exception of the 2019 MST cohort, each group had at least one area of concern.

While the review of our EAS scores was underway, in June 2020, after several weeks of Black Lives Matter protests, academics began to discuss options for how to engage in antiracist work and invited those interested to participate in a Zoom book study. We met each week that summer to discuss Layla Saad's (2020) book,

Table 5.1. Educating All Students: Overall and Sub-Competency Areas, Undergraduate (UG) and Graduate (MST) Inclusive Childhood 1–6 Student Teachers, 2018–2019, and 2019–2020

	Overall Score (Mean)	Diverse Student Populations Multiple Choice (Mean)	Diverse Student Populations Constructed Response (Mean)	English Language Learners Multiple Choice (Mean)	English Language Learners Constructed Response (Mean)
UG 2018 n = 4	533	2.25	2.25	3.25	2.75
MST 2018 n = 15	517	2.6	2.13	2.13	2.13
UG 2019 n = 20	509	2.4	2.1	2.4	2.1
MST 2019 n = 7	533	2.71	2.85	3.0	2.57
UG 2020 n = 18	528	2.83	2.44	2.33	2.38
MST 2020 n = 8	532	2.28	2.25	2.75	2.5

Note: Criteria mean above 520 (overall) and 2.5 (sub-competency)

Me and White Supremacy: Combat Racism, Change the World, and Become a Good Ancestor. Before beginning Saad's book, I considered myself to be understanding of social justice and including these discussions in my courses. Until I began actively engaging in readings around anti-racism, I was unaware of the various ways I upheld white supremacy in my teaching. It was clear I needed to shift some of my thinking and framing of my courses. Since 2020, a subset of my original coalition has continuously met to discuss our successes and challenges as well as continue our reading around anti-racism.

Kleinrock (2021) stated that antibias and antiracist work "is not just for BIPOC [Black, Indigenous, People of Color] and those who are marginalized—white folx must also be a part of this movement"

(p. 95). Given that 79% of teachers in the United States are white (National Center for Education Statistics, 2020), this is an area teacher educators need to specifically address with our students. The majority of the students I work with were White students (see Table 5.2), though they might fall into other categories of traditionally marginalized populations.

Table 5.2. Percentage of White Students Enrolled in Courses

Course Cohort	Undergraduate	Graduate
2020	100%	83%
2021	100%	95%
2022	89%	71%
2023	81%	78%

I attended a collaborative conversation hosted by AAQEP and Dr. Casey Graham Brown in April 2020 to learn more about how others were addressing Standard 2D. One of the presenters from the University of Texas at Arlington, Dr. Joyce Myers, described how she was using children's picture books to help students work on their understanding of global perspectives. This sparked an idea for creating a new course project to have students use picture books focused on global perspectives as the basis for a lesson plan. Over the past three years I have refined the project and received positive feedback from students about the project.

We Need Diverse Books Project

COVID-19 restrictions provided an unexpected opportunity to pilot the class project in the fall of 2020 in place of a project intended to be in their practicum placement. Because this was a mid-semester change of plans, there was only 1 week of readings that were available to prepare them for the project. In the spring of 2021, I was able to dedicate 2 weeks of readings and in-class activities to learning about social justice and critical literacy before they wrote their plans. In the first two pilot semesters, the project focused exclusively on one picture book with global and international perspectives. For the purpose of this chapter I will concentrate on the results from 2022 and 2023 cohorts of students, who had the same assignment parameters described in the next section.

Assignment Parameters

After the two pilot iterations of the assignment, I redesigned the project to focus on both Standard 1C as well as Standard 2D. In the overview of the assignment, I describe the following:

> You will locate picture books and analyze the content and authors
> for appropriateness. The picture books will be focused both within
> the US (with a traditionally marginalized group) [focused on
> AAQEP Standard 1C] and outside of the US (focused on global or
> international perspectives) [focused on AAQEP Standard 2D]. For
> one of these picture books, you will write a lesson plan focused on
> the book that will be presented to your peers. After presenting, you
> will reflect on how your lesson plan went using prompts.

Students analyzed the appropriateness of the books and selected one book to write and deliver a lesson plan and then reflect on their successes and areas for development.

I redesigned the due dates so the book analysis was completed after engaging in class activities around analyzing books for appropriateness (with examples and non-examples) as well as analyzing authors and the content of the texts. The following week, after students engaged in designing a lesson plan in class, their draft was due for the project. I provided feedback on their draft before they presented their lesson plan. After presenting their plans, they received feedback from their peers and then completed their reflection.

After the course pilot semesters in 2020 and 2021, the point value of the overall project was increased from 20 to 30 points, which was 20% of their overall course grade. Point values were increased for the book analysis, delivery, and reflection, with an additional category of peer feedback included. The following description is focused on the last cohorts of students (spring 2022 and 2023) who had similar class experiences, readings (see Table 5.3), and used the same assessment rubric (Appendix 5.A).

Scaffolding Students After Pilot

My personal teaching philosophy relies heavily on the work of Pearson and Gallagher's (1983) conceptualization of the *Gradual Release of Responsibility*. My in-class work often follows the "I do" (I model), "We do" (student partner/small group work), "You do" (independent assignment completion) format. The scaffolding of this project followed this gradual release of responsibility format, where I modeled and scaffolded before the book analysis and lesson plan were due.

I asked preservice teachers what their two favorite picture books were the first week of classes before we discussed the importance of diverse books. Additionally, during our discussions of emergent literacy I asked them to identify books they would use in an early childhood classroom. In Figure 5.1 are the compiled results for students enrolled in 2021 to 2023.

Overwhelmingly, preservice teachers identified books that featured main characters who were animals or books that included animals, people, and/or inanimate objects (145 total books). There was a large group of students who also identified books where the

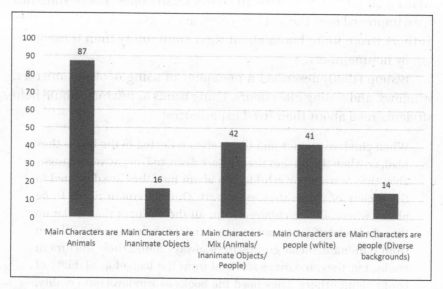

Figure 5.1. Favorite and Emergent Literacy Picture Books for Course Cohorts 2021–2023.

characters were white (41 books). Only 14 out of 200 books featured characters with diverse backgrounds and 10 of these were written by authors with diverse backgrounds.

My students' identification of books somewhat match the information in Figure 5.2 regarding the publication of children's books. Overall, published books for children and young adults in 2018 focused on white characters (50%) with 27% focusing on animals. My students did focus more on animals with their selections but also noted many books with white characters. Figure 5.1, updated each semester, has been enlightening for students. They immediately notice that their first inclination for books for a lesson plan or favorite books from childhood generally featured animals and white characters.

Part of the complication in locating diverse books is the lack of options in texts written by members of diverse communities. In class we discussed the Cooperative Children's Book Center (2023) book statistics that indicated many books are written by authors who are not members of the communities. For example, in 2022, 462 books were written by Black or African authors while 491 were written about Black or African characters/people. These statistics have improved over the last few years, and in 2022, Asian and Latinx authors wrote more books about their community than those written by nonmembers.

Bishop (1990) described a metaphor of using books as mirrors, windows, and sliding glass doors. Using books as mirrors should help students read about their lived experiences:

> When children cannot find themselves reflected in the books they read, or when the images they see are distorted, negative, or laughable, they learn a powerful lesson about how they are devalued in the society of which they are a part. Our classroom needs to be places where all the children from all the cultures that make up the salad bowl of American society can find their mirrors. Children from dominant social groups have always found their mirrors in books, but they, too, have suffered from the lack of availability of books about others. They need the books as windows onto reality, not just on imaginary worlds. (Bishop, 1990, para 4 & 5).

Books can also serve as sliding glass doors to facilitate change and action after reading (Laminack & Kelly, 2019). Figure 5.2 (Huyck & Dahlen, 2019) highlights the concept of mirrors to see who is represented in books based on publication numbers. In addition, the illustration notes the size of the mirrors, reflecting the number of books published that year. Bishop's (1990) metaphor was useful for my students in thinking about how to select books to represent the students they will have in their future classrooms but also in sharing windows into other's experiences.

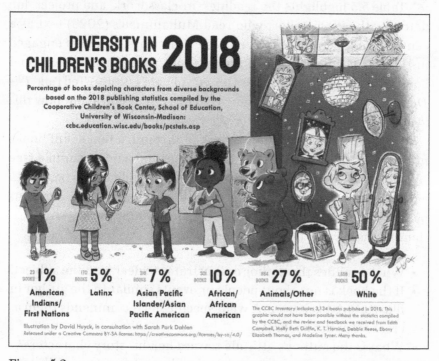

Figure 5.2.
Note: Created and distributed for Creative Commons use. Dropbox address to download original files: https://www.dropbox.com/sh/7zn2logbx7hrvko/AADB87N9rK1qmQn-sMCdUXa5a?dl=0

A recommendation made by Miller and Sharp (2018) and Hass (2020) is to be cautious about only using books that center diverse characters in conflict about injustices. A further concern when selecting books is that they are often set in the past, indicating these issues have been settled and are no longer relevant (Hass, 2020). When I reviewed my book collection, the work I owned heavily focused around past injustices. I have worked to include various books that center and celebrate joy in the everyday experiences of people with diverse backgrounds in my personal library. Each week during the 2022 and 2023 semesters I shared diverse book recommendations, generally focused on positive representations and joy for my students, so they regularly hear about books written by authors they may not be familiar with.

Table 5.3 highlights the readings, in-class work, and project due dates for the 2023 cohort who read Muhammad's (2023) text as a central book to prepare for this project. In class, students engaged in the discussions described above about their favorite texts and book publishing statistics. We viewed Adichie's (2009) TedTalk *The Danger of a Single Story* and engaged in a discussion about how this idea linked to their readings for the week.

In the first week, students worked through a text set of books provided as an example of a book to select and a non-example (see Appendix 5.B). The book sets were focused on Indigenous people. In each set was a book written (and often illustrated) by an Indigenous person and one written by a white person. Groups were given questions to answer about the books such as:

- What qualifies the author or illustrator to deal with the subject?
- If the book is not about people or events similar to the author or illustrator's background, what specifically recommends them as creators of the book?
- What is the author's attitude toward her/his story characters?
- Are the images accurate and do the illustrators respectfully render the people in the story?

After answering the questions, students determined the book that would best fit the parameters of the project. Then they answered questions similar to those posed for the book analysis project focused on the accuracy of the lived experiences in the text, reviewed for stereotypes and misrepresentations, and whether the text provided windows/mirrors for their future students. This element of class mimicked the process they would engage in during the book analysis portion of their assignment and allowed them to hear some feedback in class before writing independently. The next week the analysis portion of their assignment was due.

Table 5.3. Weekly Readings, Experiences, and Assignment Due Dates for Project

	2023 Cohort
Week 1 Readings/Experiences	• Muhammad (2023) • Laminack & Kelly (2019) selection • Miller & Sharp (2018) selection • Bishop (1990) • Social justice standards (Learning for Justice, 2022)
Week 1 In-class Scaffolding	• Adichie (2009) *Danger of a Single Story* • Diverse books discussion • Example/non-example of diverse authors • Book analysis questions
Week 2 Readings/Projects Due	• Muhammad (2023) • Ahiyya (2022) selection • Kleinrock (2021) selection • Book challenge information (i.e., Potter, 2022) • Book Analysis due
Week 2 In-class Scaffolding	• Example lesson plan • Case study – Book challenge • Create lesson plan in Muhammad (2023) format
Week 3 Project Due	• Lesson plan draft due
Week 4 Project Due	• In class presentation of lesson plan (small group) • Feedback provided to peers
Week 5 Project Due	• Reflection on lesson plan due

In the second week focused on this project, the book analysis was submitted, and students read about lesson planning around diverse books and book challenge information. In 2021, attempts to ban books reached their highest point since the American Library

Association began to track challenges 20 years ago (Harris & Alter, 2022). The top 10 books targeted in 2021 focused on Black and LGBTQ+ characters. Preservice teachers may find themselves reluctant to select books that parents or community members may raise concerns about. I felt strongly that I needed to adapt 2023's reading list to include how they can handle attempts to ban books before entering their future classrooms. In class we discussed a case study focused on parents challenging a book and how they could handle a similar situation.

In that same class period, students engaged in my modeled lesson plan using Muhammad's (2023) format featuring the book *We Are Water Protectors* (Lindstrom, 2020). These lesson plans address:

1. Identity: Helping students to make sense of who they are and to learn about diverse cultural lives and identities of others.
2. Skills: Helping students to develop proficiencies across the content areas and state learning standards.
3. Intellect: Helping students to gain new knowledge that connects to the context of the world where they can apply the skills and standards.
4. Criticality: Helping students to name, understand, question, and disrupt oppression (hurt, pain, and harm) in the world and within the self, and to work to make the world a better place.
5. Joy: Helping students to uplift beauty, aesthetics, truth, ease, wonder, wellness, solutions to the problems of the world, and personal fulfillment. Joy is the ultimate goal of teaching and learning, not test prep or gradation (Muhammad, 2023, p. 17).

After observing my model plan, in class they wrote a lesson plan around a diverse book, and I provided feedback to them. In the subsequent weeks, students completed their draft, implemented the lesson plan, provided feedback to their peers, and reflected on their planning/implementation.

Results and Discussion for 2022–2023 Cohorts

Overall, students are successful on this project, earning averages above 26/30 (see Table 5.4). Generally their lesson plans are well prepared and focused on the Social Justice Standards (Learning for Justice, 2022). They are also generally detailed in their feedback to peers (providing both glows and grows) and reflecting on their lesson planning/implementation with detailed commentary.

Table 5.4. 2022–2023 Average Results for Undergraduate and Graduate Cohorts

	Book Analysis (5 points)	Lesson Plan Draft (2 points)	Lesson Plan (6 points)	Lesson Delivery (6 points)	Feedback to Peers (5 points)	Lesson Reflection (6 points)	Total (30 points)
Spring 2022 Undergraduate Cohort (n = 8)	4.63	1.69	5.6	5.31	5	5.5	27.72
Spring 2022 Graduate Cohort (n = 7)	3.86	1.86	5.58	4.79	4.71	5.5	26.29
Spring 2023 Undergraduate Cohort (n = 16)	4.56	1.81	5.6	5.13	4.75	5.86	27.72
Spring 2023 Graduate Cohort (n = 18)	4.61	1.75	5.72	5.42	4.75	5.42	27.67

An area I am hoping to focus on for future growth is in the implementation of the lesson. (Averages range from 4.79–5.42 out of 6 possible points). While I have modeled dialogic discussions, as students presented their lessons there was a great deal of teacher talk and limited dialogue between "students" in the lessons. Based on my review of the data I will focus on this idea and possibly increase the number of weeks for the project so we can directly discuss the importance of open-ended discussion questions for the 2024 cohort.

Table 5.5 notes the scores on the Educating All Students exam for students who completed the pilot versions of the project as well as the 2022 course cohort. The fall 2020 pilot cohort completed student teaching in spring 2021 and the spring 2021 pilot cohort finished student teaching in spring 2022. The course cohort who engaged in the first 30-point version of the assignment just completed student teaching in spring 2023. The most recent cohort who completed this course will student teach in spring 2024 and have not taken the exam yet.

The concerns noted in Table 5.1 from our previous completers have improved in almost all areas for the cohorts after they engaged in this project. There are two cohorts (from the pilot versions of the assignment) who had mean scores in two sub-competency areas below our cut score. Overall I am pleased to see the improvement of these scores from the previous three cohorts of completers in our program and feel the focus on diverse books and social justice in our class discussions have likely helped to increase scores.

Along with my review of the EAS exams, several students provided feedback on this project, 6 months after completing the course. These three comments are all from white, undergraduate students:

> As for the We Need Diverse Book projects, I feel as though it was one of the most applicable and helpful assignments thus far in this program. Being able to examine a variety of books from the lens of a culturally responsive teacher and choose one autonomously was an important takeaway. I feel as though it was a good practice for the future. Combining that with the presentation of a lesson itself was all the more relevant as we prepare to be future teachers in the world of literacy as well.

Another student shared:

> All over social media we see pictures and videos of kids excited over seeing characters that look like them. Images like Chadwick Boseman as Black Panther or Mirabel in Encanto are what children

Table 5.5. Educating All Students: Overall and Sub-Competency Areas, UG and MST Inclusive Childhood 1–6 Student Teachers, 2020–2021, 2021–2022, and 2022–2023

	Overall Score (Mean)	Diverse Student Populations Multiple Choice (Mean)	Diverse Student Populations Constructed Response (Mean)	English Language Learners Multiple Choice (Mean)	English Language Learners Constructed Response (Mean)
UG 2021 (Fall 2020 Pilot) n = 9	539	2.89	2.78	2.55	2.56
MST 2021 (Fall 2020 Pilot) n = 11	534	1.91	2.82	2.72	2.91
UG 2022 (Spring 2021 Pilot) n = 9	534	2.56	2.78	2.33	2.67
MST 2022 (Spring 2021 Pilot) n = 15	537	2.93	2.67	2.6	2.87
UG 2023 (2022 Cohort) n = 6	535	2.5	3	3	2.5
MST 2023 (2022 Cohort) n = 6	542	3	3	2.67	2.67

Note: Criteria mean above 520 (overall) and 2.5 (sub-competency)

connect to. Through this project we are able to introduce children to characters like them, find a connection for them, and just maybe encourage the ability to read with the love to read.

A third student shared:

In my opinion, that was the most engaging and relevant lesson I have done so far. The concept of the lesson was not to teach AT students about incorporating diverse books into the classroom is needed and why rather, I was learning WITH the students about why we should be curious about other cultures and how we can pique that curiosity through books. Additionally, I like how we researched books that had positive diverse themes associated with them instead of negative ones. I think it is important for all students to understand that as students are developing their sense of self-identity in a school setting, they are also working on embracing their culture. Overall, the lesson plan and presentation were beneficial to not only my students but me as well. We all learned the benefits of incorporating books and diversity in the classroom.

These students' comments illustrate the results on the EAS, and I am pleased with how this project has developed and the pedagogical skills we are able to focus on throughout the assignment.

Future Considerations for Continuous Improvement

A point I have noticed in the past 2 years since broadening the book analysis to include traditionally marginalized populations in the United States, along with books focused on global and international perspectives, is my students will often select to use the book set in the United States, for their lesson plan. I will likely revise my assignment parameters to refocus on a text with global and international perspectives beginning in 2024 to refocus on this standard.

My sabbatical project in fall 2023 is to revise our literacy courses for our preservice teachers in grades 7–12. Similar to the scores reported in Table 1 for completers of our elementary programs, our adolescent candidates have similar struggles with the sub-competencies of the EAS exam. I intend to develop a project using Muhammad's (2023) lesson plan format focused on global and international perspectives within their content areas. My 2023 cohort commented that they preferred this lesson plan format, with one White graduate student stating:

I found the overall format of planning to be easier to navigate through, as well as offer a different outlook on the lesson itself. I personally enjoyed the learning goals prompts because they encouraged us to dive a little deeper into the connection between the content and our students.

As a department, the next steps we will need to engage is to follow up with our students during student teaching and after graduation to determine how this course assignment impacted their understanding of global and international perspectives. Further, we will need to see ways they are integrating these ideas into their future classrooms. As of right now, this has not been a consistent focus of our conversations with completers.

Appendix

Appendix 5.A. Assignment Rubric

Analysis of Bias/Stereotypes (5 points) **AAQEP Standards 1c & 2d**	Books are appropriate for use in a read aloud to develop "mirrors" for students to see themselves in texts OR "windows" into others' experiences and perspectives. Book avoids bias/stereotypes and shows new perspectives/experiences to students. Analysis is clear and detailed. **(4–5 points)**	Books are mostly appropriate for a read aloud for developing "mirrors" for students to see themselves in text OR "windows" into others' experiences and perspectives. Book generally avoids bias/stereotypes and shows new perspectives/experiences to students. Analysis provides information but is lacking details. **(1–3 points)**	Book is not appropriate for read aloud to develop "windows" into others' experiences and perspectives. Does not avoid bias/stereotypes. Details are lacking in description. **(0 points)**
Draft of Lesson Plan (2 points) **AAQEP Standards 1a, 1c, 1d & 1e**	Draft is fully complete, materials provided, and submitted on time. Provides clear details and plans. **(2 points)**	Draft is incomplete (missing multiple parts) but submitted on time. Materials may not be submitted. Some details are unclear. **(1 point)**	Draft is not submitted or is submitted late. **(0 points)**
Lesson Plan (6 points) **AAQEP Standards 1a, 1c, 1d & 1e**	Each portion of lesson plan has detailed thoughts to prepare for giving the lesson. Plans for the lesson engage students in discussion and activities with detailed explanation. **(5–6 points)**	Portions of the lesson plan may be lacking detail or information and may need clarity for an outside reader to understand the lesson. **(1–4 points)**	Multiple portions of the lesson plan are missing or incomplete. It would be difficult for someone else to implement the lesson plan based on the provided details. **(0 points)**

Lesson Plan Delivery (6 points) AAQEP Standards 1a, 1c, 1d & 1e	Delivery engages peers throughout and focuses on social justice standards and exploring the topic through the read aloud. Submitted copies of student work. **(5–6 points)**	Delivery engages peers at times, other times is focused on teacher talk only. Mostly focused on social justice and exploring the topic. Peers are engaged in discussion or activity during some of the lesson. May not have submitted copies of student work. **(1–4 points)**	Delivery rarely engages peers and is mostly teacher talk. May focus on social justice but does not engage peers in discussion or activity for the majority of the lesson. Did not submit copies of student work. **(0 points)**
Feedback to Peers (5 points) AAQEP Standards 1a, 1c, & 1f	Provides detailed feedback to each group member on his or her presentation, both on areas of strength and development. These can include comments on pedagogical methods or implementation. **(4–5 points)**	Provides a few key points of feedback to each group member on his or her presentation, both on areas of strength and development. These can include comments on pedagogical methods or implementation. Lack of details or information provided. **(1–3 points)**	No feedback provided to peers. **(0 points)**
Lesson Plan Reflection (6 points) AAQEP Standards 1a, 1c, 1d, 1e, & 1f	Each prompt answers all portions of question with clear and accurate details. Thoughtful analysis of teaching provided, not just describing the moment. **(5–6 points)**	Some prompts are answered with details and responses to each portion of the prompt. Some prompts lacking information or details. Prompt responses describe teaching with no analysis. **(1–4 points)**	No attempt at providing answers to prompts. **(0 points)**

Appendix 5.B. Text Sets

Examples Authors and Illustrator Tribal Affiliation provided when appropriate		Non-examples All books found on Reese & Mendoza's (2022) list for books to avoid about Thanksgiving
Sorell, T. (2022). *Powwow Day*. Charlesbridge.		George, J. C. (1993). *The first Thanksgiving*. Puffin.
Author: Traci Sorell- Cherokee Nation	Illustrator: Madelyn Goodnight- Chickasaw Nation	
Maillard, K. N. (2019). *Fry bread: A Native American family story*. Roaring Books Press.		Melmed, L. K. (2001). *The first Thanksgiving day: A counting story*. Harper Collins.
Author: Kevin Noble Maillard- Seminole Nation	Illustrator: Juana Martinez Neal	
Child, B. J. (2018). *Bowwow powwow*. Minnesota Historical Society press.		Stanley, D. (2004). *Thanksgiving on Plymouth Plantation*. Harper Collins.
Author: Brenda J. Child- Red Lake Ojibwe Ojibwe Translator: Gordon Jourdain- Lac La Croix First Nation	Illustrator: Jonathan Thunder- Red Lake Ojibwe	
Lindstrom, C. (2023). *My powerful hair*. Abrams Books for Young Readers.		Gibbons, G. (2004). *Thanksgiving is . . .* Holiday House.
Author: Carole Lindstrom- Turlte Mountain Band of Ojibwe	Illustrator: Steph Littlebird- Confederated Tribes of Grand Ronde	
Goade, M. (2022). *Berry song*. Little Brown Books for Readers.		Greene, R. G. (2002). *The very first Thanksgiving day*. Atheneum.
Author- Michaela Goade- Tlingit Nation	Illustrator: Michaela Goade- Tlingit Nation	
Harjo (J). (1983/2023). *Remember*. Random House.		Hennessey, B. G. (1999). *One little, two little, three little pilgrims*. Viking.
Author: Joy Harjo- Mvskoke Nation	Illustrator: Michaela Goade- Tlingit Nation	

References

Adichie, C. N. (2009). *The danger of a single story*. [Video]. TedGlobal. https://www. ted.com/talks/chimamanda_ngozi_adichie_the_danger_of_a_single_story/c

Bishop, R. S. (1990). Multicultural literacy: Mirrors, windows, and sliding glass doors. *Perspectives: Choosing and Using Books for the Classroom, 6*(3). https://scenic regional.org/wp-content/uploads/2017/08/Mirrors-Windows-and-Sliding-Glass-Doors.pdf

Cooperative Children's Book Center. (2023, May 4). *Data on books by and about Black, Indigenous and People of Color published for children and teens*. School of Education, University of Wisconsin-Madison. https://ccbc.education.wisc.edu/ literature-resources/ccbc-diversity-statistics/books-by-about-poc-fnn/.

Harris, E. A., & Alter, A., (2022, April 4). *Book banning efforts surged in 2021. These titles were the most targeted*. The New York Times. https://www. nytimes.com/ 2022/04/04/books/banned-books-libraries.html#:~:text=Attempts%20to%20 ban%20books%20in,people%2C%20the%20association%20said.

Hass, C. (2020). *Social justice talk: Strategies for teaching critical awareness*. Heinemann.

Huyck, D., & Dahlen, S. P. (2019, June 19). Diversity in children's books 2018. *Sarah Park*. Created in consultation with Edith Campbell, Molly Beth Griffin, K. T. Horning, Debbie Reese, Ebony Elizabeth Thomas, and Madeline Tyner, with statistics compiled by the Cooperative Children's Book Center, School of Education, University of Wisconsin-Madison: https://ccbc.education.wisc.edu/ literature-resources/ccbc-diversity-statistics/books-by-about-poc-fnn/. Retrieved from https://readingspark.wordpress.com/2019/06/19/picture-this-diversity-in-childrens-books-2018-infographic/.

Kleinrock, L. (2021). *Start here start now: A guide to antibias and antiracist work in your school community*. Heinemann.

Laminack, L., & Kelly, K. (2019). *Reading to make a difference: Using literature to help students speak freely, think deeply, and take action*. Heinemann.

Learning for Justice (2022). *Social justice standards: The Learning for Justice Anti-Bias Framework*. https://www.learningforjustice.org/sites/default/files/2022-09/LFJ-Social-Justice-Standards-September-2022-09292022.pdf

Lindstrom, C. (2020). *We are water protectors*. Roaring Books Press.

Miller, D., & Sharp, C. (2018). *Game changer: Book access for all kids!* Scholastic.

Muhammad, G. (2023). *Unearthing joy: A guide to culturally and historically responsive teaching and learning*. Scholastic.

National Center for Education Statistics. (2020, September). *Race and ethnicity of public school teachers and their students*. Institute of Education Sciences. https://nces.ed.gov/pubs2020/2020103/index.asp

Pearson, P. D., & Gallagher, M. C. (1983). The instruction of reading comprehension. *Contemporary Educational Psychology, 8*(3), 317-344. https://doi.org/10.1016/ 0361-476X(83)90019-X.

Potter, K. (2022, September 8). *7 ways to make a case for a challenges book in the classroom.* Lee and Low Books Blog. https://blog.leeandlow.com/ 2022/09/08/ 7-ways-to-make-a-case-for-a-challenged-book-in-the-classroom/

Reese, D., & Mendoza, J. (2022). *Oyate's list of Thanksgiving books to avoid.* American Indians in Children's Literature. https://americanindiansinchildrens literature.blogspot.com/2014/11/oyates-list-of-thanksgiving-books-to.html

Saad, L. (2020). *Me and white supremacy: Combat racism, change the world, and become a good ancestor.* Sourcebooks.

CHAPTER SIX

Classroom and Behavior Management: A Case Study in Using Data to Revise a Course and Better Prepare Novice Teachers

HEATHER ANN BOWER

Our Context

Chartered in 1891, Meredith College continues to be one of the largest independent private women's colleges in the United States. The mission of the College is to educate and inspire students to live with integrity and provide leadership for the needs, opportunities, and challenges of society. The Meredith College community is dedicated to the specific core values of integrity, intellectual freedom, academic excellence, responsible global citizenship, personal development, religious diversity, and relevance, as it meets "society's needs by educating students in programs that prepare them for the future."

This study focused on the initial licensure portions of our teacher preparation program. At the undergraduate level, teacher education is a professional program, not an academic major; students, faculty, and administration share a campus-wide commitment to teacher preparation. Students pursuing elementary licensure can major in any one of the 40-plus majors offered and complete a professional studies component in the elementary licensure area. Students interested in pursuing middle, secondary, or a K-12 teaching license major in the academic area that is related to their teaching field and supplement that major with the professional studies component. Qualified seniors who are interested in pursuing a teaching license in special education, English as a Second Language, or elementary education can take up to two specified graduate courses in the Master of Arts in Teaching (MAT) during their senior year and then transition into the full MAT program the following year.

At the graduate level, Meredith College offers the MAT in three specialty areas: elementary education, English as a second language, and special education (general curriculum). The MAT program was developed in response to North Carolina's need for teachers in 2008. The MAT program has been successful in preparing committed adults with little or no background in the education profession to be full-time teachers in North Carolina.

All education faculty teach at both the undergraduate and graduate level. Furthermore, no one faculty member "owns" any course. All major curriculum decisions or course revisions are decided by the consensus of the department based on numerous data sources, including faculty observations, exit surveys, completer surveys, student teaching data, and feedback gathered from cooperating teachers and school administrators.

Initial Data

All of the department's data are reviewed each fall at the department's opening retreat. At the fall 2019 retreat, classroom and behavior management was a consistent relative concern across all data sources. While some of this data are to be expected, such as at the midpoint of the student teacher semester, others were more concerning. Both exit surveys, which are utilized at the end of the student teaching semester, and completer surveys, which are utilized in September of students' second and fourth years in the classroom, indicated that students felt unprepared to establish routines and procedures and manage problem behavior.

Informal data also pointed towards this concern. At each meeting of the department's Teacher Education Committee, which is comprised of faculty, candidates, completers, and PK-12 partners, the final item on the agenda is "Notes from the Field," which is an opportunity for stakeholders to share what they are seeing in their classrooms and schools. Classroom and behavior management was consistently named as a struggle for beginning teachers.

All of these data were particularly concerning because students take a classroom and behavior management course during their student teaching semester. For undergraduates, it is a focus of their student teaching seminar. MAT students take an entire stand-alone course on classroom and behavior management. Furthermore, classroom and behavior management objectives are woven into introductory and methods courses at both levels.

Based on these preliminary data, the department realized a more thorough exploration of the problem was necessary.

Creating and Conducting the Case Study

Two faculty designed and implemented a case study to develop an understanding of the perceived needs of beginning teachers (BTs) in regards to classroom and behavior management from the perspectives of administrators, BT coordinators, experienced teachers, and BTs themselves. The key research questions were

- What skills do beginning teachers bring to the classroom in regard to classroom and behavior management?
- What skills do they lack?
- How can these perceptions inform our teacher education program?

A semi-structured interview protocol was developed for phone interviews.

- What strengths do beginning teachers bring to classroom management?
- What challenges do beginning teachers face in terms of classroom management?
- What recommendations do you have for our program regarding classroom management?
- What strengths do beginning teachers bring to behavior management?
- What challenges do beginning teachers face in terms of behavior management?

- What recommendations do you have for our program regarding classroom management
- Is there anything else you would like to tell us?

At the beginning of these interviews, the researchers defined classroom management as the routines, procedures, and norms that guide a classroom to maximize learning and ensure a safe and equitable environment. Behavior management was defined as how teachers prevent, respond to, and shift problematic behavior for individual students.

Once the protocols were defined, the entire faculty brainstormed a list of 75 administrators, beginning teachers, and experienced teachers who had unique experiences with classroom and behavior management. Some of these potential participants had previously shared challenges or successes. Some had been observed and were considered master teachers or administrators in the area *or* were known to have struggled with one or both of these areas. Some were BT coordinators or coaches who had a unique perspective on the lived experiences of BTs in the classroom.

Twenty-seven participants from eight districts participated in phone interviews with one of the researchers. The participant pool was equally balanced among the three roles and building levels (elementary, middle, and high). These interviews were recorded and transcribed verbatim.

Analyzing the Data

Once all of the data were collected, the primary researchers read the responses by question. Observations that appeared three times or more across subgroups were considered salient themes and brought forward to the department for discussion.

Classroom Management Themes

Strengths of Beginning Teachers

Beginning teachers brought significant strengths to classroom management. All types of participants (administrators, experienced teachers, and BTs) articulated that BTs have a keen awareness of the need for routines, procedures, and participation protocols. Administrators and experienced teachers also commented that BTs brought excitement and thoughtfulness about setting up the physical space as well as an awareness of the significance of building relationships. Administrators also noted that BTs had an open-mindedness to new ideas and strategies—often more so than more experienced teachers. This awareness and foundation knowledge allows BTs to enter the classroom prepared for a strong beginning with their students.

Challenges for Beginning Teachers

Although BTs had some strengths in classroom management, several significant challenges were noted. All participant types noted that BTs often struggle to find their teacher identity and voice, often wavering between being too nice/too firm or too fun/all business. Similarly, they often struggle with finding the right systems and procedures for their students, either changing too quickly or holding on too long. Experienced teachers and administrators noted that BTs often rush establishing classroom management and norms to delve into the curriculum; they also wait too long to ask for help from mentor teachers or administrators when classroom management systems are not working. BTs noted that the lack of a cooperating teacher to receive consistent feedback from resulted in a lack of confidence in their ability and decisions. Administrators also noted that our program completers specifically come in very focused on one system of classroom management that had been stressed in their classroom management course; however, very few schools in the area were implementing that model.

Behavior Management Themes

Strengths of Beginning Teachers

Administrators and experienced teachers noted several strengths of beginning teachers in relation to behavior management. BTs reflect the overarching shift in perspective from negative approaches to behavior management towards conscious discipline, restorative justice, and assets-based approaches to behavior management. They also tend to implement school-wide systems with higher fidelity than more experienced teachers. BTs believed they capitalize on their relationship with students and have personal conversations with students to understand the why of the behavior. This asset- and relationship-based approach allowed BTs to stay more positive toward all students and persevere in the face of challenges.

Challenges for Beginning Teachers

All participant groups thought behavior management, in general, was the largest struggle BTs face. Primarily, BTs struggle with consistency, finding their authority, and lack of confidence to fol- low through on consequences. Furthermore, they also tend to not ask for help quickly enough—especially in the face of trauma and extreme behavior. They are slow to enlist family support due to fear over their reactions, and they often think the behaviors are intracta- ble and they just have to "cope."

Making Data-Informed Decisions

The themes discussed above were compiled by the two researchers, and a series of suggestions for the classroom management courses and the program as a whole were put forward to the department.

The classroom and behavior management courses were com- pletely redesigned. Rather than emphasizing a specific model, the course now provides an overview of all models currently being used in the area and emerging trends in best practice. Students analyze the strengths and challenges of each model and then analyze what their student teaching placement site utilizes both as a whole school and in their individual classroom. The course also provides readings and discussions about engaging families, partnering with admin- istrators, and specific tools for addressing problematic behavior. This work culminates in students completing a functional behav- ior assessment for an individual student in their student teaching classroom.

Suggestions for the duration of the entire programs are outlined in the change charts below; numbers are specific courses in the pro- gram. These changes were proposed by the researchers and then vet- ted and supported by the entire faculty and the Teacher Education Committee.

Table 6.1. Undergraduate Change Chart

Throughout	During Internship
Every course: Classroom and Behavior Management Observation Protocol Tool	*Review collection of protocol tools to see trends and strategies*
234: Learning Environments—Intro current frameworks (conscious discipline, restorative justice, trauma-informed teaching)	*Use real case studies from our grads: what happened, what they did, what they wish they did*
232: Culture—Culturally sustaining pedagogy as classroom management; In-equity in terms of response to behavior	*During the first week, use of protocol tool in student teaching classroom*
All Other Courses: Debriefing protocol tool in light of specific methods and content areas	FBA of a focus student (maybe one of the focal students for the PPAT)
	Mock conferences and phone calls

Table 6.2. MAT Change Chart

Throughout	During Internship
Every course: Classroom and Behavior Management Observation Protocol Tool	*Review collection of protocol tools to see trends and strategies*
700: Learning Environments—Intro current frameworks (conscious discipline, restorative justice, trauma-informed teaching)	*Use real case studies from our grads: what happened, what they did, what they wish they did*
700: Culture—Culturally sustaining pedagogy as classroom management; In-equity in terms of response to behavior	*During the first week, use of protocol tool in student teaching classroom*
All Other Courses: Debriefing protocol tool in light of specific methods and content areas	FBA of a focus student (maybe one of the focal students for the PPAT)
	Mock conferences and phone calls

The department is still in the process of implementing the changes that are italicized in the change charts—largely because the study was completed just before the outbreak of the COVID-19 pandemic. While the course revisions were easy for individual instructors to implement in the 2020–2021 and refine in the 2022–2023 academic years, the changes across the entire program were tabled due to time and energy constraints. The program will continue to implement these changes in the 2023–2024 academic year.

Most Recent Data

Even though the changes have not been fully implemented, data demonstrate the changes that have been implemented have been successful. Classroom and behavior management have not surfaced as areas of concern in the past two cycles of exit and completer surveys. PK-12 partners have also expressed a noticeable shift in our completers approach and confidence in both areas. Completers have more specific tools to address behaviors when they arise, and they are better able to analyze the "why" of the behavior to prevent further instances. Furthermore, completers are less hesitant to ask for assistance or share concerns early instead of waiting for behaviors to escalate to dangerous levels.

Final Thoughts

While this particular study led to changes in specific courses and a thread throughout the program, the process utilized can be a model of data-based decision-making.

First and foremost, a culture of continuous improvement and data analysis is critical. The initial data scores were all between 3 and 3.5 on a 4 point scale, but the target is 3.6 on each of these scales. Rather than "settling" for scores above 3.0, the higher threshold challenges the program and individual faculty to reflect and fine-tune in order to produce highly qualified and well-prepared teachers.

Second, survey data is just a starting point. It was only by delving into the secondary study and having focused conversations with stakeholders that a clear picture of the problem emerged. It is also critical that the entire faculty is involved in the analysis of data and development of a plan—even if the study is conducted by a subset of faculty. Implementing change is significantly easier if all stakeholders have a thorough understanding of the data and a voice in the planning.

Third, not all change has to occur simultaneously. While the revisions outlined above could certainly all be implemented in a year, going slow to go fast is often a wise strategy. Rather than pressing ahead when faculty focus and energy must be concentrated on an emerging situation, waiting so that the revision can be implemented well results in higher quality programs. The change charts help the department track implementation and increase accountability for change over time. Implementing change in smaller segments also allows better connecting of outcome data to discrete changes.

Finally, the cycle is continuous. Survey data and Teacher Education Committee feedback will still be collected about behavior and classroom management. Revision is not the end; it is just a new beginning.

CHAPTER SEVEN

Continuous Program Improvement through an Integrated Student Support System

HOPE G. CASTO AND VIRGINIA R. LEE

Introduction

This chapter tells the story of the creation of an application process for students to enter the certification program in an undergraduate teacher education program at a small liberal arts college. We offer this story as an example of how a shift from a compliance-based approach to accreditation to a process of data analysis for continuous improvement has returned agency to program faculty. In addition, we describe how the development of the application process rooted in our program's mission statement became the centerpiece to an integrated and program-wide student support system. For faculty, this process has been reflective and recursive as we led with individual student stories and progressed to cohort-level analyses to understand student experiences within the program context. We mirrored this process by creating an application process that would allow students a reflective moment as they decide to commit to the teacher education program. Similarly, the development and use of a professional dispositions assessment tool has created the opportunity for faculty and students alike to grow and learn. In particular, we found that through this process, faculty have demonstrated professional dispositions in our programmatic stance toward accreditation and continuous improvement. In these ways, faculty's work in the accreditation process of using data analysis for continuous improvement mirrors the multifaceted and integrated student support system within the teacher education program.

Context: Skidmore College's Education Studies Department

Skidmore College is a small, liberal arts college in upstate New York. The average enrollment is 2,700, including students from across the country and the world. Skidmore's traditional liberal arts disciplines (40+ departments and programs) are enhanced by preprofessional programs, including a teacher education program. Although a small proportion of the teacher education programs in the United States are in liberal arts colleges, these programs play an important role in educating preservice teachers in intellectually rigorous environments to be well-prepared professionals for today's schools (Bjork et al., 2007; Mule, 2010). The principle-based approach in liberal arts colleges (LaBoskey & Kroll, 2007) is evident in our college's mission of creative, inclusive, multifaceted, and engaging education (see the inner ring in Figure 7.1).

The Education Studies Department at Skidmore College prepares undergraduate students to become elementary teachers with initial certification (grades 1-6) in New York State. The department graduates an average of 15 students each year. As described in this chapter, most of these students complete the teacher education program, while a smaller group elect or are counseled to complete a non-certification major. The program's mission statement describes the program's commitments to constructivist pedagogies and social justice in schooling. The mission statement is aligned with professional standards, New York State expectations, and the accreditation agency, AAQEP's standards. Figure 7.1 illustrates the essential aspects of the program mission, and the complete mission statement can be found at https://www.skidmore.edu/education_studies/mission statement.php.

Our Story: The Creation and Revision of a Certification Program Application

We start our story about the creation of an integrated student support system, by sharing three students' stories. These stories created

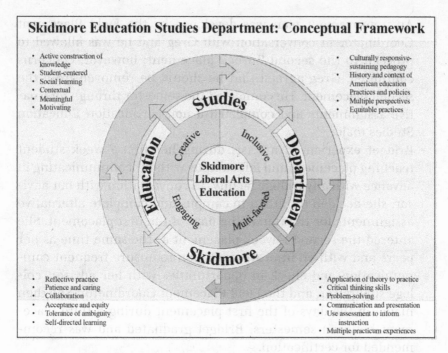

Figure 7.1. Skidmore Education Studies Department: Conceptual Framework.

a sense of concern among faculty. It was these stories, in combination with a need to revise a compliance-driven application process, that led to what has become an integrated student support system. The stories of these three students motivated conversation among program faculty about the ways in which the program welcomed students into the teacher certification program, created a moment for students to reflect on their commitment to the field of elementary school teaching, and offered a structured support system for students as they progress through the program.

- Greg (all student names are pseudonyms) entered the student teaching semester with a passion and commitment to teaching, or at least to working with children. Through his first 7-week placement, he had conversations with his cooperating teacher, college supervisor, and the Field Placement Coordinator due to concerns around timeliness, the enactment of high-quality teaching, and the maturity and professionalism needed for success.

An improvement plan was developed by the Field Placement Coordinator in conversation with Greg and he was allowed to proceed to the second 7-week placement; however, concerns continued. Greg agreed that he should be removed from the second placement. He completed the semester through alternative assignments and completed a non-certification Education Studies major.

- Bridget experienced a crisis during her first 7-week student teaching placement and left campus without communicating in advance with any college faculty. In conversation with her advisor, she decided to return to campus and complete alternative assignments for the remaining days of the first placement. She entered the second 7-week placement at the same time as her peers and with an improvement plan to ensure frequent communication and check-in opportunities with her advisor, college supervisor, and the Field Placement Coordinator. She then made up the days of the first placement during a third placement between semesters. Bridget graduated and was recommended for certification.

- Howard experienced common challenges during his first 7-week student teaching placement and was placed on an improvement plan focused on timeliness, complete and detailed lesson plans, and evidence of the use of feedback from the college supervisor and cooperating teacher. Howard continued to his second 7-week placement with a different college supervisor and a different cooperating teacher. Although everyone involved was made aware of the challenges during the first placement, no additional concerns were raised during the second placement. Howard graduated and was recommended for certification. However, in analysis conducted after the fact, it became obvious that Howard's average score on the Student Teaching Evaluation Tool (STET) from the end of his second placement was lower in each of the six domains than the cohort average (see Table 7.1).

The department was left with these concerns and questions:

1. How can the program better support students in their process of making a decision to enter a teacher certification program?

Table 7.1. Final STET (Student Teaching Evaluation Tool) Ratings: Comparing Howard to Cohort

STET Domain	Final STET Rating Domain Average: Howard	Final STET Rating Domain Average: Cohort
1: Knowledge and Application: Knowledge of Learner and Content	2.83	2.93
2: Planning & Preparation for Learning	2.5	2.93
3: Delivery of Instruction	2.44	2.91
4: Student Assessment & Data-Informed Decision Making	2.25	2.89
5: Learning Environment	2.0	2.87
6: Professionalism	2.64	2.95

2. How can the program ensure that the students who are admitted are ready and supported to face the challenges and opportunities, as well as the expectations and responsibilities of a teacher education program and elementary classroom placements?

While we had created the application to the certification program due to the requirements of our accrediting agency at the time, we took the opportunity to refine this process so it could meet the needs of students and the program.

Creating the application process

The department created an application to the certification track distinct from the college-wide declaration of the major process. The timing of these two events was separated with the major declaration occurring in the spring of the students' sophomore year (the same timing for all majors across the college) and the application to the certification track occurring in the fall of the students' junior year. Among other reasons, this delay in the application moment allowed for the grades from the second semester of the sophomore year and midterm teacher evaluations from the students' first classroom placement in the college's laboratory school to be considered with the application materials. This timing allowed for students to reflect on their decision to pursue teacher certification separate from the pressure to declare a major and with the knowledge and experience gained from a few weeks of their first classroom placement.

This application process involves students submitting an essay on their commitment to teaching in connection to the department's Mission Statement and a resumé. In addition, the materials include a faculty disposition assessment, the student's disposition self-assessment, the student's Early Childhood Center (ECC) placement teacher's evaluation, and the student's transcript. Students are admitted or conditionally admitted to the certification track. While the department's goal is not to deny admission, the admission to the certification track process has created the space for reflection on the part of candidates and advising conversations that can lead to a candidate's decision not to apply. Continued monitoring of students' progress occurs through grades in EDS required coursework, disposition assessments, student support meetings among faculty, advising meetings between advisors and students, office hour meetings between students and instructors of EDS courses, and the use of Academic Alerts issued by faculty for students who fail to attend class or who submit coursework that fails to meet expectations (see Figure 7.2).

Implementing the application process: Year 1

In the first year of the new application process, the department faculty divided up the students' materials with two faculty reviewing each student's application, met to discuss the applications, and decided which students would be admitted with no reservations and which would be admitted with conditions. The department chair sent acceptance letters to all students, and for those who were admitted with conditions the letter included information regarding each area where it was determined that support may be needed. As noted by a faculty member when we brought the process to our Advisory Council for feedback, some of these letters were quite long! The department had not carefully considered how best to convey a conditional admission to a student. Part of this communication

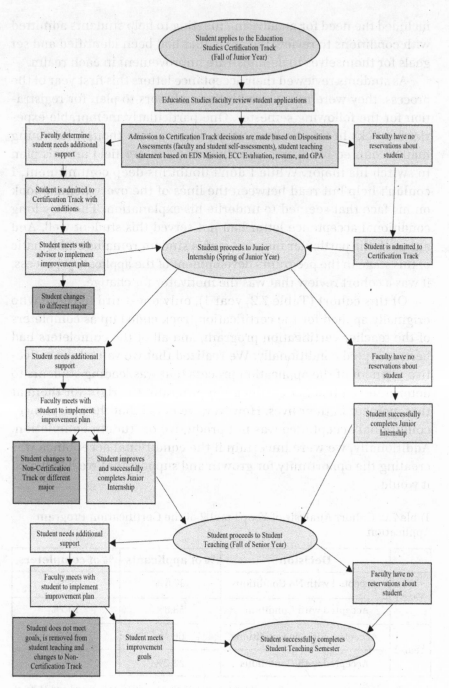

Figure 7.2. Pathways in the Multifaceted Student Support System.

included the need for an advising meeting to help students admitted with conditions to review the areas that had been identified and set goals for themselves to demonstrate improvement in each realm.

As students reviewed their acceptance letters this first year of the process, they were meeting with their advisors to plan for registration for the following semester. One particularly memorable experience sticks in this author's mind, when a very thoughtful young man recounted his deep commitment to another field and his plan to switch his major. While I don't doubt his deep commitment, I couldn't help but read between the lines of the overwhelmed look on his face that seemed to underlie his explanation. The very long conditional acceptance letter had not served this student well. And although the particular moment with a student remains emblematic of this stage in the program's development of the application process, it was a cohort review that was the motivator for change.

Of this cohort (Table 7.2, year 1), only one-third of those who originally applied for the certification track ended up as completers of the teacher certification program, and all of the completers had been accepted conditionally. We realized that we valued the reflective moment of the application process that was leading students to determine if a teacher certification program was right for them at that moment in their lives. However, we noted that the acceptance/conditional acceptance was not predictive of student completion. Additionally, we were uncertain if the conditional acceptance was creating the opportunity for growth and support that we had hoped it would.

Table 7.2. Cohort Analysis of Year 1 and 2 of the Certification Program Application

	Decision	**% of applicants**	**% of completers**
Year 1	Accepted with No Conditions	17.6%	0%
	Accepted with Conditions	58.8%	100%
Year 2	Accepted with No Conditions	66.7%	100%
	Accepted with Conditions	22.2%	0%

Note: These percentages do not sum to 100% because 23.5% of applicants in Year 1 and 11.1% of applications in Year 2 did not complete the application process or were denied admission.

Learning from Year 1: Year 2 of the application process and program improvements

In the following year (Table 2, year 2), we maintained the same review process for students; however, we accepted a greater proportion of students without reservations. This likely was the result of a number of changes and contextual factors. It could be that it was a stronger cohort of students. However, the program also improved the communication with students by clarifying the instructions with the application materials and hosting an information session on the application process. In addition, the program informed students of the professional dispositions earlier by including a description of the dispositions in the syllabi of required courses and by posting the dispositions in large format on the walls of the college classroom where Education Studies classes are held, which could allow faculty to reference and hold discussions of the dispositions in the context of the college course content. Due to it being the second year of the application process, it was also likely a more honed review process since faculty were more familiar with the application materials and the disposition instrument.

The development and improvement of the application process has led to the following program improvements:

- Increased faculty agency. Adapting what began as a program application created due to accreditation requirements allowed faculty to take ownership over the process and make the application useful for students and the program. This increased faculty agency and was an overall improvement for the program.
- A reflective moment for students. The design of the application process allows students time to reflect on their commitment to teacher education. It aids in their understanding of the expectations of teacher certification and offers a chance to see themselves in the work of elementary teaching.
- Learning about students. Advisors and supervisors have the chance to learn about students through the application process and offer targeted support throughout students' college coursework and classroom placements.

- Unity and coherence through faculty conversation. The application process and resulting integrated support systems create opportunities for enhanced faculty conversation on the topic of our most shared commitment: our students. The integrated student support system brings out the shared commitment to preservice teachers in our teacher education program. This coherence is essential for program improvement.

Implications for Other Programs in Other Contexts

This process of continuous improvement through the implementation, reflection, and revision of an application process to the certification track has benefited our program, our students, and our P-12 partners. While some characteristics of this process are specific to our context, there are several key takeaways that could benefit other teacher education programs as they engage in this ongoing work. We learned that maintaining a focus on program improvement and quality, rather than compliance, is the key factor, and one that may need to be brought to the forefront throughout the self-study process. When considering programmatic improvement, a compliance mentality is misguided and can derail the self-study within the program's unique context. Instead, a strengths-based approach to program needs can position programs to address areas for improvement with agency. There are many ways to accomplish these types of collaborations for continuous improvement, but here are some examples.

- Create an application to the certification process in the semester following the declaration of major in order to provide an additional point of reflection for students. This process directs students to take the time to focus their attention specifically on the expectations of the teaching profession, and to determine their commitment to a teacher education program. Students submit an essay highlighting their commitment to teaching in connection to the department's Mission Statement, and they submit a resume highlighting their past job experiences and responsibilities. As part of this application process, students complete a self-assessment of their own professional dispositions and faculty complete disposition assessments for each of the applicants. Each of these components is reviewed by faculty, along with the students' Early Childhood Center (ECC) evaluations and transcripts, during the fall of the students' junior year. This gives students an additional summer and another semester to consider the expectations of the Education Studies major and the certification track. Long-held beliefs have viewed the early declaration of a college major with student persistence and on-time graduation; however, recent findings have dispelled this myth (Spight, 2020), leading to an understanding of the importance of allowing students time to consider and explore their interests prior to an academic commitment, so this extra time is important.

- Conduct regular student support meetings among faculty as an aspect of the multifaceted ways we support teacher candidates. Our student support meetings began as conversations during regular department meetings centered around students in their placements who were struggling and could benefit from additional support; however, as we developed the application process, we became increasingly aware that support could and should begin prior to entering the certification track, while students are completing their education courses. Eventually faculty determined that separate student support meetings focused solely on our struggling students would improve the ways that we could support them both in the college classroom as well as in their placement classrooms. These regularly scheduled meetings in addition to the use of the disposition form at other times (Disposition Concern Form) allowed us to discuss shared or differing perspectives on students across the program. Students who are struggling in education courses, internship, or student teaching placements can be discussed in order to obtain multiple perspectives and to brainstorm support opportunities for those in need of them. Following each student support meeting, for any student who may be in need of support the student's advisors and/or course instructors can meet with them to incorporate their perspectives as they make plans for improvement and support.

- Have a comprehensive program mission statement and refer back to this often when designing processes and choosing or designing measurement tools. This is not to say that programs determine their own standards, but rather that they approach the professional standards with well-founded programmatic goals and values informing the decisions and practices of the teacher preparation program at each juncture. Practices such as these have been described as having:

  > . . . *coherence around a vision of practice grounded in what we know about deeper learning and productive development; modeling of powerful teaching practices in university coursework, along with the provision of concrete strategies and tools for practice; demonstrated connections between theory and practice and between coursework and clinical work; extended, well-planned, carefully supervised clinical training in sites that also instantiate these practices.* (Darling-Hammond, 2020, p. 65)

  As we designed our application process, we determined that a focus on our mission was relevant and important, so as part of the application, students reflect on the Education Studies Department Mission Statement as they write an essay about their personal commitment to the teaching profession. Our mission incorporates aspects of pedagogical and content knowledge, as well as themes of inclusive teaching, reflective practitioners, constructivism, and the social context of education.
- Incorporate instruments that are designed to be completed from multiple perspectives. For example, as part of our admission to the certification process, dispositions surveys are completed by faculty as well as by the students themselves. Additionally, our laboratory school teachers complete evaluations of candidates' in their placement classrooms. These varied perspectives provide opportunities for faculty discussion as well as educative moments of self-reflection for the students as they begin to consider the ways they will develop and enact the professional behaviors of a teacher. Additionally, the multiple perspectives provide points of discussion and potential areas for targeted support when they do not align with one another.

- Consider data at different units of analysis. While individual student's stories and experiences can be an excellent source of ideas for program improvement, data analysis at the cohort level and over time can lead to data-informed decision-making for continuous improvement. In addition, a balance between individual student experiences and cohort-level analyses can be found in disaggregated data analysis. This allows programs to consider the experiences and success of students of varied social identities including gender, race and ethnicity, nationality, language background, and first-generation college student status. Even in programs with small cohort sizes like ours, faculty can look for patterns in disaggregated data over time.
- Organize collaborative opportunities such as an advisory board to meet with P-12 partners, current students, alumni, and local district parents to discuss and get feedback on program policies, instruments, processes, and challenges. This feedback can be used to inform programmatic improvements. Our Advisory Board reviewed our application process and provided feedback and suggestions. They have also reviewed some of our assessment instruments and have given us guidance and suggestions for their use. The accreditation process can be especially fruitful when collaboration is valued as a component of "democratic accountability," founded on discussions and participation of multiple perspectives of the varied stakeholders involved in teacher education (Cochran-Smith et al., 2018). Such discussions are rich and resourceful when the voices of faculty are joined by P-12 teachers and administrators, the teacher candidates themselves, external reviewers, program graduates, and employers of program graduates. The process can be enhanced by regular, organized meetings of group of programs who share ideas, successes, and questions to tackle together.

Conclusion

Self-study is an important inquiry-based process that tells your story as a teacher education program. But what is your story? How do you tell it? Our most recent self-study has highlighted the ways that this

is a recursive process, beginning with a well-articulated programmatic mission statement that is aligned with the values and expectations of the profession. Who are you as a program? What are your
theoretical underpinnings? What are your core values? Collaborating
with faculty to create a comprehensive mission statement can serve
as a firm foundation for future decisions, such as which instruments
and data will best inform your path forward. For example, does this
instrument measure what we know to be valuable and useful skills
or behaviors for teaching? Another key question is, who are your
students? What can you know about them as individuals? What can
you know about them as cohort groups? Data collection and analysis
play important roles in these understandings, along with personal
connections and voices from multiple perspectives. Once you know
who you are as a program, and know who your students are, you are
in a position to determine which instructional and programmatic
processes align. An important question at this juncture is, how can
you use data to inform programmatic decisions and to determine
competency of your completers? What can data tell you about your
students, your faculty, and your instructional sequence? How can
data help you understand competencies as aligned with the core values of the profession and of your program? Each of these questions
points us back to who we are as a program, and who our students
are. This cycle of inquiry is the basis for continuous improvement.

The process of creating an application to the teacher certification program has played a significant role in our understanding,
reflecting, and shifting our practices to improve our own teacher
education program. Originally this process was implemented from a
standpoint of compliance; however, after having shifted to a standpoint of quality and program improvement, this process has enabled
us to use this application process as a means for reflection and
growth. The application process, as it relates to program improvement, is both implicit and explicit. Implicitly, it is a manifestation of
the dispositional stance we encourage among our own students of
being reflective practitioners, identifying areas for personal growth,
implementing feedback, and taking intellectual risks by trying out
thoughts and ideas. Explicitly, this process has provided us with data
to inform our support and guidance of students.

By shifting our attitude toward program accreditation from a compliance-based approach to one of data analysis for the purpose continuous improvement has improved the experiences of faculty and students alike. It has allowed us to explore our own story and lead our program improvement efforts from a place of examining our strengths. We have taken what began as a compliance-motivated application process and revised it through reflective and recursive work to make it a centerpiece of a multifaceted student support system. We have created a reflective moment for students to better understand their own commitment to a teacher education program. Through these practices we have honed our understanding of our program's commitments and better conveyed these to students. In these ways, we have better articulated who we want to include in the program and designed a system to support them. While there are many opportunities for data-informed decision-making in our program, we have highlighted how a cohort-level analysis of the application process in connection to who completes the program shed light on how our application process was working (or not) as we revised it in years one and two of the implementation. Overall, this chapter elucidates the ways in which faculty's work in the accreditation process mirrors our work with students. Through our programmatic stance toward accreditation and continuous improvement we have engaged in three of our professional dispositions that we have articulated for our students: (1) identifies areas for personal growth; (2) willingly accepts and implements feedback; and (3) takes intellectual risks by trying out thoughts and ideas. By modeling these practices in our work, we can coach and support students to meet with success through enacting these same professional behaviors.

References

Bjork, C., Johnston, D. K., & Ross, H. (Eds.) (2007) *Taking teaching seriously: How liberal arts colleges prepare teachers to meet today's educational challenges in schools*. Paradigm Press.

Cochran-Smith, M. (2021). Rethinking teacher education: The trouble with accountability. *Oxford Review of Education, 47*(1), 8–24. https://doi.org.lib-proxy01.skidmore.edu/10.1080/03054985.2020.1842181

Cochran-Smith, M., Carney, M., Keefe, E. S., Burton, S., Chang, W. C., Fernández, M. B., Miller, A. F., Sánchez, J. G., & Baker, M. (2018). *Reclaiming accountability in teacher education.* Teachers College Press.

Darling-Hammond, L. (2020). Accountability in teacher education. *Action in Teacher Education (Routledge), 42*(1), 60–71. https://doi.org.lib-proxy01.skidmore.edu/1 0.1080/01626620.2019.1704464

LaBoskey, V. K. & Kroll, L. R. (2007). Principles-based teacher education: A liberal arts contribution. In C. Bjork, D. K. Johnston, & H. Ross (Eds.) *Taking teaching seriously: How liberal arts colleges prepare teachers to meet today's educational challenges in schools* (pp. 119–131). Paradigm Press.

Mule, L. W. (2010). *Teacher education, diversity, and community engagement in liberal arts colleges.* Lexington Books.

Spight, D. B. (2020). Early declaration of a college major and its relationship to persistence. *NACADA Journal, 40*(1), 94–109.

CHAPTER EIGHT

Developing a Five-Layer Dispositional Assessment System in a School of Education

VINCENT GENAREO

In teacher education programs, monitoring and developing candidates' professional dispositional factors, such as beliefs, values, and attitudes, can improve program and teacher quality (Martin et al., 2013). If assessed correctly, these data provide valuable insights into factors associated with teacher candidates' potential for classroom teaching success, including cognitive and affective characteristics, strengths, and areas for growth. Education programs should use dispositional data to identify potential issues throughout the program that can lead to targeted candidate or program interventions and support, when needed. For example, if a teacher candidate exhibits questionable attitudes toward a particular group of students, philosophical approaches, or pedagogies, these might be addressed through specific curricular or pedagogical modifications, through reflective clinical experiences, or through conversations or coaching. Additionally, monitoring dispositional data can help teacher education programs identify candidates who may not be a good fit for the profession, which can lead to better outcomes for both teachers and students (Martin et al., 2013), or it can identify particular strengths of programming on attitudes, behaviors, and beliefs.

A dispositional data system designed for program improvement requires a commitment to ongoing data monitoring across various levels and through the perspectives of multiple stakeholders. It requires dedicated, consistent efforts to collect, track, and share results. This chapter will present the Five-Layer Dispositional Assessment System used for monitoring, reporting, and program improvement at Salisbury University. The system being discussed was developed based on the needs of multiple program types and partially in response to post-COVID-19 challenges.

University Context

Salisbury University enrolls approximately 7,000 students, of which about 6,200 are undergraduates. It is positioned on the Eastern Shore of Maryland in Salisbury, part of the Delmarva (Delaware-Maryland-Virginia) Peninsula. Salisbury University's Seidel School of Education contains four departments that offer undergraduate and graduate degrees in education and educational leadership fields. As of 2022, the School of Education enrolled over 800 students across programs. About 630 students were undergraduates, over 120 were master's-level, over 40 were Doctor of Education students, and the rest were post-master's or postgraduate certificate students. All initial licensure programs and two advanced programs offered through the Seidel School of Education are accredited by AAQEP. Each of these, in addition to the other programs not accredited by AAQEP, needed assessment systems revised to monitor candidate dispositions and make program improvements, particularly in relation to AAQEP Aspect 1f, which asks for evidence of student dispositional data. Faculty and staff on the School Assessment Committee and Dean's Office were committed to identifying best dispositional data practices and building those into the School of Education data system.

Types of Dispositional Data

Three types of dispositional data are typically collected by teacher preparation programs: self-report measures, observational data, and performance-based assessments (Drucker, 2013). Self-report measures rely on candidates' evaluations of their personal and professional attributes, including motivation, communication skills, and cultural responsiveness. Observational data are collected by observing candidates' interactions with students, peers, and colleagues, as well as their professional classroom behaviors and demeanors. Performance-based assessments involve candidates completing teaching tasks, such as developing lesson plans or delivering classroom instruction, which are evaluated based on criteria associated with dispositional benchmarks.

There is not a consensus on whether dispositions can be accurately measured (Johnston et al., 2018), but validated instruments exist to evaluate educator dispositions. The 24-item Teacher Disposition Scale (TDS) was constructed to assess five factors: teaching motivation, teaching efficacy, willingness to learn, consciousness, and interpersonal and communication skills (West et al., 2020). The Teacher Dispositions Index (TDI) assesses dispositions of teacher candidates in relation to effective attributes outlined in the Interstate New Teacher Assessment and Support Consortium (InTASC; Schulte et al., 2005). The Educator Dispositions Assessment (EDA; Almerico et al., 2011) assesses candidates on a number of professional criteria using a Likert-type ratings system and open-ended comments. There are also dispositions assessments for teacher leaders and those in other education roles, such as the Educational Leadership Disposition Assessment (EDLDA; Wilson et al., 2020). Though validated dispositional assessment instruments can provide teacher education programs with information about candidates' personal and professional qualities, homegrown instruments may also be effective, given careful development and psychometric strategies to analyze their technical adequacy.

Context of Dispositional Revitalization

In the Seidel School of Education at Salisbury University, a Dispositional Assessment System had historically been in place, but conditions necessitated a need to assess the Seidel School's policy, procedures, and practices around dispositions. Due to challenges in hiring an assessment specialist, the Dispositional Assessment System functioned but was not critically evaluated between 2019 and 2021. In the midst of this timeframe, the COVID-19 pandemic policies forced learning to be done largely online, which complicated the entire assessment system in the Seidel School of Education, including the functions of the dispositional assessment system. In the post-lock-down timeframe from 2021 to 2022, unique candidate dispositional issues emerged that were not covered under the existing policy. The newly promoted Assistant Dean for Program Assessment—this chapter author—took this as an opportunity to rethink the Dispositional Policy and the entire system to function as a safeguard to allow input from internal and external stakeholders, as well as a way to monitor and coach dispositional issues, report results to programs for monitoring and improvement, and to screen candidates who exhibited major dispositional violations through a due process hearing. The revised Five-Layer Dispositional Assessment System took 2 years to fully implement.

Five-Layer Dispositional Assessment System at Salisbury University

Layer 1: Dispositional Policy and Violations

Programs should have clear policies and procedures in place for addressing dispositional violations, including providing students with opportunities for remediation and support. As a result of a complicated dispositional issues with candidates, the Dean's Office determined the existing Dispositional Policy needed to be revised to be more broadly encompassing of candidate dispositional violations that occur in courses, clinical placements, and university-sponsored events. The previous version of our policy was developed by the Seidel School of Education's Unit Assessment Committee in consultation with university legal associates. This policy is our first and foundational layer of our Dispositions Assessment System.

We discovered that important procedural steps were missing from the Dispositional Policy. If candidate dispositional violations are recurrent or severe enough to require a hearing with the Faculty Discipline Committee, a faculty committee established to review filed dispositional violations, the process did not provide guidance for certain timelines or personnel involvement. One reason these gaps were not discovered earlier is that there had not yet been a hearing.

Hearings have since increased in frequency, likely due to another, pragmatic revision to the Dispositional Policy: a digital Dispositions Violation Form.

The previous Dispositions Violation Form was a PDF copy that needed to be downloaded, filled out by hand, and scanned back to digital form. This was tedious and likely prevented dispositions violations from being reported by stakeholders. A new form, done using Microsoft Forms, was created. Though much easier to use, faculty needed robust training to understand what dispositional violations were, when they should file, who should file under certain conditions, and the type of corrective action they should refer to the Faculty Discipline Committee. Violations are received and monitored by the Assistant Dean, who also chairs the Faculty Discipline Committee. A descriptive flowchart was created to walk faculty and stakeholders through scenarios and ways they could be handled according to the Dispositional Policy, ranging from classroom remediation to reporting major violations for a hearing.

As explicated in the Dispositional Policy, descriptive data of filed Dispositional Violation Forms are reported annually at schoolwide Seidel School of Education faculty retreats. Data are reported overall and by program, according to numbers and types of dispositional violations and corrective actions taken. Currently, we are on our second year of the new policy, so longitudinal data will continue to be monitored and reported. Moving forward, we will have discussions about schoolwide and program-specific curricular and assessment practices and needs in relation to dispositional violation trends we identify.

Layer 2: Dispositional Priming

The second layer of our Dispositional Assessment System relates to priming and preparing candidates for our expectations. Candidates must be aware of dispositions and expectations early in their programs. To provide candidates with this information, we posted a webpage to our Seidel School of Education website that included the policy, forms, and expectations. This webpage was linked on all department sites. Additionally, we shared with faculty a revised, substantive syllabus policy with a link to the webpage, and we checked all syllabi to ensure the common syllabus statement was present. At a faculty retreat, departments also discussed what the dispositions meant for their programs, as well as opportunities prior to or early in the programs that dispositions could be presented and discussed. Many programs now discuss examples of dispositions and our expectations as early as recruitment events for prospective students. It has taken a year or more of deliberate discussions to help faculty understand processes, but faculty buy-in was nearly immediate. All faculty want students aware of dispositional expectations and also saw the benefit of a formal process to monitor strengths and needs of candidates in their programs.

Layer 3: Early Program Dispositional Self-Assessments

The final three layers involve gathering data on candidate dispositions from multiple sources across the program timeframe. The third layer of our Dispositional Assessment System involves candidate self-assessments. Candidate self-assessed dispositions can provide valuable insight into their own attitudes, beliefs, and values and can be an effective tool for promoting self-reflection and self-awareness in the learning process (Gao & Moyer, 2018). Candidates across all programs, even those not under the AAQEP umbrella, are required to self-evaluate their dispositions as part of their program application process in licensure programs, or the first semester of enrollment in other programs.

In initial licensure programs, program candidates self-assess using a homegrown, Qualtrics-based instrument. The instrument was designed with items aligned to Salisbury University's Academic Misconduct Policies, the Code of Ethics of the Association of American Educators and the National Education Association, and InTASC standards. On the assessment, candidates assess their current dispositions in five factors evaluating their Commitment to: the Ideals of the Profession; Students; Professional Knowledge; All Stakeholders; and Professional Colleagues, Faculty, and Fellow Students. This assessment takes candidates approximately 25 minutes to complete. Each factor includes five, Likert-type items rated from Unacceptable to Exemplary and open-ended items for candidates to describe their strengths and challenges in each factor. Advanced programs and the

Outdoor Education Leadership programs have developed similar self-assessment instruments that are aligned with their professional standards, using Watermark's Student Learning and Licensure platform through an observational form template assigned to candidates.

Data are presented each semester to faculty in an assessment report. The data include descriptive tables with frequencies and means of Likert-type items, open-ended responses, and trends from previous cohorts. Faculty have discussions about the results and recognize that one challenge of self-assessed dispositions instruments is that candidates may lack the self-awareness or understanding of what constitutes a desirable disposition (Sumsion & Goodfellow, 2016). To assist with this, the instrument includes many observable behavior examples for each item that may indicate if a candidate would exhibit strength in that area. Being the second year of using this instrument in our updated assessment system, we will run validation strategies on the instrument, including factor analysis and Pearson correlation coefficient analyses to determine the content and criterion validity. Initial testing with limited data has been promising.

Another challenge of self-assessed dispositions is that candidates may be motivated to present themselves in a favorable light, leading to potential bias or overinflation of their own abilities and dispositions (Wagner et al., 2014). Surprisingly, data have indicated many candidates do not rate themselves highly in all areas. Interesting patterns have emerged that demonstrate high and low scores vary uniquely by candidate program. Perhaps requiring candidates to reflect on and write about personal challenges for each factor has shown that we do not expect perfection. Faculty recognize these self-reported data challenges, but we present results to them with the prompt, "These are the candidates in your next cohort. What might they need?"

Many innovations resulted from these conversations. It is common for faculty who teach the same cohorts to look at self-assessment data and make plans for assisting dispositional development across their courses. In one case, faculty noticed self-assessments showed generally low perceptions of candidates feeling connected to families and communities. These faculty created a clinical activity in which mentor teachers aided students in meeting families, holding conversations and planning individualized student experiences in a more deliberate, guided way than had been done before. Programs have built faculty-developed case studies of common dispositional issues into introductory and early courses, including updated contexts such as hypothetical candidates' use of TikTok during clinical placements and artificial intelligence programs with classroom assignments. Students and instructors read and discuss these cases in relation to professional and ethical expectations. There is some discussion about developing online training modules for all students in some programs using this case study approach. Several faculty have requested aggregate summaries of their students' dispositional self-assessment results to identify dispositional needs, which they use to build in course videos or readings that can support understanding and development of candidates' professional dispositions. One such faculty discovered their candidates felt disconnected from professional organizations and built into the syllabus time to guide candidates to explore and join a relevant professional organization and use its resources in the classroom. We have allowed faculty in programs to be flexible and responsive in their approach to using these results.

Layer 4: Instructor Dispositional Assessment

Instructor assessment of teacher candidates' dispositions can be an important part of teacher education programs (Collie et al., 2018). The fourth layer of our Dispositional Assessment System involves an evaluation of each candidate's dispositions by a faculty member in a select course for each program. All evaluations are efficiently done using Student Learning & Licensure. In a faculty retreat, programs identified a course early in the program that would house this assessment. For the initial licensure programs, faculty chose a course in the first semester after program acceptance that all students took, and most often from the same instructor as to encourage rating reliability. For the graduate programs, faculty selected a core required course for the programs that would be taken in the first year by all candidates. Due to the nature of the graduate programs' students, who often take courses in a more part-time or less rigidly structured format than traditional undergraduates, faculty identified a course for their programs that served a role as a required and/or prerequisite early in the program sequence.

To lessen the burden on instructors, a slimmed-down, course-based observational rubric is used to evaluate candidates. It includes 13 items scored using a 4-level rubric ranging from Unacceptable to Target. Items include assessing candidates on their Respect for Diversity, Self-Reflection, Empathy, Response to Feedback, Engagement, Collegiality, Punctuality, Initiative, and more. Using Student Learning & Licensure for assessment provides an easily accessible platform for faculty, and detailed reports can be generated by aligned standards, such as AAQEP 1f, and by rubric lines.

The data resulting from this assessment are used in multiple ways. First, candidates have immediate access to view the ratings they received from their instructors and are encouraged to have discussions about the results. If candidates have concerns about ways they were rated, and some do, they can meet with instructors to discuss behaviors or issues that led to that concern. Furthermore, faculty have used these results to confer with colleagues about conflicting dispositional expectations amongst stakeholders. One notable conversation occurred at a department meeting when a colleague, who had just completed an assessment of their candidates, stated, "How can we expect our students to understand appropriate cell phone use when some of their mentor teachers are on their cell phones during class?" Colleagues did not come up with a solution, but found it necessary and helpful to introduce this same discussion with the candidates.

Next, department chairs and program directors have been added as Student Learning & Licensure administrators, giving them access to review and download aggregated dispositional data directly from Student Learning & Licensure at any point they need it. They can share these with faculty and monitor candidates with ratings of concern. Finally, I aggregate and share data annually with faculty, by program, who discuss areas of strengths or concern and how they might address them with individuals or programmatically. I share descriptive data, including frequencies and mean scores by item.

Moving forward, we will run correlation analyses to determine if areas of candidate self-reported data and faculty data are significantly similar, which could indicate criterion validity between instruments. If some item results diverge, we will have conversations about faculty or candidate rating reliability, challenges with one or both forms of dispositions assessment, or further revisions needed on one or both instruments. Still, by incorporating instructor assessments into teacher education programs, our candidates can receive targeted feedback and support to help them develop and improve their dispositions (Collie et al., 2018), which we hope will lead to more effective classroom teachers.

Layer 5: Internship Self-Assessment Dispositional Triad

The fifth layer of our Dispositional Assessment System is our Dispositional Triad, which is a three-source triangulation of dispositional data done twice during final internship (student teaching). We refer to it as a triad because the same instrument used in our Dispositional Assessment System Layer 4 is evaluated by the mentor teacher, university supervisor, and intern (student teacher). Similar to Layer 4, it is done on Student Learning & Licensure. We implemented the Dispositional Triad during the 2022–2023 school year.

The major goal of triangulating these data was to compare sources to confirm or corroborate dispositional data results (Mertler, 2014). Comparing dispositional data from multiple sources can provide a more comprehensive understanding of an intern's dispositions and can inform decisions about their readiness for the teaching profession. For example, if a teacher candidate rates themselves highly in a particular disposition, but their mentor teacher and supervisor both rate them lower, it may indicate a lack of self-awareness, an overinflation of their abilities, a gap in their ability to effectively demonstrate their dispositional strengths, or a potential bias in how the candidate is being assessed by the mentor teacher and/or university supervisor. On the other hand, if all three sources rate the candidate similarly, it may provide a more accurate and reliable picture of the candidate's dispositions. We require these results to be discussed at a meeting between the three individuals in the school setting.

We recognize the challenges of mentor teachers assessing the dispositions of interns. First, they may have limited time to observe and assess dispositions, particularly as they are responsible for doing other, time-consuming evaluations of their interns (Eisenman & Condon, 2015). They may be subjective in their assessments (Zeichner & Liston, 2014) or concerned about giving negative feedback about interns (Wang et al., 2008). There is potential for evaluation bias (Milner, 2010). They may also not have enough opportunities to observe their interns across settings, which can make it difficult to comprehensively assess dispositions accurately (Korthagen et al., 2006).

University supervisors may face the same challenges. Additionally, they might have limited opportunities for observation (Hammerness & Darling-Hammond, 2012), limited contact with interns (Feiman-Nemser, 2001), and different expectations than mentor teachers for interns' dispositions (Zeichner & Liston, 2014). Our university supervisors generally visit interns once a week for roughly an hour as they review lesson plans, observe an intern's teaching, and provide feedback.

The Dispositional Triad produces a vast amount of data. Being a new assessment process, we first presented it to faculty in the form of program-specific reports and a presentation to help them understand our findings. We shared data in a three-column, color-coded table that displayed mean rating by item for each of the three stakeholders—mentor teacher, university supervisor, and intern. Each cell of the table included the item mean, and colors represented the stakeholders who rated the item highest (green) and lowest (yellow). Additionally, we presented Pearson r and probability values from our correlation analyses to indicate strength of similarity across scorers. In the first year, we found item means demonstrated that mentor teachers rated nine items highest, supervisors rated two items highest and 10 lowest, and interns rated three items highest and four lowest. Mentor teachers' and interns' overall rating scores across the instrument were nearly identical, whereas the supervisors' overall scores were significantly lower by nearly 4%. At a faculty retreat, we discussed whether this indicated different perspectives, different expectations, different opportunities to observe, or whether more explicit communication about dispositional expectations and scoring was necessary for all scorer types.

As we gather more dispositional data, we hope to use them to identify patterns that may not be currently noticeable. Perhaps a regression analysis may indicate Layer 3 or Layer 4 data; course grades, signature assessment rubric items, or other data might predict Layer 5 results or show how programming affects candidates' dispositional trends over time. We hope further analysis will indicate if Layer 3 self-assessments correlate with other layers of dispositional data; if they do, it will indicate their importance and a deeper discussion of those results to provide necessary interventions. If they do not, perhaps we reconsider revising Layer 3 to help candidates understand and reflect upon professional dispositions in more effective and reliable ways.

Conclusion

In this chapter, I described the Five-Layer Dispositional Assessment System used in the Seidel School of Education at Salisbury University, Maryland. The system employs multiple measures, including candidate self-reflection early and end-of program, observations of candidate dispositions in the university classroom, and observations of intern dispositions and performance during the final internship. Salisbury University candidates are provided with feedback on their dispositions by course faculty, university supervisors, and mentor teachers. This system has demonstrated marked improvements in our programming. First, faculty and stakeholders are more aware of the Dispositional Policy and have initiated the dispositional violation process numerous times over the previous year. This has led to closer monitoring and reporting of results, student remediation and coaching, and some students reconsidering the teaching profession to one that better aligns with their strengths. When dispositional violation cases get sent to the Faculty Discipline Committee for review, the common dispositions syllabus statements and candidate self-assessment system ensure evidence exists that candidates have read and understand the policies and expectations of the Seidel School of Education.

Next, all programs have more relevant and methodical practices of introducing, teaching, and building upon professional dispositions in ways that align with program and student needs. We have seen faculty be creative in ways they modify or create course and clinical placement activities to develop candidates' areas of needs. When our candidates discuss case studies, engage with professional organizations, or work with teachers on guided projects related to their dispositions, they are better prepared for a successful career. Lastly, all programs are now engaged in the dispositional process and have access to actionable data from stakeholders across the programs. We have noticed more interest from faculty in discussing the student dispositional results, the relation of those results to program content and curricula, and the extent to which programs and clinical placements supplement or, in some cases, might diverge in efforts to form and develop professional dispositions. Our Five-Layer Dispositional Assessment System aligns with goals and outcomes of the Seidel School of Education, that we offer meaningful and relevant practices and assessments to provide skills and knowledge that candidates need to become effective teachers, and base our program improvement decisions in actionable data from multiple perspectives.

References

Almerico, G., Johnston, P., Henriott, D., & Shapiro, M. (2011). Dispositions assessment in teacher education: Developing an assessment instrument for the college classroom and the field. *Research in Higher Education Journal, 11*, 1–19.

Collie, R. J., Shapka, J. D., Perry, N. E., & Martin, A. J. (2018). Teacher candidate dispositions: An international systematic review of the empirical literature. *Teaching and Teacher Education, 72*, 34–52.

Drucker, P. F. (2013). Observing and assessing growth in dispositional learning. In A. L. Costa & B. Kallick (Eds.), *Dispositions: Reframing teaching and learning* (pp. 94–124). Corwin Press.

Eisenman, L. T., & Condon, C. (2015). The challenges of mentoring and assessing dispositions in teacher education. *Teaching and Teacher Education, 49*, 35–44.

Feiman-Nemser, S. (2001). From preparation to practice: Designing a continuum to strengthen and sustain teaching. *Teachers College Record, 103*(6), 1013–1055.

Gao, L., & Moyer, J. (2018). Student self-assessment of dispositions: A useful tool for teacher education. *Journal of Education and Learning, 7*(1), 119–127.

Hammerness, K., & Darling-Hammond, L. (2012). Evaluating teacher effectiveness: How teacher performance assessments can measure and improve teaching. *Kappan Magazine, 94*(4), 16–21.

Johnston, P., Wilson, A., & Almerico, G. M. (2018). Meeting psychometric requirements for disposition assessment: Valid and reliable indicators of teacher dispositions. *Journal of Instructional Pedagogies, 21*, 1–12.

Korthagen, F. A., Loughran, J. J., & Russell, T. (2006). Developing fundamental principles for teacher education programs and practices. *Teaching and Teacher
Education, 22*(8), 1020–1041.

Martin, N. K., Snow, D. A., & Franklin, T. W. (2013). Measuring teacher dispositions: An overview of the dispositions assessment system. *Journal of Teacher
Education, 64*(4), 340–352.

Mertler, C. A. (2014). *Action research: Improving schools and empowering educators*
(4th ed.). Sage Publications.

Milner, H. R. (2010). Teacher dispositions reconsidered: Implications for teacher
preparation programs. *Journal of Teacher Education, 61*(1–2), 72–86.

Schulte, L., Edick, N., Edwards, S., & Mackiel, D. (2005). The development and validation of the Teacher Dispositions Index. *Essays in Education, 12*(1), 7.

Sumsion, J., & Goodfellow, J. (2016). Teacher professional standards and Australian
early childhood education and care: Issues and tensions. *Australian Journal of
Early Childhood, 41*(4), 4–11.

Wagner, L., Friend, C., & Taylor, M. J. (2014). Teacher candidate dispositions: An
examination of self-assessment and faculty evaluation. *Teacher Education
Quarterly, 41*(3), 95–112.

Wang, J., Odell, S. J., & Schwille, S. A. (2008). Effects of mentor pedagogical skills on
student teachers' performance, attitudes, and career commitment in the United
States and China. *Teaching and Teacher Education, 24*(8), 2143–2154.

West, C., Baker, A., Ehrich, J. F., Woodcock, S., Bokosmaty, S., Howard, S. J., & Eady,
M. J. (2020). Teacher Disposition Scale (TDS): construction and psychometric
validation. *Journal of Further and Higher Education, 44*(2), 185–200.

Wilson, A., Almerico, G. M., Johnston, P., & Ensmann, S. (2020). Examining educational leadership dispositions: A valid and reliable assessment of leadership dispositions. *International Journal of Educational Leadership Preparation, 15*(1),
17–28.

Zeichner, K., & Liston, D. (2014). *Reflective teaching: An introduction*. Routledge.

CHAPTER NINE

Enhancing Quality Program Practices Through a Qualitative Student Teacher Feedback Survey

JOSEPH HAUGHEY, ASHLEY STRICKLAND,
TRAVIS DIMMITT, EVERETT SINGLETON,
JENNIFER WALL, MIKE MCBRIDE, AND TIM WALL

Introduction: Gathering Student Teacher Qualitative Feedback

Northwest Missouri State University has conducted a qualitative feedback survey during student teacher call-back days since the fall 2019 semester to understand student teacher perspectives and glean ideas for continuous program improvement by soliciting and listening to teacher candidate perspectives. All Northwest candidates complete at least 550 hours of clinical field experience, including a 16-week culminating student teaching experience, and as part of their student teaching experience, candidates return from their clinical placement to campus for 2 callback days. In these, they reflect on their challenges and successes in student teaching. Because Northwest is in rural Missouri, serving teacher candidates from Missouri, Nebraska, Iowa, and Kansas, many candidates complete student teaching more than an hour from campus: in the Kansas City, St. Joseph, Omaha (NE), and Des Moines (IA) metropolitan areas, as well as through several dozen rural partnerships across the four-state region. As a result, the mood for both callback days takes on a festive and social nature as candidates celebrate these last two reunions before graduation. For most, these 2 callback days culminate their face-to-face, on-campus experiences.

The Northwest Professional Education Unit (PEU) decided in 2019 that these callback days might prove an opportunity to collect meaningful qualitative feedback from the field on 1) which elements from programs were working well for candidates and 2) what elements candidates saw as weaknesses upon which programs could improve their preparation. We ask the students for honest feedback, and our school Dean makes a simple yet essential statement to frame the data collection process: "I promise that we will use your feedback to improve programs and make things better." When we honor candidates' knowledge and perceptions, they provide honest and meaningful information that we use for continuous improvement. Candidate voices are a significant part of our university-wide culture of evidence for ongoing improvement. Such feedback enhances quantitative data collected before and during student teaching: the Missouri General Education Assessment (MoGEA); a general education assessment required for admission in all Missouri EPPs; the Missouri Content Assessment (MOCA), a content-based assessment required for state certification taken right before student teaching; cumulative and content course-based GPA; the Missouri Educator Evaluation System (MEES), a performance assessment comprised of nine teacher preparation standards also used to measure classroom teachers' performance; and Likert scale–based surveys meant to assess student teaching sent to candidates, supervisors, and cooperating teachers.

Faculty coordinating the callback days scheduled a 1-hour block each semester, generally held on the second callback day. Approximately 110 student teachers return to campus and gather face to face for the event in the university ballroom, one of the Northwest campus's largest indoor spaces. After a morning of learning and reflection activities, including employer panels, training on Kagan learning structures, and classroom management sessions, candidates meet with faculty program coordinators within their disciplines. The mood is social. Candidates know their feedback will be heard, increasing commitment and modeling a process worthy of emulation in their classrooms with students.

Other than graduation commencement ceremonies, this will be the last time they gather as one group. Candidates over 4 years have forged deep relationships across the whole group and within their specific disciplines. They have learned together, for some 4 years, taken classes together, and transformed together from students into educators. They have seen one another both struggle and triumph, and at this moment, they sit together one last time just weeks before the finish line.

Candidates reconvene after lunch for the feedback survey. The method is straightforward. One faculty member takes 5 minutes to introduce the instrument, explaining that students will be asked to free-write for 10 minutes and then gather in large groups to discuss their responses afterward. The lead faculty member emphasizes that the survey responses will be used to improve programs for future candidates. Candidates are engaged in the process, and participation is strong. The prompt is then introduced, and students write:

> What elements of your preparation program were particularly useful in your student teaching? What do you think would have been useful in your program that would have prepared you better for student teaching? (In other words, what did your program do well to get you ready for student teaching, and could it have done it a bit better?)

Candidate responses in previous semesters were collected through Canvas, the campus LMS (Learning Management System), and then through an online form beginning in the spring of 2023. Students are also asked to identify their program so that data can later be disaggregated. Responses are otherwise anonymous.

After writing, candidates gather in groups of 8 to 12, though group size varies. Candidates usually have self-selected to sit according to their program throughout the day—there is no assigned seating for the callback days—and typically remain in these groupings for the survey. Smaller groups are combined. At this point, a faculty or staff member joins each group to facilitate conversations and take notes, which Northwest's Quality Assurance Team (QAT) will combine with the candidates' writing for analysis.

Once in groups, candidates share their thoughts aloud. Often, a comment from one will spark insights in others. When multiple programs are represented within one group, the other students agree or disagree with what others have said. A candidate often will comment that a topic had been addressed, but it was too early in the program, and they had forgotten it. "Oh yeah, that's right." Often, if students find many areas of improvement, someone will say, "You know, it seems like we have a lot to complain about, but really, we are prepared. These are just things that we could have had better." The conversations generally are upbeat. Sometimes, as student teachers discuss their program and what they wish they had more experience with, they realize they are gaining the necessary experience during student teaching and will be prepared when hired as full-time teachers.

Combined with faculty and staff notes, the qualitative survey responses generate 100 to 150 pages of candidate feedback. Identifying information is removed from the data, and the anonymous responses are then reviewed by the QAT, led by Northwest's assessment director and composed of faculty from across the PEU. To further protect candidate anonymity, as some student writing is recognizable to faculty in their area, raw candidate responses are not distributed outside of the QAT. At its final meeting for the year in April, after both fall and spring student teacher feedback has been collected, the QAT spends 90 minutes analyzing the candidates' feedback and faculty notes. The pages are divided among the QAT members, some 20 to 25 pages each, and each member reads their assigned pages, noting trends they find in their data. This takes some 30 minutes, and the group then spends the next hour discussing the findings in the data and generating a list of trends they find across the data.

That list is then used to craft a two- to three-page document, which is disseminated to faculty before the end of the academic year for use in their planning for the fall. It is then disseminated again in department and committee planning meetings before (and shortly after) the start of the fall semester as a guide to PEU discussions and work toward continuous improvement. Over the past four years, student teacher feedback has led to several significant programmatic and course improvements, to be described in more detail in the following sections. Results are further evaluated by the School of Education (SOE) Leadership Team; the Northwest PEU

Advisory Committee, which consists of partner school leaders; and the Council on Teacher Education (COTE), the chief policy-making faculty shared governance committee. Northwest supports ongoing program improvement by listening to students in our programs and multiple voices to provide context.

An Assessment Lens: Disseminating Aggregated Data for Program Improvement

The Northwest QAT meets several times a semester to analyze and discuss candidates' comments and other data, then crafts a plan to best disseminate that data to the rest of the PEU to support continuous improvement. Critical analyses and results are shared with the COTE and other stakeholders. The QAT meets to work through the student teacher qualitative survey results as part of that ongoing work. The first analysis of candidates' qualitative writing happened in person in an on-campus conference room in the fall of 2019. The raw data were printed out, and the QAT divided up approximately 100 to 125 pages of writing amongst the group. The group read the pages silently to themselves and used color highlighters to mark trends using open coding techniques. After everybody had time to read and highlight their pages, the team reconvened to list the common trends they saw throughout the data, which was then written on a whiteboard at the front of the room. This was condensed into a one-page document and disseminated to faculty that semester before the holiday break.

The following semester, in the spring of 2020, no qualitative student teacher feedback was collected because of the COVID-19 pandemic. Callback days were held virtually, and the feedback process was suspended. Only candidates' written data were collected when the process was reinstated in the fall of 2020 for the second round of data. The after-writing discussions were again suspended. The QAT met through Zoom to analyze its second set of candidate responses. The semester data revealed candidates' struggles in preparation because of the pandemic. Student teachers had not been able to have typical in-class experiences. This limited their development, and the learning gap featured prominently in their qualitative comments.

The data collection model instituted in 2019 resumed in the spring of 2021, but the QAT continues to meet and analyze data virtually through Zoom.

For each data collection cycle (fall 2019, fall 2020, spring 2021, 2021–2022, and 2022–2023), the QAT has developed a summary document as described in the previous section, outlining the candidates' perceptions of program strengths and weaknesses. The most recent version of the document is included as an appendix. Candidates' feedback has fed unit-wide improvements, cross-departmental benchmarking, idea sharing, and collaboration. If specific themes require program-level discussion, this can be done through meetings between the Dean of the School of Education and program coordinators. The question then becomes, what does this qualitative feedback typically yield? This can include quick-hitter improvements or insights requiring deeper, unit-wide discussions. Faculty advisors and program coordinators appreciate knowing precisely what was perceived by teacher candidates as useful during the student teaching experience, and when the PEU holds a retreat about these data, they arrive with openness to all feedback.

Many times, the feedback can be difficult to hear: "This didn't work," "I felt unprepared for . . . ," "this was covered in another class—seemed repetitive," "this was not covered." We get better, though, when we know. And when we know better, we can do better. It takes courage to ask, "How can we better meet your needs," and "What are we doing that we should keep or do away with." This set of candidate listening sessions promotes assessment literacy, the use of data for program improvement, continuous quality improvement of courses and programs, and a unit-wide commitment to fearlessly gathering and using helpful information to tweak what we do and get better. To help the next generation of teacher candidates be optimally prepared with relevant curriculum and experiences. This models the approach our school partners promote and demonstrates deep reflection for our teacher candidates by their faculty, staff, and administration. The following section reveals the process of acknowledging significant challenges in the teacher candidate feedback and closing the loop on improvement.

Closing the Loop: Highlighting Opportunities, Tough Conversations, and Implications for Accreditation

After analyzing the feedback from student teachers, Northwest faculty use candidates' recommendations to implement changes. Some changes are realized quickly, while others require programmatic, curricular changes. For example, some candidates indicated they did not feel prepared for some of the elements of the MEES, particularly Standard 7, which addresses student assessment and data. Professors had long provided assignments in methods courses that aligned with the assessment standard, but candidates had not connected that work to the MEES standard. Professors responded by changing the name of those assignments to MEES Standard 7 Analysis of Student Data and intentionally connecting the course work to the MEES expectation.

Another example involves curriculum; early feedback from candidates indicated a trend in which candidates felt their programs overemphasized creating unique curricula and lessons at the expense of learning to use their districts' curricula in student teaching. Candidates explained that in their student teaching, they were expected to follow a standardized curriculum and textbook and desired deeper preparation in using such resources in their everyday teaching.

Up to that point, a customary practice in methods courses had been to assign students to write lesson and unit plans. After hearing feedback from the student teachers and completers, though, several methods course professors changed these assignments. For example, in "Math in the Elementary School" and "Methods in Secondary School Mathematics," candidates are now assigned a section or chapter from a K-12 math textbook. The focus shifted to determining what pieces of the textbook resources to utilize in the lesson and how best to supplement these with external content-based resources (e.g., NCTM Illuminations, Open Middle, Illustrative Mathematics).

In "Methods of Teaching English 5-12," candidates previously completed a unit plan as the culminating project for the course, including 12 to 15 formal lesson plans. Instead, candidates now complete a textbook interrogation activity in which each student selects a standard middle or high school textbook from the Northwest library's curriculum collection and analyzes its selections and assignments. Candidates compare their findings with one another in class, evaluating the merits of each text, and then select one reading selection from their text from which they craft a microteaching lesson, which now serves as the culminating project for the course. Course comments in both cases thus far have been positive.

Another example of meaningful change derived from candidates' qualitative feedback was in the middle school and secondary classroom and behavior management class, which continues to evolve. One of the critical pieces of feedback we have received since schools have returned to face-to-face learning as the novel coronavirus recedes has involved trauma-informed practice, especially regarding classroom management. In response, we have incorporated more information and activities that explain and encompass Adverse Childhood Experiences (ACES). This includes preservice teachers examining, taking, and reflecting on the ACES test, how the scores might correlate with their own educational experiences, and what implications ACES might have on management and discipline in their observation settings and future classrooms.

Some completers also indicated the need for more experience implementing Individualized Education Plans (IEP) in all classrooms. Faculty members adjusted course content to include specific IEP instruction, score report analysis, and implementation ideas. Candidates read an IEP and determine how the student's IEP would impact them in their future classrooms. Also, candidates, as part of their coursework, now analyze an English learner's score report from WIDA ACCESS, a summative English language proficiency assessment. Using the score report, candidates determine what the leveled scores mean for the student and the lessons the candidate is preparing. Additionally, the candidates review student case studies, an ELL student, and a Special Education student and offer modifications/accommodations based on a previously written lesson plan and the IEP or WIDA scores.

The PEU also made a programmatic change based on feedback from these qualitative data gatherings. Student teachers indicated a need for knowledge in trauma-informed practices. One program designed and implemented a course in trauma-informed instruction that their program completers now take. Other programs responded to the need by redesigning pre-existing courses to infuse trauma-informed instruction into the course content. Over the last four years, feedback from students that initially identified programmatic needs now identifies programmatic strengths. Overwhelmingly, program completers now feel prepared to implement trauma-informed practices in their classrooms.

Sometimes, through conversations with student teachers, it becomes evident that one program had a particular experience that the other program did not. Maybe one program's students had more experience with microteaching or observing IEP meetings. Hearing the values of these experiences in specific programs allows PEU faculty to collaborate and implement changes. Faculty can indicate what works well with one group and offer ideas on what can be included in the other programs in the future.

As student comments and qualitative data are condensed, the QAT can sift through some of the more critical comments. The discussions among QAT allow them to determine which comments are isolated complaints and which are worthy of more inspection. If the comments are echoed by multiple students or restate anecdotal comments heard during office hours or advisement, these qualitative data are beneficial as the QAT and Director of Teacher Education can use these data as a springboard to approach faculty or programs requiring immediate change. Thus, the data support closing the loop on the qualitative improvement cycle and provide evidence for tough conversations.

On occasion, an issue becomes known that allows the QAT to visit with faculty and administrators to garner additional feedback from students to frame critical conversations about courses, faculty, or programs. While these can be difficult conversations, Northwest's culture of continuous quality improvement based on data makes these conversations evidence based and less confrontational. One example percolated in the thematic analysis of student teacher comments related to a discrepancy in perceptions about the value of content-specific examples provided in an education course. Specifically, the data revealed that many of our teacher candidates

in one content area felt that their education courses lacked significant examples germane to their content area. In speaking with the
education methods instructors, members of the QAT and the dean
could leverage these comments to reframe the examples used in
class. Using the candidates' feedback was essential for nudging faculty to make needed changes.

When using candidates' feedback, the improvement process is
much more ground up than top down. Such work is fundamental
to meeting AAQEP national accreditation Standard 3, which calls
on EPPs to use stakeholder feedback, including that of candidates,
to improve programs. Standard 3 requires EPPs to prioritize highly
impactful and robust assessment systems. By aspiring to use meaningful evidence of candidate and program effectiveness, Northwest
supports a continuous conversation about quality assurance with
multiple measures of both qualitative and quantitative data. Using
candidate reflections gathered at precisely the right time (near the
conclusion of the student teaching semester) supports innovation.
Our university staff and faculty eagerly seek ongoing feedback from
multiple stakeholders to continuously support innovative ideas and
courageous conversations, all of which are one of several kinds of
evidence that Northwest uses to meet standard three.

Looking Forward: Focus Groups for Studying Teacher Resilience and Retention

As the qualitative feedback teacher process continues to evolve,
Northwest intends to use candidate feedback to gain even deeper
insights valuable toward continuous improvement and a starting
point for addressing other issues in teacher preparation. In its most
recent incarnation of the survey, in the spring of 2023, two quantitative questions were added to the survey regarding teacher resiliency and retention. The first asks candidates about their short-term
career plans, and whether they intend to enter the field as an educator after student teaching. The second asks candidates about their
long-term career plans and whether they see themselves working
in education as either educators or administrators 5 to 10 years into
the future. Of 68 responses, only two indicated they planned to leave

the field of education. Research suggests, though, that the actual number of students who will endure in education beyond 5 years is much smaller, and the research team at Northwest intends to begin work to understand better the teacher retention problem facing education.

Ongoing continuous quality improvement is vital for education preparation program success, and gathering and using essential information from our candidates and our faculty will be a significant part of continuous improvement efforts to improve programs. Yet further research in teacher resilience, retention, and sustainability within the profession is necessary. The nation's K-12 schools are experiencing a teacher shortage, a well-acknowledged but poorly understood crisis (Garcia and Weiss, 2019). Thus, it is critical to examine teacher perceptions regarding the fidelity of teacher preparation programs in providing essential training. Northwest researchers are currently developing a study to better understand teacher resiliency among Northwest completers. The study will use a mixed-methods phenomenological approach via a survey and focus group, with an in-depth analysis of the experiences and perceptions of Northwest completers. Data will be collected through 30-minute focus group questions and a brief survey. The rationale is to contribute to research and the national dialogue concerning the current teacher shortage crisis nationwide and provide guidance to specific programs to improve curriculum that impacts resiliency in the profession. This will assist Northwest and other institutions in further unpacking why teacher candidates decide to stay in the profession and why they choose to leave the field. The guiding question for the study is: "What things in our program impact your sustainability, resilience, and retention as a new educator?"

The aim is to study teacher candidates in their final semester and first-year teachers' perceptions and understanding of teacher preparation program experiences that impact sustainability, resilience, and retention within the teaching field. Additionally, the goal is to acquire data and information on current factors that affect the continued teacher shortage. Because of Northwest's ongoing commitment to data collection, analysis, program revision, and improvement, it is part of our culture to continue this work to see how we can keep teachers in the profession longer. Northwest has been evaluating our programs quantitatively and qualitatively and will continue to do so, focusing on preparing teachers to be effective for many years into the future.

References

García, E., and Weiss, E. (2019). The Teacher Shortage is Real, Large and Growing, and Worse than We Thought. Economic Policy Institute.

CHAPTER TEN

Strengthening Social, Emotional, and Culturally Sustaining Teaching Practices: A Study of Oregon Educator Preparation and New Teacher Perceptions

KRISTIN RUSH, SHARA MONDRAGON,
REBECCA BAHR, KIRSTEN PLUMEAU, SUSAN BOE,
DEIRDRE HON, JULIE SAUVE, AND LINA DARWICH

Students, caregivers, and educators are entering schools with increasingly diverse and complex needs. These needs were exacerbated due to the COVID-19 pandemic and the post-pandemic landscape. According to Bhatnagar and Many (2022), teachers report feeling burnt out and exhausted due to increased job demands and meeting student needs in this time of trauma. "Teachers' own balance in such a context was [is] closely tied to the issues of the community, students' social-emotional health, and systemic or equity-related resource challenges" (Bhatnagar & Many 2022, p. 528). Teaching is a stressful profession under typical circumstances and the sustaining effects of heightened stress levels can impact teaching quality, teacher health, and well-being, and lead to higher attrition rates from the profession (see, e.g., Bakker et al., 2014; Clunies-Ross et al., 2008; Eblie Trudel et al., 2021; Harmsen et al., 2018; Maulana et al., 2014; Skaalvik & Skaalvik, 2015).

According to a recent survey conducted by the National Education Association, 55% of educators plan to leave the profession earlier than they anticipated because of burnout and increases in job expectations (Walker, 2022). Oregon's retention numbers suggest an even more bleak situation. The Oregon Department of Education (ODE) Staff Position Report (2021) states that approximately 61% of our first-year teachers did not return to their positions a second year; as shown in Figure 10.1, this retention pattern has become progressively worse between 2019 and 2022, leaving our state apprehensive of the future.

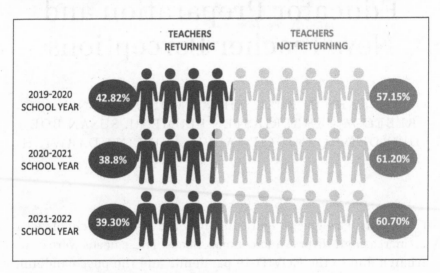

Figure 10.1. Teacher Retention by Year.
Note: Image retrieved from the 2022 Oregon Educator Equity Report.

To counteract this alarming forecast and the realities occurring presently in our state, research supports developing socioemotionally competent educators so they can better manage the stressors of the modern learning environment, including self-care (Yang et al, 2021). According to Donahue-Keegan, Villaegas-Reimers, and Cressey (2019), "Mounting research evidence points to why it is vitally important for teachers, in all types of schools and at all levels, to develop culturally responsive social-emotional learning (SEL) skills, beginning with preservice training" (p. 151). Fostering culturally responsive SEL skill development in teacher preparation programs supports new teachers to develop foundational competencies for (a) maintaining their own health, well-being, and emotional resilience—to avoid burnout (Jennings, 2018); (b) fostering students' SEL skills through strength-based, rigorous academic learning; and (c) engaging in authentic culturally responsive teaching, to equitably reach and teach students with a range of backgrounds (e.g., cultural, racial, socioeconomic) and social identities (Gay, 2002; Hammond & Jackson, 2015; Yang et al., 2021).

Teachers play a vital role in creating the kind of classroom environment that promotes SEL and positive social-emotional development among students, including sustainable practices that support their own retention; however, when the Oregon Teacher Standards and Practices Commission (TSPC) evaluated the retention trends in our own state, it was determined that reevaluating our SEL requirements and outcomes was necessary.

Purpose of the Study

This case study leans on the research of Schonert-Reichl et al. (2014). These researchers set out to better understand how well incorporated SEL is in teacher training requirements. "According to [the] Collaborative for Academic, Social, and Emotional Learning (CASEL) report, a whopping 83 percent of teachers stated that they want training in social-emotional learning (SEL) skills" (p. 1), inferring that they did not receive SEL as part of their training or professional development, or that the training was not comprehensive enough to meet their needs. Further, a recent scan of U.S. teacher education programs conducted by Dr. Kimberly Schonert-Reichl and Dr. Shelley Hymel showed that very few U.S. preservice teachers are actually receiving training in SEL (2017). In that report, Dr. Schonert-Reichl proposed a conceptual framework for SEL that includes three components of well-rounded SEL: The Learning Context[1], SEL of Students[2], and SEL of Teachers[3] as shown in Figure 10.2.

Given Schonert-Reichl's findings, TSPC sought to delve into our own teacher preparation outcomes to better understand how our Educator Preparation Providers (EPPs) are performing in these

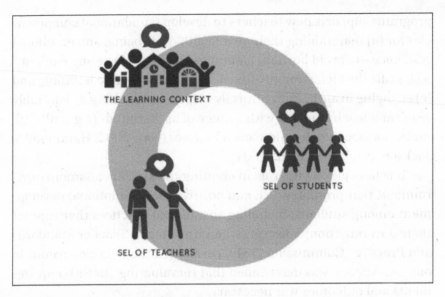

Figure 10.2. Social and Emotional Learning Conceptual Framework.
Note: Image retrieved from Schonert-Reichl et al., 2017.

areas (e.g., developing foundational SEL competencies among their candidates) and how TSPC may support them with the barriers or challenges their programs may be experiencing in carrying out this important work. The purpose of this chapter is to describe how TSPC is working to bridge the gap between SEL theory and practice implementation in K-12 by supporting EPP reconceptualization of SEL integration in teacher preparation programs.

Nature of the Situation

Before conducting the case study presented here, which is focused on the results of an SEL Survey of Newly Licensed Teachers, the TSPC partnered with other Oregon state agencies to review the needs of and alignment to student learning standards related to SEL resulting in a framework. After the completion of the framework, it was evident that there was a need to investigate the extent to which Oregon education preparation providers integrate whole child practices, more specifically SEL and trauma-informed practices, into their programming.

Oregon Educator Preparation Program SEL Framework

Driven by the need to support Oregon K-12 students and their social and emotional well-being, the ODE, with consultation from TSPC and in collaboration with other education partners, created a framework and standards for K-12 students. In alignment, TSPC developed a framework and standards that specifically address the unique needs of teacher preparation to support new teachers as they embark in the K-12 system. Oregon's vision for SEL focuses on the social and emotional elements of learning, teaching, and cultivating affirming school cultures through a transformative approach. A framework for SEL that bridges the K-12 and EPP systems will be critical for the universal integration of SEL across settings. Given that most districts and Education Service Districts (ESDs) in Oregon, as well as the state's Early Learning and Kindergarten Guidelines (2016), align their SEL practices and programming with the CASEL framework, it was important to TSPC that our educator SEL framework align with CASEL as well.

Oregon Educator Preparation Program SEL Survey

As TSPC embarked on work related to whole child and whole educator practices, it was important to identify current practices related to social, emotional, and cultural competency within Oregon EPPs. While all of Oregon's programs are accredited regionally and nationally, each has a unique lens for preparing qualified teachers for the classroom. As a result, there was a lack of consistency across providers as to where and how SEL was evident within programs. For clarity, TSPC surveyed EPPs requesting they self-identify in which courses SEL typically occurs in their programs. This Educator Preparation SEL Survey was sent in January 2022 to the Deans and Directors, and those who would best identify SEL-supporting concepts and strategies within their programs. Of our 16 Oregon preparation programs, 10 responded.

Qualitative responses were coded into minor categories and then grouped into major categories. Findings identified Teaching Methods, and Classroom Management/Environment/Behavior courses as where SEL is most likely to be taught across all Oregon EPPs as shown in

Table 10.1. When the courses were analyzed using Dr. Schonert-Reichl's conceptual framework, courses primarily aligned to (1) the Learning Context and (2) Student SEL. A gap identified a need for increased focus on Educator SEL. However, we know that while preparation programs may cover content, there is often a gap between what is learned in a teaching program and whether it can be applied in a teaching setting by a new teacher (Rovio-Johansson, 2019). It was important to TSPC that we surveyed new teachers to understand their Oregon preparation program experience and how prepared they feel to implement SEL in K-12.

Table 10.1. Count of Courses by Major Category

Major Category	**Conceptual Framework Area**	**Count**
Teaching Methods	Learning Context	11
Classroom Management/Environment/Behavior	Learning Context	10
Cultural/Diversity/Inclusive Practices	Student SEL	6
Humanistic Theory/Whole Child Practices/Overall Wellness	Student SEL	6
Learning Theory	Learning Context	5
Field Experience	Learning Context	5
SEL Integrated into All Coursework	All	1
Educator SEL	Educator SEL	1

Case Study

While working through the process of drafting the framework and standards for SEL in EPPs, we noted a misalignment between what EPPs are currently teaching to teacher candidates, and what new teachers are reporting they need in the field. However, all the information that existed in Oregon on new teachers' needs was qualitative reporting from district staff (e.g., SPED workforce shortage summit). It was determined that TSPC would survey new teachers on their experience of SEL in their teacher preparation programs and how prepared they felt to be new teachers. The hypothesis was that new teachers would agree that EPPs covered SEL for Students and SEL in the Learning Context adequately, but that SEL for Teachers was lacking.

Participants

Our first step in understanding how to best support EPPs was to survey new teachers, with "new teacher" being defined as any teacher who completed an Oregon EPP and was granted their first preliminary teaching license between 2017 and 2022. Evidence suggests that the first five years of teaching is a critical time for targeted retention efforts. The National Association of Secondary School Principals reported in 2020 that nearly half of new teachers leave the classroom in their first five years of teaching, with 9.5% leaving within the first year (Abitabile, 2020).

For this survey, new teachers were identified through Program Completion Reports submitted by Oregon EPPs. Individuals were removed from the participant list if they completed a nonteaching license program (e.g., personnel services, administrators), or if they had received an add-on endorsement during that period (e.g., were initially licensed before 2017). An initial email invitation to complete the survey was sent in spring 2022 to 4087 individuals that included the survey link through Qualtrics, and two follow-up reminders to complete the survey were sent once per month following. Of those who responded, most identified as female (71.38%) and held a master's degree (73.19%).

Method

The survey, named the New Teacher Survey, was designed by TSPC in partnership with the University of Portland and Lewis and Clark Graduate School of Education. The New Teacher Survey included 43 questions to gain the perspective of new teachers' experience with SEL in their Oregon educator preparation program, followed by 16 demographic questions (e.g., length of time they have been in a licensed position, highest degree earned). The questions on the survey were patterned after other large-scale surveys that had been recently distributed. These include The American Teacher Panel Survey (Hamilton et al., 2019), the Albany Survey of Former New York City Teachers (Boyd et al., 2006), and the British Columbia Teachers' Council New Teacher Survey (BC Teachers' Council, 2015). Most questions asked the candidates to respond using a five-point Likert scale to indicate how well their program prepared them in each of the areas investigated; the Likert scale and corresponding point values are provided below.

- Very Poorly Prepared – 1
- Poorly Prepared – 2
- Prepared – 3
- Well Prepared – 4
- Very Well Prepared – 5

Our case study analyzed the following questions from survey Section 3, Feelings of Preparedness in SEL: As you began your teaching career, how well do you feel your teacher preparation program prepared you to: (refer to survey question 12)[4]

1. Know how to develop and maintain a caring and supportive learning environment where the social and emotional development of students is nurtured? (e.g., Learning Context, refer to survey question 12_2).
2. Develop your own social and emotional skills and capacity so that you can successfully manage the challenges and stressors of teaching? (e.g., Teacher SEL, refer to survey question 12_6).
3. Know how to provide SEL-based instruction to students? (e.g., Student SEL, refer to survey question 12_1).

Survey Results and Discussion

While overall participation was low (n = 276; 6.75% participation rate), all Oregon teacher preparation providers were represented in the results, and participation rates reflect the proportion of completers we would typically see from each program. Of those surveyed, 125 held a Multiple Subjects endorsement (e.g., typically elementary level), 95 held a Single Subjects endorsement (e.g., typically secondary level), 33 held a Special Education (SPED) endorsement, and 6 reported holding an "Other" endorsement (e.g., substitute, private school, K-8, and early learning related endorsements).

Responses to our focused questions (e.g., exploring the extent that teachers felt prepared to create SEL-focused learning environments, manage the challenges and stressors of teaching using their own SEL skills, and support the SEL development of their students), revealed some interesting trends. Overall, about 70% of individuals surveyed felt prepared (Prepared, Well Prepared, or Very Well Prepared) to create an SEL-supportive learning environment (see Figure 3). However, only about 50% of individuals reported feelings of preparedness to develop their own SEL skills to manage the challenges and stressors of teaching (48%) and provide SEL-based instruction to students (49%) (see Figures 10.4 and 10.5).

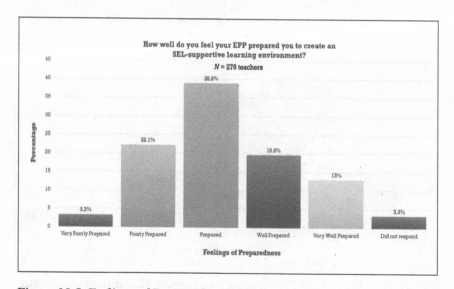

Figure 10.3. Feelings of Preparedness.
Note: The survey item reads as follows: "How well do you feel your EPP prepared you to create an SEL-supportive learning environment?" (Image retrieved from Sauve et al. 2023).

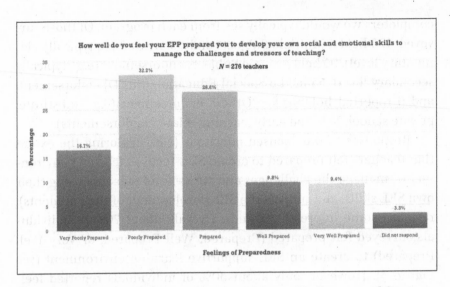

Figure 10.4. Feelings of Preparedness to Manage Challenges and Stressors of Teaching.
Note: The survey item reads as follows: "How well do you feel your EPP prepared you to develop your own social and emotional skills to manage the challenges and stressors of teaching?" (Image retrieved from Sauve et al., 2023).

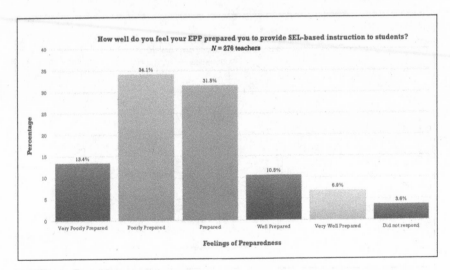

Figure 10.5. Feelings of Preparedness to Provide SEL Instruction to Students.
Note: The survey item reads as follows: "How well do you feel your EPP prepared you to provide SEL-based instruction to students?" (Image retrieved from Sauve et al., 2023.

Table 10.2 shows the average response of candidates by license endorsement area for each of the Likert scale questions included in this study. On average, regardless of license endorsement level, teachers reported that they felt well prepared for teaching SEL in the Learning Context ($M = 3.17$); however, all teachers felt less prepared on average to manage the stress of teaching using Teacher SEL strategies and skills ($M = 2.55$) and serve individual Student SEL needs ($M = 2.60$).

Table 10.2. Feelings of Preparedness in SEL by Endorsement Area

License Endorsement	Learning Context	Teacher SEL	Student SEL
Elementary	3.15	2.61	2.69
Secondary	3.18	2.48	2.52
Total	3.17	2.55	2.60

Supplemental Findings

Upon analysis of the initial survey findings, two additional interesting results surfaced: increased feelings of preparedness in SEL for special education teachers, and a lack of explicit coursework in SEL in EPP programming. Regarding special education teachers, on average, individuals with a SPED endorsement noted higher reported feelings of preparedness in managing the stresses of teaching using Teacher SEL strategies skills ($M = 3.03$) (see Table 10.3).

Table 10.3. Feelings of Preparedness in SEL for Special Educators

License Endorsement	Learning Context	Teacher SEL	Student SEL
SPED	3.15	3.03	2.61

The data identified in Table 10.3 led the authors to ask additional questions, "What might be contributing to the differences in outcomes between SPED program participants and general education teachers (e.g., elementary and secondary level) as reported by new teachers?" The authors theorize that SPED teachers may receive more preparation in SEL to prevent burnout due to the high demands of the position, or SEL has been integrated into SPED programs for a longer period in relation to other program types. Exploring these theories was beyond the scope of this case study, but worthy of note for future research opportunities.

Additionally, TSPC noted that new teachers surveyed reported not having explicit coursework in SEL in their EPP (76.09%) (see Figure 6). Of note, despite EPPs reporting that SEL content is occurring in all their programs (see Table 10.1).

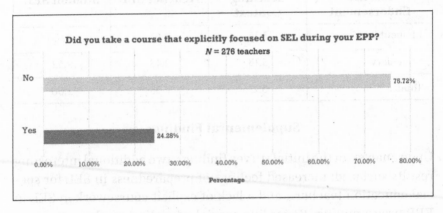

Figure 10.6. Explicit SEL Coursework.
Note: The survey item reads as follows: "Did you take a course that explicitly focused on SEL during your EPP?"[5] (Image retrieved from Sauve et al., 2023).

These findings did not vary significantly by endorsement area, with secondary teachers reporting less SEL-explicit coursework than elementary teachers (Elementary: 74.4%; Secondary: 78.13%). Special Education teachers reporting did not vary significantly from elementary or secondary teachers (75.76%) (see Table 10.4).

The data in Table 10.4, alongside the results from the Oregon Educator Preparation Program SEL Survey, indicate variations between EPP and new teacher reporting of SEL-explicit coursework and integration within programs.

Table 10.4. Percent of Teachers Who Report Whether or Not They Received Explicit Coursework in SEL

License Endorsement	Yes	No
Elementary	25.60%	74.40%
Secondary	21.88%	78.13%
Special Education	24.24%	75.76%
Total	23.90%	76.09%

Summary and Next Steps

This case study, although limited in scope, highlights that a large majority of Oregon teachers report that they did not receive explicit coursework in SEL. Schonert-Reichl (2017) states "that warm classroom environments and positive teacher-student relationships promote both academic learning and SEL. Hence, teachers do not just need to know how to explicitly teach social and emotional skills; they also need the knowledge, dispositions, and skills for creating a safe, caring, supportive, and responsive school and classroom community." Our Oregon experience supports this research and indicates that there is a need for both explicit and integrated approaches to training future teachers. The implications for practice are vast, especially as we look toward meeting the needs of our students in the K-12 classroom while also supporting the teacher along their career pathway. Oregon TSPC's mission is to ensure Oregon schools have access to well-trained, effective, and accountable education professionals so all students are well-equipped to pursue and achieve their goals. Oregon EPPs must adhere to a set of administrative rules, including standards, and design programs to meet those specifications while utilizing a continuous improvement lens to support the ever-changing educational landscape on their pathway to compliance.

Well-established and emerging research, including the case study in our own state, supports the need for SEL preparation and a review of the related standards on which EPPs rely. The State Standards for SEL in Educator Preparation were completed by TSPC in March 2023, and EPPs have already started identifying how well-rounded SEL can be better integrated into their programs. One high-level example of this identification can be found in a program matrix produced by an Oregon university. This matrix outlines where SEL competencies are currently embedded within coursework, experiences, and assessments. The competencies are displayed as column headers, and there are rows for knowledge, modeling, practice, and reflection, with the supporting evidence at the points of intersection. This structure allows for a visual representation for the university to see where SEL is adequately covered in programs, and identifies gaps where additional coverage is needed.

Additionally, in the fall of 2024 K-12 SEL standards will go into effect and EPPs will need to demonstrate growth toward those standards through self-reflection and program analysis. The results from this case study highlight specific areas where EPPs can intentionally target SEL instruction to better meet the identified needs of new teachers and reinforces the important work EPPs need to do to strengthen SEL in teacher preparation. As a result, TSPC is designing a scaffolded plan to support Oregon EPPs in intentionally integrating SEL into teacher preparation. Oregon TSPC will support EPPs in the implementation of these standards through the following:

1. Collaboration between EPPs through the continued work of the Oregon Collaborative for SEL in Educator Preparation (OCSEP).
2. Creation of a communal space for SEL resources (e.g., sample syllabi, literature library).
3. Collaboration with ODE on Professional Development and other professional learning resources for teachers.
4. Creation of a system of evaluation and accountability.

In recognition of the Association for Advancing Quality in Educator Preparation's (AAQEP)'s twin aims of quality assurance and continuous improvement, TSPC seeks a local process that is formative, collaborative, and in keeping with Oregon's unique context.

Implications for Future Research

Schoolwide Culture and Climate

"TSPC envisions a teacher's context to be an interconnected web of systems which coordinate to shape learning, development, and experiences" (Oregon Teachers Standards and Practices Commission SEL Framework, 2022, p. 9). When students learn and teachers work in an environment that is safe and supportive, they are more likely to develop the social and emotional competencies they need to be successful in school and in life (CASEL District Resource Center, 2021). The social and emotional skills that develop and are fostered within the classroom can increase student resiliency, improve attendance, and decrease behaviors that often lead to exclusion. Additionally, research has shown that "SEL approaches not only provide benefits to a student's social-emotional skills, but these approaches also provide benefits to student academic success" (Oregon HB 2166 Phase II SEL Advisory Group, 2023). Beyond the classroom, improved schoolwide culture and climate has been shown to improve teacher well-being including increased job satisfaction and improved teacher retention (see, e.g., Bryk, 2010; Moore Johnson et al., 2012; Papay & Kraft, 2017), begging the question of whether a direct and intentional focus on improving school climate and culture could change the current trajectory of the state of the teacher workforce.

The School Leader's Role in SEL Implementation

Kendziora & Yoder (2016) note that educational leaders play a significant role in providing the support and guidance needed to implement effective SEL programming and ultimately play a key role in cultivating a schoolwide culture and climate that comprise successful SEL programming. Moreover, principals in districts that place a high emphasis on SEL report greater levels of success in developing students' social and emotional skills, as well as greater implementation across a host of benchmarks. Key strategies include SEL integration into curricula, all teachers being expected to teach SEL, and having a SEL planning team in place to support SEL (Atwell & Bridgeland, 2019). Additionally, an explicit focus on teacher wellness enhances the capacity of the classroom teacher to implement the strategies envisioned by the leadership. Ongoing training for administrators enhances their ability to support schoolwide practices, develop relevant professional development activities that support SEL learning, and practice SEL strategies that support teacher wellness.

Endnotes

1. Examples include communication styles, school climate, policies, performance expectations, etc.
2. Defined as the process by which K-12 students apply knowledge, attitudes, and skills in the five CASEL competency areas (responsible decision-making, relationship skills, social awareness, self-awareness, and self-management).
3. Defined as a teacher's own social-emotional competency and overall well-being.
4. For a survey copy, email kristin.rush@tspc.oregon.gov
5. The research team acknowledges the possibility that new teachers interpreted this question to indicate a single course while EPPs may have reported content across multiple courses.

References

Abitabile, A. W. (2020). *Making teachers stick: January 2020*. NASSP. https://www.nassp.org/publication/principal-leadership/volume-20/principal-leadership-january-2020/making-teachers-stick-january-2020/

Atwell, M., & Bridgeland, J. (2019). Ready to lead: A 2019 update of principals perspectives on how SEL learning can prepare children and transform schools. A Report for CASEL.

Bakker, A. B., Demerouti, E., & Sanz-Vergel, A. I. (2014). Burnout and work engagement: The JD-R approach. *Annual Review of Organizational Psychology and Organizational Behavior, 1*(1), 389-411. https://doi.org/10.1146/annurev-orgpsych-031413-091235

Bhatnagar, R., & Many, J. (2022). Teachers using social emotional learning: Meeting student needs during COVID-19. *International Journal of Technology in Education* (IJTE), *5*(3), 518-534. https://doi.org/10.46328/ijte.310

Boyd, D., Grossman, P., Hamilton, L., Loeb, S., & Wyckoff, J. (2006). *Albany survey of former New York City teachers*. Stanford University. https://cepa.stanford.edu/sites/default/files/2006%20Albany%20Survey%20of%20Former%20NYC%20Teachers_060301.pdf

British Columbia Teachers' Council. (2015). *New Teacher Survey*. https://www2.gov.bc.ca/assets/gov/education/kindergarten-to-grade-12/teach/

teacher-regulation/teacher-education-programs/bctcteachersurvey-2015
results.pdf

Bryk, A. S. (2010). Organizing schools for improvement. *Phi Delta Kappan, 91*(7), 23–30. https://doi.org/10.1177/003172171009100705

Clunies-Ross, P., Little, E., & Kienhuis, M. (2008). Self-reported and actual use of proactive and reactive classroom management strategies and their relationship with teacher stress and student behaviour. *Educational Psychology, 28*, 693–710.

Collaborative for Academic, Social and Emotional Learning. (2021). SEL Framework. from https://casel.org/casel-sel-framework-11-2020/

Collaborative for Academic, Social and Emotional Learning. (2021). District Resource Center. https://drc.casel.org/promote-sel-for-students

Donahue-Keegan, D., Villegas-Reimers, E., & Cressey, J. M. (2019). Integrating social-emotional learning and culturally responsive teaching in teacher education preparation programs. *Teacher Education Quarterly, 46*(4), 150–168.

Early Learning and Kindergarten Guidelines. (2016). Oregon Department of Education Early Learning Division. https://www.oregon.gov/ode/students-and-family/Transitioning-to-Kindergarten/Documents/ODE_EarlyLearning Standards_final.pdf

Eblie Trudel, L., Sokal, L., & Babb, J. (2021). *Teachers' voices: Pandemic lessons for the future of education. Journal of Teaching and Learning, 75*(1), 4–19. https://doi.org/10.22329/jtl.v15i1.6486

Gay, G. (2002). Preparing for culturally responsive teaching. *Journal of Teacher Education, 53*(2), 106–116. https://doi.org/10.1177/0022487102053002003

Hamilton, L., Doss, C., & Steiner, E. (2019). *Teacher and Principal Perspectives on Social and Emotional Learning in America's Schools: Findings from the American Educator Panels.* https://doi.org/10.7249/rr2991

Hammond, Z., & Jackson, Y. (2015). Culturally responsive teaching and the brain: Promoting authentic engagement and rigor among culturally and linguistically diverse students. Corwin, a SAGE Company.

Harmsen, R., Helms-Lorenz, M., Maulana, R., & van Veen, K. (2018). The relationship between beginning teachers' stress causes, stress responses, teaching behaviour and attrition. *Teachers and Teaching, 24*(6), 626–643. https://doi.org/10.1080/13 540602.2018.1465404

Jennings, P. A. (2018). *Trauma informed classroom: Building resilience with compassionate teaching.* W. W. Norton.

Kendziora, K., & Yoder, N. (2016). When districts support and integrate social and emotional learning (SEL): Findings from an ongoing evaluation of districtwide implementation of SEL. Washington, D.C.: American Institutes for Research. https://casel.org/wp-content/uploads/2017/04/When-DistrictsSupport-SEL-Brief.pdf

Maulana, R., Helms-Lorenz, M., & van de Grift, W. (2014). Development and evaluation of a questionnaire measuring pre-service teachers' teaching behaviour: A

Rasch modelling approach. *School Effectiveness and School Improvement, 26*(2), 169–194. https://doi.org/10.1080/09243453.2014.939198

Moore Johnson, S. (2012). Build the capacity of teachers and their schools. *Phi Delta Kappan, 94*(2), 62–65. https://doi.org/10.1177/003172171209400215

Oregon Department of Education (2021). Staff Position Report. https://odedistrict.oregon.gov/CollectionsValidations/Collections/Documents/21-22%20Staff%20Position%20Audit%20Manual.pdf

Oregon House Bill 2166 Phase II SEL Advisory Group. (2023). Social and emotional learning framework and Standards. In press.

Oregon Teacher Standards and Practices SEL Framework. (2022). *Strengthening social, emotional and culturally sustaining teaching practices A framework for Oregon educator preparation.* https://www.oregon.gov/tspc/EPP/Documents/Oregon%20TSPC%20Educator%20SEL%20Framework%20%26%20Standards.pdf

Papay, J. P., & Kraft, M. A. (2017). Developing workplaces where teachers stay, improve, & succeed: Recent evidence on the importance of school climate for teacher success. In E. Quintero, ed. Teaching in Context: *How Social Aspects of School and School Systems Shape Teachers' Development and Effectiveness.* Cambridge, MA: Harvard Education Press.

Rovio-Johansson, A. (2019). Reinvestigating the theory and practice gap in Participatory Educational Research. *International Journal for Lesson and Learning Studies, 9*(1), 1–10. https://doi.org/10.1108/IJLLS-01-2020-094

Sauve, J., Rush, K. J., Darwich, L., & Hon, D. (2023). *Opportunities for SEL in Oregon's teacher preparation programs: What do early career teachers think?* Presentation delivered at the Oregon Association of Teacher Education.

Schonert-Reichl, K. A. (2017). Social and emotional learning and teachers. *The Future of Children, 27*(1), 137–155. https://doi.org/10.1353/foc.2017.0007

Schonert-Reichl, K. A., & Weissberg, R. P. (2014). Social and emotional learning during childhood. In T. P. Gullotta & M. Bloom (Eds.), *Encyclopedia of primary prevention and health promotion,* 2nd edition (pp. 936–949). New York: Springer Press

Schonert-Reichl, K. A., Kitil, M. J., & Hanson-Peterson, J. (2017). To reach the students, teach the teachers: A national scan of teacher preparation and social and emotional learning. A report prepared for the Collaborative for Academic, Social, and Emotional Learning (CASEL). Vancouver, B.C.: University of British Columbia

Skaalvik, E. M., & Skaalvik, S. (2015). Job satisfaction, stress and coping strategies in the teaching profession—what do teachers say? *International Education Studies, 8*(3). https://doi.org/10.5539/ies.v8n3p181

Walker, T. (2022). Survey: Alarming number of educators may soon leave the profession. NEA. https://www.nea.org/advocating-for-change/new-from-nea/survey-alarming-number-educators-may-soon-leave-profession

Yang, C., Manchanda, S., & Greenstein, J. (2021). Educators' online teaching self-efficacy and compassion fatigue during the COVID-19 pandemic: The dual roles of "connect." *School Psychology, 36*(6), 504–515. https://doi.org/10.1037/spq0000475

CHAPTER ELEVEN

Redesigning Principal Preparation Programs: A Continuous Improvement Culture Using Bambrick-Santoyo's Data Meeting Conceptual Framework

STEPHANIE ATCHLEY AND SHARON ROSS

Clinically-based principal preparation programs need updated coursework and curricula that reflect the real-world skills needed by principals in 21st-century schools.

—The Wallace Foundation

Overview: Changing Policy in Educator Preparation

State Policy and Organizational Views

Educator preparation changes are driven by state policymakers. These policymakers utilize levers as key items in the policies that are adopted. For many states, these key levers include certification standards, test options, and certification test tracking. In some states, like Texas, the education code defines the required courses, and often the requirements an educator must meet to be a principal. Thus, these levers prove significant as decisions surrounding the importance of each lever, or the extinction of levers, are made. This ultimately impacts the principal preparation program and certification outcomes for individuals as programs bend to make needed changes to meet mandated requirements from policymakers (Gates et al., 2020).

Effective policies should incorporate elements such as mentoring, coaching, focus on instructional leadership, networking, and simulation exercises to provide individualized support to new principals, ultimately contributing to improved leadership effectiveness and student outcomes (Abdelrahman et al., 2022; Darling-Hammond et al., 2007). Darling-Hammond (2022) pointed out the crucial role of policy in shaping the quality of principal learning programs. Successful programs aligned with high standards and supported by robust policies have demonstrated improvements in principal learning quality. While many states and districts have adopted standards for principal certification and program accreditation, not all have fully embraced other effective policies such as rigorous selection processes, clinically rich internships, district–university partnerships, or performance-based assessments for licensure.

Policymakers must work alongside universities to prepare the best, skilled school leaders spurred by improvements that are written into policy and enacted through levers. As university officials move to institute state-mandated improvements, the door opens for a more robust, stronger program to produce leaders ready to excel in schools.

Policy Impact on Principal Preparation

In 2016 the Texas State Board of Educator Certification re-designed the principal standards. With the re-design came new certification requirements that included the Principal as Instructional Leader (PAIL) certification test and the Performance Assessment for School Leaders (PASL) certification tasks. Both requirements reflect the skills new principals need to be successful instructional leaders. These new certification requirements were implemented on September 1, 2019.

Local Level Superintendent Input

While researchers continue to examine the need to improve and redesign principal preparation programs for various reasons, Davis

(2016) found that 80% of 408 surveyed district superintendents in 42
states shared dissatisfaction with quality and output based on the
effectiveness of those hired to lead campuses and indicated the need
for improvement in university programs. Davis further reported that
preparation program representatives from the colleges and universities agreed there was room for improvement. Those superintendents cited instructional leadership as being one of the lowest among
other responsibilities for which principals were prepared. Preparing
principal candidates requires understanding what superintendents
and districts look for during recruitment and what those individuals
will need for their jobs.

Conceptual Framework

The conceptual framework for this case, developed by Bambrick-
Santoyo (2016), was the weekly data meeting template. The framework emphasizes the iterative process of improvement through data-
driven decision-making, intentional practice, and targeted feedback.
Further, Bambrick-Santoyo (2019) suggests successful instructional
leaders intentionally build processes and systems to conduct deep,
quality analyses of previous work. The work done right is defined
as a common best practice (Bambrick-Santoyo, 2019). To meet
the new challenges of leadership, common best practices must be
taught in principal preparation programs. Not only does Bambrick-
Santoyo's conceptual framework yield high-leverage actions and
results for the day-to-day operations of campus leadership, it further improves the principal candidate's ability to move from theory
to practice when institutions of higher learning include the model
into the curriculum.

   To understand the vision of moving from theory to practice, a
working definition of data meetings is necessary. Data meetings are
as implied, data conferences held between campus leaders and teachers. Under Bambrick-Santoyo's (2016) design, these were not the traditional conferences held after an evaluation to discuss an observation. Data meetings were designed to look at results from a previous
assessment, or the work from the week prior, and change the culture and outcomes by focusing on the highest-leverage actions and
strategies that would yield different results. During these interim

meetings, both teacher and administrator are able to analyze, assess, and discuss data to increase accountability and enhance effectiveness. This framework is a blueprint for shifting gears. The campus leader coaches teachers into shifting gears in data meetings, creates a calendar in which the meetings and feedback are more frequent, and leads teams of teachers and other campus leaders to focus on getting better faster by taking action differently.

For school leaders, the highest leverage action for change is taking an observation and changing it to an interim assessment analysis meeting. Bambrick-Santoyo (2018) provides an example of effective data-meeting steps and what they might look like when applied by a principal. Following the See It, Name It, Do It steps, a principal would first prepare by analyzing data prior to the meeting and ensuring the standards being addressed are readily available for participant teachers. Bambrick-Santoyo suggests having a timer, chart paper, upcoming lesson plans, and samples of student work that range from low to high to discuss misconceptions and opportunities for reteaching. The leader is now prepared with materials and ready to begin coaching and leading a meeting averaging around 30 minutes of quality conversation.

Beginning with the See It and Name It steps of the framework, the leader can impact necessary changes. See what? See the exemplar first to understand where the rest of the students should be going. The principal will also want to review the exemplar and standard side by side, according to Bambrick-Santoyo (2018) to promote the use and requirement of the academic language describing student thought processes. The second step is to See the Gap between the exemplar responses and those responses that did not master concepts. Bambrick-Santoyo (2018, p. 62) provides sample questions to guide a leader's meetings such as:

- What does a student need to know and be able to do to master this standard?
- How does the exemplar response connect to the standard?

In seeing what students have done and what they need, all members of the team can collaboratively reach consensus on the next steps for student improvement. After the team sees the need, they can name the exemplar and the gaps noted by writing down their notes of students' misunderstandings, or misconceptions. Now the principal is ready to lead the team into the Do It step and shift the discussion to asking the teacher how he or she will reteach. The reteach is articulated but most importantly, planned, scripted, and practiced prior to implementation. At this step, the principal uses more prompts to ask key questions about the reteaching plans and whether the teacher wants to add more to the plan. The principal is ensuring the effective practice of the reteach so teachers and students can be successful.

Prior to the end of the meeting, teachers are asked to schedule a follow-up meeting to review action items and assess the reteaching. These interim data assessment meetings continued consistently, create a culture of continuous improvement, and shift theoretical leadership structures to daily practice. Bambrick-Santoyo (2018) provides a sample guide of the Weekly Data Meeting. Successful principals schedule weekly meetings but also ensure professional development is provided to ensure a greater understanding and the highest leverage strategies are considered. A meeting once a year will not yield high-impact results as seen in the schools using the model with fidelity.

A New Approach

The first submission window for the PASL certification tasks opened in the fall of 2019. The score reports for the first submission were released the following semester. For all students submitting PASL tasks, the Texas Education Agency (2022) reported a 76.41% first-attempt pass rate for the 2019–2020 administration and a 69.69% first-attempt pass rate for the 2020–2021 administration. Based on data reported by the Texas Education Agency, the instructors began implementing curriculum changes across the program to better prepare students to not just pass the PASL tasks but to also address the ever-evolving responsibilities and requirements of the principalship.

To address the marginal passing scores, instructors in the program sought to utilize a continuous improvement cycle. Garet et al. (2021) described continuous improvement as practitioners engaging in iterative cycles of inquiry by identifying problems of practice, implementing interventions, analyzing the results, and improving upon those interventions. This type of iterative cycle would allow the instructors to model data-driven best practices for the students as well as provide individualized feedback. The Bambrick-Santoyo data meeting template (2016) was already being used by students in the principal preparation program to target and address instructional issues at the campus and district level so it made for an easy transition to adapt the template to address individual student data for the PASL certification tasks.

Adapted Bambrick-Santoyo Data Meeting Template for Principal Preparation

Implementation of the adapted template began following the release of the first round of PASL score reports. While the Bambrick-Santoyo Data Meeting Template is typically used at the school or district level for analyzing student data collectively, its principles and steps were adapted to address low-performing ratings on the Performance Assessment for School Leaders certification tasks. Table 11.1 includes a step-by-step description of implementing the template for individual student data analysis.

Table 11.1. Adapted Template

Adapted Steps for PASL Tasks	Activity	Guiding Questions
Step 1: Pre-meeting Preparation	Introduce the purpose and benefits of the Bambrick-Santoyo Data Meeting Template to the student. Provide an overview of the data meeting process and its role in informing instructional improvement. For this meeting, the assessment results from three PASL-like tasks will be the focus of the data meeting. Ensure that participants have access to the instructor-developed rubric and score report.	Guiding Questions Prior to the meeting, students need their individual ratings from the three PASL-like assignments.

Adapted Steps for PASL Tasks	Activity	Guiding Questions
Step 2: Determine Objectives and Key Questions	Determine the key objectives and questions to be addressed during the data meeting. Create an agenda that outlines the topics, data points, and discussion points to be covered. Ensure that the meeting stays focused and productive. Meetings should be conducted in a 30-minute time period.	What successes have you recently experienced in the content area to build on? What do you need to know and do to master the PASL-like activities? Review the exemplar.
Step 3: Data Analysis	Facilitate a collaborative analysis of the data by guiding participants through a structured process. Start by presenting an overview of the data, highlighting key trends, patterns, and areas of concern. Encourage participants to contribute their observations, insights, and interpretations of the data.	Are there any gaps or differences between your work and the exemplar? What does this tell you about your understanding or misunderstanding?
Step 4: Identify Focus Area	Engage students in identifying patterns and trends in the data, focusing on both strengths and areas that require improvement. Facilitate a discussion to determine the most significant needs or priorities that emerge from the data analysis. Encourage participants to consider the implications of the data for instructional strategies, interventions, or professional development opportunities.	What are the gaps you see between the activity steps with a high rating and the steps with a lower rating? What is the highest leverage misconception to fix? What does the data tell you is the highest leverage step? What specific task and step do you plan to target?
Step 5: Develop an Action Plan	Guide students in developing action plans based on the identified needs and priorities. Ensure that action plans are specific, measurable, attainable, relevant, and time-bound.	What are the Principal as Instructional Leader Domains and Competencies that address the target area? When will you submit the revised step?

Adapted from *Get better faster: A 90-day plan for coaching new teachers* (pp. 231–232), by P. Bambrick-Santoyo, 2016, Wiley Inc. Copyright 2016 by Jossey-Bass. Reprinted with permission.

Sustaining the Continuous Improvement Cycle

Implementing a systematic approach to identifying, analyzing, and implementing improvements for student performance on PASL certification tasks is ongoing. For this Texas public university, the task force team modeled a culture of continuous improvement to sustain momentum. Program instructors and coordinators implemented the adapted template in their courses with fidelity and the task force team continues to meet on a regular basis to assess and evaluate student performance as it pertains to the PASL certification tasks. Finally, the task force solicits feedback from instructors, students, and industry professionals to inform the continuous improvement process.

Lessons Learned

Faculty members coordinating principal preparation programs must not wait to be guided by university department heads or other officials who may or may not know the program requirements, or needs. Program coordinators and other educational leadership department faculty should be the leaders arming others in their departments, college, and university with recommendations based on data-driven decision-making from audits, certification changes, and/or legislative/policy changes from national, state, and local levels.

Looking back, the following lessons were learned the hard way; however, they are now recommendations for others to use during the beginning redesign stages:

- Include a coaching module or unit in the curriculum
- Add additional time to Data Meetings Module to ensure understanding
- Create opportunities for principal candidates to practice with each other (model) the Data Meetings from beginning to end prior to using in the practicum
- Require principal candidates to conduct at least two data meetings in practicum for two different content areas
- Create an exemplar video of professors modeling a data meeting
- Ensure all adjuncts understand the curriculum requirements and have regular meetings regarding the new curriculum changes.

Recommendations for Creating a Network to Sustain Continuous Improvement

Adapted from The Wallace Foundation (Davis, 2016)

- Review/Revise Selection process—recruitment (specific candidate performance assessments, interviews, leadership readiness exercises, specific certification/teaching experience, specific degree requirements
- Ensure internships that integrate the curriculum, promote meaningful mentorships/supervision, and include authentic, reflective experiences when logging activity hours that are based on state standards and local needs.
- University/district partnerships that include intentional meetings/collaboration from candidate selection, and program design, to graduation/completion.
- Program oversight that includes feedback from all parties to improve practice
- Curriculum review and alignment with state standards and state assessments for certification
- Regularly scheduled feedback from students/university/district partners to inform practice and effectiveness
- Use certification test results to determine the quality and effectiveness of program knowledge (low but passing; mid-range; high scoring)
- Train new faculty on curriculum requirements and course non-negotiables such as Bambrick-Santoyo Data Meeting Template

Research Implications

Longitudinal studies should be conducted to assess the long-term effects of implementing the adapted framework in principal preparation programs. Possible topics for examination might include career trajectories and the success of certified principals. This research can provide insights into the framework's sustainability and its influence on principal retention, leadership development, and overall school improvement.

Comparative studies have the potential to inform practice for principal preparation programs. Comparative research can compare principal certification programs that utilize the adapted framework with those that do not, evaluating the differential outcomes on pass rates on the PASL certification tasks.

Discussion and Conclusion

Implementing a systematic approach to continuous improvement is essential for principal preparation programs seeking high-quality instruction and preparing principal candidates for future success. By following the steps outlined above, this Texas principal preparation program established a culture of continuous improvement and set clear goals and objectives. Creating a culture of continuous improvement is crucial as it encourages students to actively participate in identifying problems and developing solutions. When students feel empowered and supported in this process, they become more engaged and motivated to contribute their ideas and expertise. This collaborative, iterative approach has fostered innovation and continues to drive positive change throughout the program.

References

Abdelrahman, N., Irby, B. J., Lara-Alecio, R., & Tong, F. (2022). The influence of university principal preparation program policies on the program internship. *SAGE Open, 12*(3). https://doi.org/10.1177/21582440221117110

Bambrick-Santoyo, P. (2016). *Get better faster: A 90-day plan for coaching new teachers*. Jossey-Bass; A Wiley Brand.

Bambrick-Santoyo, P. (2018). *Leverage Leadership 2.0: A practical guide to building exceptional schools*. Jossey-Bass; A Wiley Brand.

Bambrick-Santoyo, P. (2019). *Driven by data 2.0: A practical guide to improve instruction*. Jossey-Bass; A Wiley Brand.

Darling-Hammond, L., LaPointe, M., Meyerson, D., Orr. M. T., & Cohen, C. (2007). *Preparing school leaders for a changing world: Lessons from exemplary leadership development programs*. Stanford, CA: Stanford University, Stanford Educational Leadership Institute

Darling-Hammond, L., Wechsler, M. E., Levin, S., Leung-Gagné, M., & Tozer, S. (2022). Developing effective principals: What kind of learning matters? [Report]. Learning Policy Institute. https://doi.org/10.54300/641.201

Davis, J. (2016). *Improving university principal preparation programs: five themes from the field*. The Wallace Foundation. https://www.wallacefoundation.org/knowledge-center/Documents/Improving-University-Principal-Preparation-Programs.pdf

Garet, M., Mitrano, S., Eisner, R., Kochanek, J., Jones, K., Ibis, M., & Estrada, S. (2021, August). *Continuous improvement in education settings - air.org*. American Institute for Research. https://www.air.org/sites/default/files/2022-03/Continuous-Improvement-in-Education-Settings-A-Literature-Review-August-2021.pdf

Gates, S. M., Woo, A., Xenakis, L., Wang, E. L., Herman, R., Andrew, M., and Todd, I. (2020). *Using state-level policy levers to promote principal quality: Lessons from seven states partnering with principal preparation programs and districts*. RAND Corporation. https://www.rand.org/pubs/research_reports/RRA413-1.html. Also available in print form.

Texas Education Agency. (2022). *PASL Annual Report 2021-2022*. Texas Education Agency. https://tea.texas.gov/media/document/351911

CHAPTER TWELVE

Using a Data-Driven Dialogue Protocol for Continuous Improvement

KRISTEN M. DRISKILL

When our institution switched our accrediting body to Association for Advancing Quality in Educator Preparation (AAQEP), there were great things happening at the time in terms of curriculum and assessment. We had established and grown school-university partnerships, updated curricula across all programs, and aligned all initial certification programs so candidates had similar experiences, just to name a few. This was no small feat in that we are a small, private institution with limited resources, including faculty. Although warranted, none of those updates were part of a formal, documented quality assurance system. Of course, faculty communicated regularly with one another as well as our stakeholders, which is what brought about most of the changes made. However, a consistent system for this continuous improvement was lacking.

What was also lacking was data-driven decision-making. Given that a formal quality assurance system was not solidly in place, documentation for any changes made simply did not exist. Rather than collecting data to show the need to make curricular or structural program changes, and then collecting data to show the impact of such changes, all the work being done appeared to be done randomly. Of course, that was not the case, and all changes made were justified and certainly needed. But none of the improvements made could be traced back to data or any documentation.

We know the value of using data to inform our instructional decisions and the positive impact it has on student achievement (Bambrick-Santoyo, 2010). Data, therefore, became the foundation of our quality assurance system. Creating a system to collect and organize data, analyze data regularly, use and document data to inform decision-making, track data over time to assess progress, and integrate data into our regular department discourse was sorely needed. As a new leader, I worked with the department to embrace data and allow it to drive all that we do for our teacher candidates. This involved a major climate shift, the adoption of a data-driven dialogue protocol, and a change to how the department met and worked together for the purpose of student achievement.

Shifting to a Data-Driven Climate

I had just come to higher education from the P-12 world, where data-driven instruction is non-negotiable. Every day, teachers use data to make nearly every decision they do. I had been an instructional coach and, therefore, led schools and districts to use their state and local data to make instructional decisions on a regular basis. Data-driven instruction seemed like common sense in the field of education. So, as I moved into the role of Program Director of one of the initial certification programs at my institution, I assumed the same could be said in higher education. I began my time as a Program Director by looking closely at the data that were being used across all programs so I could be sure I was adequately using program-specific data. What I realized was that I had assumed incorrectly. The department had quite a bit of data available, but it was not being used in any consistent or systematic way across programs. That is not to say that data were not reviewed. Rather, there was not a system in place for data to be reviewed collaboratively or consistently. I saw this as a significant gap, yet one that could be simple to address. At the very least, we had access to data from state certification exams. In addition, we were in the process of defining and refining our program key assessments. It only made sense to me that we more intentionally use data within our quality assurance system to inform continuous improvement efforts.

Therefore, I began using data regularly within my program steering committee meetings, which met once a week. The program is a degree-completion, nontraditional, cohort-based initial certification program. Over the course of a semester, we would analyze all state certification exams, student teaching rubrics, professional dispositions rubrics, and GPA for a given cohort and would, in turn, use our findings to inform any updating that was warranted. For example, one of the first pieces of data analyzed in my program steering committee was edTPA data. Upon analysis, it was clear that candidates in the program struggled with writing skills. We, therefore, reordered courses in the program so that the first course candidates would take is a writing course, and we revised it to better address professional writing. The steering committee felt that this would better set teacher candidates up for success in the program, and subsequent data analysis verified this. In my time as Program Director, many changes were made to the program including adding in courses where teacher candidates needed more instructional time or practice with content, removing courses that were redundant or not helpful, lengthening the student teaching experience, and hiring new adjuncts who were current instructional leaders in the P-12 space. Specific curricular changes were made as well such as integrating more coursework around diversity, equity, and inclusion, integrating the state standards more intentionally, switching out texts and materials to include diverse perspectives and current resources used in local schools, and better addressing how to work with English Language Learners. None of these changes would have been made had they not been informed by data.

The impact the changes had was significant, which was proven by the data collected, not simply hunches. Not only did candidates' passing rates on exams improve, but the reputation of our program did as well. The teacher preparation programs at my institution rely heavily on word-of-mouth and networking as our primary method for marketing. The program I was directing, in particular, received very little attention and was not well known at the time. Given the changes made and their impact on our teacher candidates, our program grew at a time when enrollment in other local teacher preparation programs was flat or in decline. In fact, the program

I was directing tripled in size within the first year that many of the above-mentioned changes were made.

When I became Chair of the Department of Teacher Education at my institution, the need for consistent data-driven dialogue across the department was evident. While I had been using it with my steering committee in my program, I realized that the department overall was not using data to inform decisions around continuous improvement, or they were not doing so in a consistent, formal, well-documented way. Mine was only one of seven programs, so there were many missed opportunities to engage in data analysis. Of course, we needed to establish a solid quality assurance system for our new accreditors. But going through the process of our self-study helped propel a shift in the climate of the department to one that values data.

Data-Driven Dialogue Protocol

Data can be scary to many educators. This was a common theme in many of my interactions with teachers as an instructional coach in P-12 settings, and I assumed that higher education would be no different. Therefore, as our quality assurance system was built, I chose a protocol for looking at data that were user-friendly, made data visually accessible, and would keep any analysis focused on facts rather than hunches. This was the process I used in my program steering committee that yielded positive results, and I knew it was a powerful tool for continuous program-specific improvement. Therefore, it only made sense that it be used across all programs within the department. Data-driven dialogue is a process for data analysis that helps one suspend any preconceived notions or judgments and simply look at what the data are saying without any biases (Wellman & Lipton, 2004). This protocol also shifts discussions away from identifying symptoms and more toward identifying possible causes of student performance, which is a much more proactive approach to program improvement (Wellman & Lipton, 2004). Finally, this protocol allows educators to make shared decisions about data and do so with confidence (Wellman & Lipton, 2004).

The data-driven dialogue process involves four phases (Wellman & Lipton, 2004). First, before even looking at the data, participants *predict* what they may expect to find. Second, participants *go visual* by making a graph or chart, or using some other means of making the data simple to read. Third, participants *observe* what the data say. Finally, participants *infer* why the data show what they do and ask questions to do some further investigating. See Figure 12.1 for a summary of the four phases of data-driven dialogue.

Predict	Occurs before looking at data
	Focuses on generating predictions the data may show
	Gets concerns out on the table
	Eliminates or reduces any bias
Go visual	Makes the data visually understandable
	Ensures everyone is speaking about the data in the same way
	Makes the data accessible to all
Observe	Simply observe and record what the data says
	No inferring
	No "because" statements
Infer/Question	Make "because" or explanation statements related to observations
	Look for possible causes
	Make inferences about what the data shows
	Generate questions prompted by the data for follow-up

(Wellman & Lipton, 2004).

Figure 12.1. Four Phases of Data-Driven Dialogue.

This protocol was shared with the entire department, including both faculty and staff, at a fall semester retreat the year we changed accrediting bodies and began to establish a quality assurance system. I was a new Department Chair, we had new accreditation standards to work toward, and we had a quality assurance system to formalize, so it was the perfect time to begin to shift the climate of the department to one that is data driven. During that fall retreat, each phase of the protocol was explicitly taught, and then the department worked together to use the tool to analyze edTPA data from the previous year.

Predict

The first phase of the data-driven dialogue protocol is to make predictions before even looking at any data. This phase is powerful and important not to skip, which may be tempting for some to do. Focusing on making predictions about what the data may show can maximize the analysis that will ensue. This phase serves several purposes. First, it allows participants to access their prior knowledge, either of the assessment or the students who were assessed. Second, it allows participants to get any concerns out on the table, rather than allowing those concerns to cloud their judgment when looking at the data. Finally, it reduces or even eliminates any bias when looking at the data.

In our first use of the data-driven dialogue protocol to analyze edTPA data, the importance of this first phase was quickly evident. Even after discussing the predict phase, including its purpose at length, many faculty wanted to grab the data immediately to dig in. Instead, the data were withheld from participants, and a group discussion took place. Faculty and staff were asked what they predicted they would see in the edTPA data from the fall and spring semesters from the previous year for all department initial certification programs. I created a notecatcher to guide the data-driven dialogue process, so as the department discussed, predictions were recorded both on individuals' notecatchers as well as one projected for all to see. See Figure 12.2 for the data-driven dialogue notecatcher used. During the discussion, faculty named things like lower scores on Task 3 rubrics, struggles with academic language demands, or candidates' ability to use feedback along with students to further their learning. Department staff struggled to participate at first as they voiced not feeling responsible for candidates' scores. However, by including both faculty and staff, I was shifting the climate to one where all people are responsible for our candidates' success.

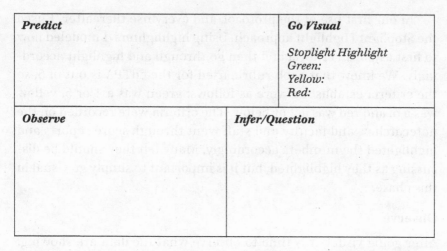

Predict	Go Visual
	Stoplight Highlight *Green:* *Yellow:* *Red:*
Observe	Infer/Question

Figure 12.2. Data-Driven Dialogue Notecatcher.

Go Visual

The second phase of the data-driven dialogue protocol is to go visual with the data. This can mean many different things and may even differ based on what data are being analyzed. Regardless, the purpose of this phase is to make it easy to sort through the data and observe what it says. A commonly used approach is the Stoplight Highlight approach (Love et al., 2008). This involves highlighting the data based on criteria established before reviewing it. Just like a stoplight, criteria are sorted into green, yellow, or red, where green shows mastery, yellow shows being close to mastery, and red shows a significant deficiency. See Figure 12.3 for an example of how one might use Stoplight Highlight to establish criteria.

Highlight Color	Meaning	Cutoffs
Green	Go! Meets expectations	100%–80%
Yellow	Caution! Below expectations	79%–50%
Red	Urgent! In immediate need of improvement	49% and below

(Love et al., 2008).

Figure 12.3. Sample Stoplight Highlight Criteria.

In our first use of the protocol, and every use thereafter, I used the Stoplight Highlight approach. Using highlighters, I modeled how to first establish criteria and then go through and highlight accordingly. We know that each rubric used for the edTPA is out of 5, so the criteria established were as follows: green was a 4 or 5, yellow was a 3, and red was a 2 or below. The criteria were recorded on the notecatcher, and faculty and staff went through score reports and highlighted the numbers accordingly. Many felt they should be discussing as they highlighted, but it is important to simply go visual in this phase.

Observe

After going visual, it is time to observe what the data are showing. Going visual truly paves the way for participants to make very clear observations. It is not a time to make inferences about what is seen or reasons why the data show what they do. Rather, it is a time to just look at what the data are saying and record accordingly. By separating observations from inferences, the analysis is much more bias-free and objective.

When the department first engaged in the observe phase, it took many reminders to faculty and staff not to make "because" statements or make inferences about the scores at hand. It was very tempting to look at anything highlighted in red, look at who the student was, and comment on why they likely struggled on a particular task. The notecatcher was key in this phase in that it was used to model what should occur while observing. Faculty and staff were encouraged to simply look at the colors and tell what they saw. The types of observations shared were things like there are more greens than yellows and reds, Task 3 has the most reds of all tasks, or students in one program have more greens than students in other initial certification programs, just to name a few. After explicitly guiding the department through this phase, both faculty and staff saw the value of going visual. They were able to look at a score report and confidently see what the colors were telling them, and then make note accordingly. It was also at this point when staff felt much more comfortable with looking at data.

Infer/Question

The last phase involves making inferences or asking questions about what was observed. This is the point when it is appropriate to make those "because" statements or infer the reasons for what has been observed. Separating this phase from the observation phase is essential in ensuring the analysis is free of biases. This is also the time to ask questions that can inform next steps or follow-up.

As the department entered the infer phase of the data-driven dialogue protocol, many commented on how difficult it was not to make inferences while observing. However, as we engaged in a discussion of what our inferences were, it became clear just how important it is to reserve any judgements for after observations are made. For example, faculty and staff had predicted lower scores on Task 3 rubrics during the predict phase. The department realized that if they were looking at the data as they had before using this protocol, they would have assumed certain students struggled with Task 3 or would have assumed they would see more 1s and 2s on those rubrics, when that may not have been what the data showed. As faculty and staff looked at the observations that were collectively recorded, this was actually a prediction that was proven false. Those students that were assumed would score lower ended up with average scores on Task 3 rubrics, and only one Task 3 rubric contained more 1s and 2s than other rubrics.

Data Meetings

After that initial data analysis, the department discussed reactions to using the protocol, and most indicated feeling that it allowed for a more informed discussion about what the data truly showed. For example, rather than looking at edTPA data and saying, "I'm not surprised at Student X's overall score" as may have happened in the past, faculty and staff were able to say things more like, "Our candidates are strong planners, which we can see with scores on the first 5 rubrics," or, "more than half seemed to struggle with pushing students toward deeper levels of thinking, which we can see by their score on rubric 8. How are we teaching that in course Y?" It also demystified some of our quantitative data, which can seem over-whelming to analyze well, especially for some of our staff. Most faculty also walked away with specific action items they could bring to the courses they taught based on what the data showed.

After that fall retreat, the rotation of weekly department meetings was adjusted, and monthly data meetings were incorporated. A sample schedule of data meetings can be seen in Figure 12.4. The purpose was twofold. First, regularly looking at data together would help that shift in culture I was looking for. Ideally, faculty and staff would see value in looking at data and would make it a habit to do so on a regular basis to inform decisions, be it at the course-level or the program-level. Second, looking at data every month would ensure that all of our data were being reviewed in a thoughtful manner. Had I only arranged to look at data once a semester, the department would not have adequate time to observe and analyze the data from all our key assessments. I wanted this to be a meaningful process, not one to get through for the sake of saying we looked at data. During each subsequent monthly data meeting that fall and spring semester, the protocol was reviewed, clarifying questions were asked specific to the protocol, and the department continued to use the tool to analyze other pieces of data collected. In time, discussions that took place at data meetings were documented, and then we looked at trends over time. We tracked changes made, including what data led to the change, as well as if/how the change impacted student achievement.

Fall Semester		Spring Semester	
Retreat	edTPA	Retreat	edTPA
September	Content-specialty tests	February	Content-specialty tests
October	Educating All Students exam	March	Educating All Students exam
November	Lesson plan/Unit plan	April	Lesson plan/Unit plan
December	Student teaching rubric, dispositions rubric	May	Student teaching rubric, dispositions rubric

Figure 12.4. Sample Data Meeting Schedule.

In Summary

Using data to inform what we do in teacher preparation is essential. Just as in the instruction-assessment cycle, we must assess what we are doing in our preparation programs to help our teacher candidates successfully enter the workforce, and then use that information to adjust as needed. While there are many ways to do so, the data-driven dialogue protocol is a helpful tool not only to analyze data, but to build a culture that is data driven. After using this protocol with the department over the past few years, we have been able to shift how data are analyzed. Rather than meet as a department to look at data, program-specific data are analyzed in each program steering committee. All Program Directors continue to use the data-driven dialogue protocol as they lead the analysis, and they track changes in student achievement over time. Then, once a semester we gather as a department to share what trends are found in the data in each program, make observations about commonalities and differences between programs, and collectively brainstorm ways in which to address areas of need. Data have definitely become the foundation of our quality assurance system, which actually frees us up to be more innovative, respond to increasing student challenges, and work toward consistent improvement.

References

Bambrick-Santoyo, P. (2010). *Driven by data: A practical guide to improve instruction.* Jossey-Bass. https://doi.org/10.1002/9781119564614

Love, N. B., Stiles, K. E., Mundry, S. E., & DiRanna, K. (2008). *The data coach's guide to improving learning for all students: Unleashing the power of collaborative inquiry.* Corwin Press.

Wellman, B., & Lipton, L. (2004). *Data-driven dialogue: A facilitator's guide to collaborative inquiry.* Mira Via.

CHAPTER THIRTEEN

Implementing the Plan-Do-Study-Act (PDSA) Cycle: Beginning to Measure Growth with Intention

AMANDA HOWERTON-FOX AND MARK A. KESSLER

Continuous Improvement Pre-PDSA

Annual or semesterly data retreats have long been a feature of the Education department's academic calendar; our accreditor required us to review student data regularly, using it to identify areas of strength and weakness to inform decisions about how we might improve our programs. We should note that "retreat" was used loosely here. As is often the case in academia, "retreat" was just another word for "really long meeting where food is served." The retreats were always on campus, in the same room where we always held our department meetings. Our small faculty of eight to 10 members sat at small tables and worked in groups of two or three to review three types of data: 1) student performance on state certification exams; 2) student performance on our internal key assessments; and 3) results of an annual administrator survey on which our graduates were evaluated on a set of accreditation-aligned attributes.

Faculty were assigned the data best aligned with their areas of expertise (e.g., Literacy, Special Education, STEM) and instructed to comb through it, noting any areas of strength or weakness. Faculty were given ample time to review the data thoroughly and discuss their noticings and interpretations in small groups before being called back to a larger departmental discussion about key findings and potential next steps. It was always a rich discussion, which tended to focus primarily on the state test data because that is where it was easiest to identify clear areas of strength and weakness. (Figure 13.1 shows how the state test data were presented for our review.)

SOCIAL STUDIES

Score Range = 400-600
Minimum Passing Score = **520**

01	United States History
02	Global History
03	Geography
04	Economics
05	Civics, Citizenship, and Government
06	Social Studies Literacy
07	Pedagogical Content Knowledge

PAST 5 YEARS

# Takers	# Pass	# Not Pass	% Pass	% Not Pass	Iona Mean	State Mean
23	22	1	96%	4%	543.1	546.1

2020-21 Completers (n = 8)

Examinee Name / SSN	Test Name	Test Code	Test Version	Test Date	Pass / Fail Status	Total Scaled	01	02	03	04	05	06	07
Barajas, Mariela (XXX-X8-7129)	SOCIAL STUDI	115	(11/16-Present)	2021-04-09	P	557	4	3	4	3	3	3	4
Carozza, Mark (XXX-X8-9655)	SOCIAL STUDI	115	(11/16-Present)	2020-09-05	P	550	4	4	3	3	3	3	3
				2021-08-17	P	524	3	2	3	3	1	2	4
				2021-07-03	F	515	3	2	2	2	1	2	4
DeVito, Victoria (XXX-X8-6516)	SOCIAL STUDI	115	(11/16-Present)	2021-05-16	F	501	2	1	1	2	1	2	4
Diaz, Alejandra (XXX-X4-1775)	SOCIAL STUDI	115	(11/16-Present)	2021-05-08	P	533	2	2	4	3	2	3	4
Gross, Jeffrey (XXX-X6-6342)	SOCIAL STUDI	115	(11/16-Present)	2021-05-28	P	573	4	4	4	4	3	4	4
Halloran-Doherty, Stephanie (XXX-	SOCIAL STUDI	115	(11/16-Present)	2021-05-27	P	563	4	4	3	4	3	4	4
Hughes, William (XXX-X8-7780)	SOCIAL STUDI	115	(11/16-Present)	2021-08-23	P	548	4	4	3	3	2	3	4
Lodespoto, Andrew (XXX-X0-5779)	SOCIAL STUDI	115	(11/16-Present)	2021-06-05	P	576	4	4	4	3	4	3	4
					80.00%	544	3.4	3	3.1	3	2.3	2.9	3.9

Figure 13.1. Example Presentation of State Test Data for Faculty Review.

The data from our internal key assessments, scored by our full-time and adjunct faculty on rubrics of 1-4 or 1-5, were less interesting because the vast majority of our students were shown to be meeting benchmark across all of our accreditor's standards and, where there was variation, it was hard to know whether to attribute it to actual differences in student performance or differences in faculty scoring practices. Likewise, while the data from our administrator survey were enlightening (typically showing potential weaknesses in our students' use of instructional technology and ability to serve multilingual learners), it was difficult to extrapolate anything concrete from it given the low N of the respondents and the low N of our program's graduates who were reviewed in those responses. (Administrators who participate review all their new teachers, rating the quality of their preparation by their respective teacher preparation programs.)

The state test data, in contrast, had the following benefits: 1) the state tests must be taken by all completers who wish to seek state certification; 2) the exams are externally validated instruments; and 3) they are scored by reviewers who don't know our students and who have received reliability training. In addition, they give us the ability to compare our students' performance to the state average. Consistently, our review of state test data has demonstrated that our students perform very well on the pedagogical subareas of the exams; when they struggle, it has been on specific content knowledge (e.g., mathematical numbers and operations, foundations of literacy development, civics and citizenship).

Over the years, we have used this data to plan improvements to our curricula and to the resources we provide to students. Specifically, we have: 1) updated the textbooks used in our foundational literacy courses; 2) integrated assessments across our coursework that mimic the structure of the state test questions; 3) added review units to courses later in our programs to help students prepare for the state exams; 4) created advising protocols to ensure that students who are struggling in their content area courses are aware of the tutoring resources and test preparation materials available on campus; 5) met with the chairs of content area departments to ensure that the courses we were requiring were aligned with the expectations of the state test; and 6) made available test preparation materials both in the library and in our department. What we have not done, until now, is collect data with the express purpose of giving us insight into how well any of these program improvements was actually working.

Implementing PDSA

The first author learned about the Plan-Do-Study-Act (PDSA, Deming & Guresh, 2011; Langley et al., 2009) cycle in an AAQEP workshop on continuous improvement in the fall of 2021. She immediately gravitated toward it since it so closely mirrored what our faculty was already doing to use data to improve our programs. We had the *Study* (i.e., annual data retreats) and the *Do* (i.e., implemented related improvements) parts down. What we were missing was the thoughtful *Planning*, inclusive of planned data collection and review, followed by focused Study of that particular data, and a subsequent choice about how to *Act* (i.e., adopt, accept, or abandon) on the intervention.

As an assistant professor positioned in a support role to the department's Accreditation Coordinator, however, she lacked the influence to enact the culture shift in the department's relationship to data that would be prerequisite to authentic engagement with the PDSA cycle. For the first time, we would be asking questions about our programs that our accreditors were not requiring us to ask, and we would potentially need to collect data about our programs that our accreditors were not explicitly asking us to collect. The shift would take time and it would take collective investment. Critically, it would also take an understanding on the part of all the faculty that the accreditation landscape had changed: Earning accreditation was no longer about producing data to satisfy an external body, but about effectively collecting, analyzing, and using data to answer our own questions.

By the spring 2023 data retreat, the first author had served as department chair for an academic year, during which time she had worked to begin developing an authentic culture of evidence by: 1) familiarizing faculty with how our internal and external measures were aligned with our departmental Student Learning Objectives (SLOs), state standards, and the Association for Advancing Quality in Educator Preparation (AAQEP) standards and aspects; 2) making our data entry and analysis processes more transparent; and 3) engaging faculty in regular rubric calibration exercises where we talked through the clarity of our own learning objectives and what kind of evidence of them we expected to see in student work. Based on this foundation, she felt confident the department faculty were ready to engage with PDSA cycle, and so she dedicated the last hour of the 4-hour retreat to that specific goal.

PDSA Cycle 1

In preparation for the retreat, the first author curated slides from AAQEP workshops to support our shift to more disciplined inquiry (see Figure 13.2).

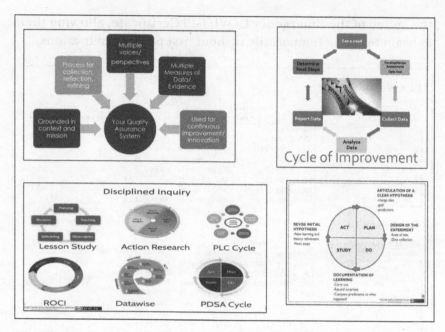

Figure 13.2. Slides from AAQEP Workshops Used in Data Retreat.

After reviewing the data on our students' performance on our internally developed key assessments and on the state tests, the department agreed that the focus of our first PDSA cycle should be students' foundational knowledge in language and literacy. Student scores on Subarea 1 (Knowledge of Language and Literacy Arts) of the state English Language Arts (ELA) assessments have consistently fallen below the benchmark score of 3, at both the Early Childhood (Birth–Grade 2) and Childhood (Grades 1–6) level, despite our efforts to improve students' knowledge in literacy foundations. The new 2022–2023 data hadn't shown any improvement in this subarea, and our overall passing rates had fallen considerably from between 94% and 100% from 2020–2022 on both assessments to 63% and 77%, respectively (see Figure 3). It is worth noting that similar dips in passing rates were seen across our students' state test scores in 2022–2023, which we believe may be due, in part, to the COVID-19-induced gap between students finishing their coursework and taking their state exams. Many of our 2022–2023 test takers completed their programs in 2020 and 2021, when they were given the option of the Emergency COVID-19 Certificate, allowing them to begin teaching temporarily without first passing their exams.

ELA Birth to Grade 2

2022-23 YTD Completers (n =8)   Retakes=2

Examinee Name / SSN	Test Name	Test Code	Test Version	Test Date	Pass / Fail Status	Total Scaled	1
	MS B-2 Part C 211		(09/14-Present)	2022-09-21	F	519	3
	MS B-2 Part C 211		(09/14-Present)	2023-01-16	P	543	3
	MS B-2 Part C 211		(09/14-Present)	2022-10-29	P	527	2
	MS B-2 Part C 211		(09/14-Present)	2023-02-18	F	508	2
	MS B-2 Part C 211		(09/14-Present)	2022-11-12	P	523	3
	MS B-2 Part C 211		(09/14-Present)	2023-02-16	P	544	3
	MS B-2 Part C 211		(09/14-Present)	2022-10-17	P	539	2
	MS B-2 Part C 211		(09/14-Present)	2023-01-21	F	516	2
					62.50%	527.4	2.5

ELA Grades 1-6

2022-23 YTD Completers (n =13)   Retakes=3

Examinee Name / SSN	Test Name	Test Code	Test Version	Test Date	Pass / Fail Status	Total Scaled	1
	MS 1-6 Part C 221		(09/14-Present)	2022-10-01	F	505	2
	MS 1-6 Part C 221		(09/14-Present)	2023-02-23	P	520	2
	MS 1-6 Part C 221		(09/14-Present)	2023-01-07	P	528	3
	MS 1-6 Part C 221		(09/14-Present)	2023-01-17	P	524	3
	MS 1-6 Part C 221		(09/14-Present)	2022-11-03	P	558	4
	MS 1-6 Part C 221		(09/14-Present)	2023-03-09	P	550	3
	MS 1-6 Part C 221		(09/14-Present)	2022-09-14	P	543	3
	MS 1-6 Part C 221		(09/14-Present)	2023-01-20	P	568	4
	MS 1-6 Part C 221		(09/14-Present)	2023-02-18	F	501	2
	MS 1-6 Part C 221		(09/14-Present)	2023-03-10	F	519	4
	MS 1-6 Part C 221		(09/14-Present)	2023-03-09	P	524	2
	MS 1-6 Part C 221		(09/14-Present)	2023-01-14	P	540	3
	MS 1-6 Part C 221		(09/14-Present)	2022-10-17	P	547	3
					76.92%	532.8	2.9

Figure 13.3. Student Performance on Subarea 1 of the State ELA Assessments in 2022–23.

Once deciding on our focus, we pulled out our PDSA worksheets and began to thoughtfully *Plan*, not only what we would *Do* to address our students' poor performance in this area, but also how we would intentionally *Study* the effectiveness of our intervention so that we could make informed decisions regarding how to *Act* going forward. We decided together on the language of our Aim Statement and on the details of our Plan: not only the specifics of the intervention, but who would be involved, when it would happen, and critically, how we would evaluate its success (see Figure 13.4).

Plan

The Aim Statement we formulated as a department was as follows: *We want to see an average score of 3.3 or above on Subarea 1 on the*

PDSA Worksheet

Complete Page 1 of the worksheet when planning your Plan-Do-Study-Act (PDSA) cycle. Multiple PDSAs can be designed in support of a single Aim.

AIM STATEMENT (Measurable goal, with a target date)

We want to see an average score of 3.3 or above on Subarea 1 on the ELA B-2 and 1-6 CSTs for test takers in 2025-26.

Today's Date: 5/16/23

PDSA Cycle #: 1

PLAN

What will you try?

EDU 370, Dr. Gmuer will introduce collaboration with the Speech department to work on the phonological foundations of literacy. In EDU 380, Dr. Gmuer will collaborate with Speech and School Psychology on best practices in literacy assessment, applying for Interprofessional Education (IPE) funding to purchase Wit and Wisdom as a curricular model. Dr. Gmuer will integrate pre- and post-, teacher-designed, CST-aligned, in-class assessments of literacy foundations in both classes.

When? This will begin in EDU 380 in Fall 2023 and continue at least through EDU 370 in Spring 2026.

Who will be involved?

Team: Drs. Gmuer, Hardigree, and Howerton-Fox (potentially Dr. Vevoda, CSD, and Dr. Zaromatidis, School Psych)

Patients: Undergraduate Childhood and Dual (ECE/Childhood) EDU majors

What do you predict will happen?

Students will demonstrate increased literacy foundations knowledge on EDU 370 and EDU 380 in-class assessments, and we will see increased Subarea 1 CST scores by May 2025.

How will you evaluate how it went?

Beginning in Fall 2023, students will be assessed in EDU 380 via pre- and post-, teacher-designed, CST-aligned, in-class assessments of literacy foundations. That assessment will continue in EDU 370 in the Spring and repeatedly through at least Spring 2026.

Who will collect the evaluation data? Gmuer - classroom data / Howerton-Fox - CST data

What do you need to do to get ready?

Dr. Gmuer: 1) design pre- and post assessments for use in EDU 370 and EDU 380; 2) Talk to Dr. Zaromatidis (School Psych) and Dr. Veyvoda (CSD) about interprofessional collaboration, and then 3) reach out to Dr. Matich-Maroney (IPE) about possible application of Cabrini grant funds to purchase Wit and Wisdom.

Figure 13.4. Completed PDSA Worksheet.

ELA B-2 and 1-6 CSTs for test takers in 2025-26. Importantly, we had to agree both on a measurable goal (i.e., a specific test score average) and a target date (i.e., 2025–2026) before we could begin to plan intentionally for its realization. This approach differed markedly

from our former approach, which had involved more vague statements about wanting to see our students "do better" on their state
exams. It also meant that we had to be realistic about what we could
achieve. For example, although we wanted to improve the foundational literacy knowledge of all students across our programs (e.g.,
undergraduate and graduate Childhood/Early Childhood Education, graduate Reading Education), our greatest concern was our
Childhood/Early Childhood majors, and the most practical approach
given constraints on personnel and time was to pilot our curricular
improvements at the undergraduate level.

   With this specific goal articulated, we were able to devise a concrete *Plan* for meeting it. Specifically, Dr. Kate Gmuer, the faculty
member teaching our Childhood Literacy sequence at the undergraduate level, would make curricular and assessment changes to
the first two courses in the three-course sequence beginning in the
fall of 2023. First, she would apply funds from Iona's grant-funded
Interprofessional Education (IPE) initiative to purchase the Wit and
Wisdom (2016) and Geodes (2019) curricula, sharing these resources
with the Speech and School Psychology departments to give students across the disciplines exposure to evidence-based curricula in
phonological development and the teaching of reading aligned with
New York's current focus on the science of reading. Second, in EDU
370, the first course in the three-course sequence, she would collaborate with the Speech department faculty to integrate a more robust
unit on the phonological foundations of literacy. In EDU 380, the
second course, she would collaborate with the Speech and School
Psychology departments to integrate a unit on best practices in literacy assessment. Finally, Dr. Gmuer would integrate pre- and post-,
teacher-designed, Content Specialty Test (CST)-aligned, in-class
assessments of literacy foundations in both classes.

Do

At the time this chapter was written, we were still in the *Do* stage
of our first PDSA Cycle. Dr. Gmuer had already put in an order for
the two new curricula and had begun conversations with faculty in
the Speech and School Psychology departments about partnering

on mutually beneficial curricular collaborations in 2023–2024. She had also begun to design the CST-aligned pre- and postassessments of literacy foundations for use in her fall 2024 course.

Study

Although we have not yet begun the *Study* phase, our use of the steps in the PDSA cycle has allowed us to develop clarity around our goals and plans such that studying the effectiveness of our innovations should be fairly straightforward. As per the *Plan* outlined above, beginning in the fall of 2023, students will be assessed via pre- and post-, teacher-designed, CST-aligned, in-class assessments of literacy foundations. That assessment will continue in the spring of 2024 and repeat in both literacy foundations courses through at least the spring of 2026. Dr. Gmuer will be responsible for collecting and analyzing the data from these assessments and presenting the results to the department so we can ascertain whether students have made measurable growth in their understanding of literacy foundations. In addition, our program completers take the Early Childhood and/or Childhood version of the state's CST in Literacy upon program completion, and their scores are shared with the department chair via Pearson. The chair will be responsible for presenting the state CST data to the department annually, at least through the spring of 2026, so that we can measure our progress toward the goal of an average score of 3.3 or above on Subarea 1 on each of the tests.

Act

We are not set to reach the *Act* stage of our first PDSA cycle until the spring of 2026. At that time, we expect to have sufficient data from our new in-class assessments and our state test data to be able to determine whether we will adopt, adapt, or abandon the curricular changes made to our first two Early Childhood/Childhood Literacy courses at the undergraduate level. If the results are promising, and if we have not done so already, we will also expand the innovations into our graduate programs in Early Childhood/Childhood Education and Literacy and study the effectiveness of the revisions to those programs, as well.

A Database to Accommodate to Our Questions

The data discussion above focused almost exclusively on or analysis of state test data. Up until now, our internal key assessment data have also been analyzed separately from external test data, so we weren't able to ask very interesting questions about the relationship between them. Over the past 2 years, we have been working to make improvements in both of these areas.

First, through regular data entry and rubric calibration sessions, we have made our internal data collection processes more transparent and begun to work through our interpretations of our department SLOs, as well as the associated AAQEP standards and aspects, and have begun to standardize how we rate the evidence of them exhibited in our students' work. Second, drawing on the computer programming and statistical expertise of our second author, whom we hired as a consultant, we have built a new database to accommodate our data from multiple sources (i.e., internal key assessments, state tests, completer/alumni surveys), coupled with student demographic data, which is allowing us to disaggregate the data in any way that interests us and to run comparisons (e.g., internal vs. external measures) and correlations (e.g., program assessments vs. completer assessments) in ways that have not been possible before.

To facilitate comparisons between cohorts (e.g., gender, race, completion year, degree/program, etc.) and investigate correlations between diverse metrics of student performance (e.g., internal vs. external measures of content knowledge, early vs. late program measures, GPA vs. content specialty test scores), we have developed a single "Measures" database containing all of our measures of student performance and student demographic information. The process of creating and populating the Measures database required three steps: 1) pulling together the data from all our internal and external measures of student performance; 2) converting each dataset into a common framework defined by a single rubric based on the AAQEP aspects and correlated with our department SLOs; and 3) associating each record of student performance with that student's demographic data.

The flexibility of our new database allows us to ask much more interesting questions about our data than we have previously been able to ask. For example, related to the focus of our PDSA cycle 1, we have asked about the correlation between our internal assessment of students' foundational literacy knowledge (e.g., course grades and key assessments) and their state test scores (see Figure 13.5). The following is a list of additional questions that were raised at our spring 2023 data retreat after faculty were shown a sample of the kinds of graphic output that are possible with the new database:

- What is the correlation between our students' overall Math GPAs and their performance on the state Math exam?
- Are students' Algebra 1 grades predictive of their performance on the state Math exam?
- Is there a relationship between students' test performance and the gap between program completion and the exam date?
- Are there gender differences between how our adolescent majors perform on our internal key assessments and on the state tests?
- Are there differences in the performance of our students who are English learners?

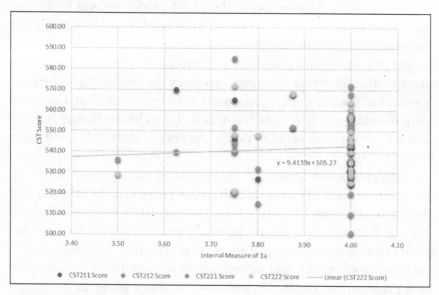

Figure 13.5. Correlation between Internal Measures of 1a and Scores on Literacy State Tests (2020–2023).
Note: CST stands for Content Specialty Test.

Next Steps

Through engaging in this PDSA process, we have begun to make the shift from a faculty who makes data-informed programmatic choices to a community authentically focused on disciplined inquiry. We have chosen both short-term (i.e., in-class pre- and post-assessments) and long-term (i.e., state test scores) assessment measures that we will review as a team at our next data retreat, scheduled for fall 2023, to evaluate the success of our planned intervention and to make decisions about whether we will adapt, accept, or abandon it. Although the basic structure of how we review and interpret data has not changed, our implementation of the PDSA cycle of disciplined inquiry represents a major shift in how we think about and use evidence to support continuous program improvement.

We have chosen to focus on a single intervention via the PDSA cycle because it is our first time using the approach, but we intend to engage in overlapping PDSA cycles as we become more comfortable with the model. In the meantime, we have not abandoned our efforts to improve our program in other areas, and as we flex our disciplined inquiry muscles through use of the PDSA model, we will look more intentionally for evidence of growth in these other areas, as well. For example, we hypothesize that our students' poor test performance might also be, in part, related to an increase in stress and anxiety we have witnessed across our programs since the beginning of the pandemic. We plan to work more closely with the Counseling Center to help us address this area of need, and also to invite alumni back to share their experiences with taking the state tests to help quell some of our students' concerns.

Regarding our students' performance on individual tests, in addition to ELA Subarea 1, Subarea 4 (Analysis, Synthesis, and Application) of the ELA state tests has consistently proven difficult for our students, and we are planning more opportunities for students to engage with questions of that type more often throughout their coursework and potentially in an additional workshop on test preparation. Relatedly, although students perform quite well on the state Social Studies assessment overall, they tend to struggle with Subarea 5 (Civics, Citizenship, and Government), so we will be looking into which Political Science course(s) at Iona might help address this gap in knowledge. Finally, our students struggle on the Math content exams across grade levels (i.e., Birth–Grade 2, Grades 1-6, and Grades 7-12), and we will be working more closely with the Advising center, the Tutoring center, and the Math department to ensure our students are taking the appropriate content area courses and getting the academic support they need to master this disciplinary content. We are also beginning to discuss the possibility of creating Methods courses for our Adolescent programs in each of the content areas, and plan to prioritize Mathematics expertise in our next tenure-track faculty hire.

The power of our new database design, coupled with our implantation of the PDSA cycle, is that we now know we have the ability to get answers to authentic and meaningful questions like those listed above. Knowing those answers are available to us will encourage us to think in a more evidence-based way about all our questions around program improvement, helping us to build a true culture of evidence grounded in disciplined inquiry.

References

Deming, W. E., & Guresh, T. (2011). Out of the crisis. *New Paradigm for Managing People, Systems and Processes, Rev, 2.*

Geodes. (2019). Great Minds.

Langley, G. J., Moen, R. D., Nolan, K. M., Nolan, T. W., Norman, C. L., & Provost, L. P. (2009). *The improvement guide: a practical approach to enhancing organizational performance.* John Wiley & Sons.

Qualis Health. (n.d.). *PDSA Worksheet.* Qualis Health. https://www.qualishealth.org/sites/default/files/pdsaWorksheet.pdf

Wit and wisdom. (2016). Great Minds.

CHAPTER FOURTEEN

Maximizing Student Outcomes: Harnessing the Power of Faculty Collaboration and Continuous Program Improvement

ALICIA KOZIMOR

Introduction

Effective data analysis and program evaluation are critical components of improving outcomes in higher education. However, the success of such initiatives depends heavily on the involvement and collaboration between all college departments and teams. For Grand Canyon University's College of Education, all faculty members, administrators, and staff must work together towards the common goal of improving student outcomes. The case study presented in the following chapter provides an example of how such collaboration can be achieved.

By analyzing student performance data, collaborating with the curriculum development department, and creating a virtual community for faculty members, the college was able to significantly improve the outcomes of its Early Childhood Education (ECE) program. This chapter underscores the importance of communication, collaboration, and a willingness to work across departments and teams. By embracing a culture of continuous improvement, colleges can ensure that their programs are constantly evolving to meet the needs of their students and the changing demands of the field of education.

Background

The Grand Canyon University (GCU) program and curriculum development process stands out for its inclusive approach, involving education stakeholders from within and outside of the university. College of Education (COE) faculty and staff collaborate to create a centralized curriculum that is comprehensive and aligned with accreditation standards and professional practices. This creates a framework that supports faculty in implementing curriculum through effective instructional practices, both online and in traditional classrooms. This approach ensures that students receive a high-quality education that is up to date with industry standards and equips them with the necessary skills and knowledge to succeed in their chosen fields.

Program and Course Development Process

The program and course development process begins by creating a centralized curriculum that serves as a foundation for program development. Faculty members act as Subject Matter Experts (SMEs) and collaborate with curriculum counterparts to design programs and courses that align with accreditation standards. These standards are derived from various sources, including industry skills and standards from the state department of education in which Grand Canyon University is located, the Arizona Department of Education.

Programmatic competencies are also developed based on accreditation standards, and these competencies are the skills that students are expected to master throughout the program. Each programmatic competency is introduced (I) and reinforced (R) throughout the program (Table 14.1), culminating in a benchmark (B) assignment in one course that demonstrates mastery of the competency.

Table 14.1. Example Competency Assessment Matrix

Competency	Course 1	Course 2	Course 3	Course 4	Course 5
1.1	I		R	B	
1.2	I	R	B		
1.3			I	R	B

These benchmark assignments serve as data points that are used to determine the effectiveness of the College of Education's programs in graduating students with the skills and knowledge required of them upon program completion. This process ensures that GCU graduates are well-prepared to succeed in their chosen fields and are equipped with the necessary competencies to meet the demands of the industry.

Instructional Autonomy

To accompany the centralized curriculum, faculty members are provided with instructional autonomy to deliver the curriculum as they see fit. This approach allows instructors to exercise their own teaching style and creativity in the classroom while ensuring that all students receive a consistent level of education. Under this model, faculty are given a curriculum framework that outlines the topics they need to cover, and the learning objectives students need to achieve. However, they are not told how to teach the material, leaving them open to share their expertise with students and employ their own teaching techniques.

This approach recognizes that every instructor has their own strengths and teaching style, and that these differences benefit students in the classroom. By allowing instructors to exercise their instructional autonomy, students are exposed to a range of teaching methods and perspectives, which help to create a more engaging and dynamic learning environment.

Plan, Do, Study, Act (PDSA) Improvement Model

The development of a centralized curriculum and the implementation of instructional styles by quality faculty are important steps in ensuring educational excellence. However, to complete the process of quality assurance, stakeholders can rely on the PDSA Improvement Model (Chang & Menzies, 2022). This model serves as the last leg of the quality assurance journey, effectively supporting and utilizing the PDSA framework.

The PDSA Improvement Model operates within an improvement paradigm, which encourages faculty members to analyze student outcomes and make informed decisions to enhance the program's effectiveness (Chang & Menzies, 2022). By employing this cyclical and iterative process, change can be planned, implemented, studied, and revised rapidly, all based on data-driven insights.

Plan: The first step in the PDSA model is planning. This stage involves developing an initial strategy for success or implementing a new plan based on previous iterations of the PDSA model. In the context of the GCU program and curriculum development process, success is planned for by designing programs that align with industry standards and involve subject matter experts.

Do: Once the planning stage is complete, the "Do" step begins, which entails putting the plan or proposed changes into action (Chang & Menzies, 2022). In the GCU process, this is manifested when faculty members implement the centralized curriculum, and data from benchmark assignments is collected to assess its impact.

Study: The next step in the PDSA Model is the "Study" phase. During this stage, faculty and staff analyze student performance data, examining various metrics to evaluate the effectiveness of the program (England, 2021). Based on this analysis, plans for improvement are developed to enhance program outcomes. A significant part of the "Study" step involves the Biannual College of Education Assessment Summit, where a comprehensive analysis of student outcomes is examined among COE faculty and staff.

Act: The PDSA model concludes with the "Act" step, wherein the improvement plan generated is implemented (England, 2021). The decision is then made to either retain the implemented changes or initiate another iteration of the PDSA cycle to continually refine and enhance the program (Chang & Menzies, 2022).

The PDSA Improvement Model serves as a crucial component of quality assurance in educational programs. By following the iterative process of Plan, Do, Study, Act, stakeholders can effectively plan for success, implement changes, study outcomes, and take action to continually improve the program based on data. Through the application of this model, educational institutions like GCU can ensure that their curriculum and instructional approaches remain effective and aligned with industry standards.

Purpose of Assessment Summit

The Assessment Summit is a vital tool in improving student learning outcomes at the COE. The purpose of the Assessment Summit is to provide a platform for the faculty and staff of the College of Education to come together biannually and review student performance data from benchmark assessments. COE stakeholders, including administrators, teachers, support staff, and researchers, attend the summit to analyze data and determine the areas in which COE students are succeeding and the areas in need of improvement. The Assessment Summit serves as a collaborative space for faculty and staff to share their knowledge and expertise, exchange ideas, and discuss strategies for enhancing student learning outcomes. The summit is designed to facilitate a data-driven approach to educational improvement, aligning with the PDSA improvement model, which involves iterative cycles of planning, implementation, evaluation, and adjustment.

During the summit, faculty and staff are grouped according to the programs in which they teach. This grouping allows for a more focused analysis of the data as it pertains to specific programs. Together, they examine the data and look for patterns and trends in student performance as it relates to programmatic outcomes. They also identify any potential gaps in the curriculum or teaching methodologies that may be contributing to the areas where students are struggling.

The insights gained from the Assessment Summit are used to develop action plans that target areas of improvement. These plans may include modifications to the curriculum, adjustments to teaching methodologies, or changes to assessment practices.

Plan: Identifying the Problem/Need

During the Assessment Summit, faculty members and staff are actively engaged in the "Plan" phase by analyzing student performance data and identifying areas where improvements are needed. During the 2021 COE Assessment Summit, faculty members teaching in the Early Childhood Education program identified a pressing need for improvement based on a review of student performance data. The Assessment Summit provided an opportunity for faculty and staff to come together and discuss the data in a collaborative and data-driven manner.

Faculty and staff were grouped by program, allowing for focused and targeted discussions on the data specific to the Early Childhood Education program. Benchmark assessment data were shared, including how students were performing on each programmatic competency. The data were broken down by performance indicator (approaching, meeting, and exceeding) and could be disaggregated by online and traditional students and other factors. Additionally, for the purposes of this Assessment Summit, the student performance was organized through "Acceptable Target" and "Ideal Target." Acceptable Target was classified as 85% of students/learners meet or exceed the Acceptable range (80%) on the competency-specific line of the rubric, while "Ideal Target" detailed 80% of students/learners will meet the Target (100%) competency-specific line of the rubric. This allowed faculty and staff to identify trends and patterns in student performance and determine if there were any specific challenges related to a particular modality in the context of ideal and target performance.

Through these discussions, faculty and staff were able to identify areas of improvement for the Early Childhood Education program. This included specific competencies where students were struggling, as well as areas where changes could be made to better support student learning and success. To better understand the competency being analyzed, faculty and staff could reference the course assigned to the competency, course description, and syllabus.

There were two identified programmatic competencies that did not yield the desired student performance data. The first, Competency 1.1, related to the theories and philosophies of early learning and development as well as making developmentally appropriate decisions. The second identified area of growth, Competency 1.2, required COE students to identify the unique characteristics of the students and utilize those to devise developmentally appropriate instruction and an effective classroom environment.

During the first group work session, the stakeholders also analyzed the initial identified competencies from a high-level. Each group was given a worksheet to guide their discussion (Appendix A).

The strengths of the program/courses were discussed, and the two highest areas of need were identified. For this initial discussion, the group shared thoughts and ideas about the areas of need.

Below is an excerpt from the group discussion.

> *B.S. Early Child Ed. - No Emphasis – ITL: ECE 300 - Most competencies that are not met have to do with child development . . . Perhaps they are not ready/understanding development at this stage in their program. The majority of students in this course are full-time online students.*

During the second session, the group worked together to analyze each competency separately and share ideas for an improvement action plan (IAP). The analysis in Table 14.1 illustrates that the improvement action plans were both instructional and programmatic.

Table 14.2. B.S. Early Childhood Education Improvement Action Plans

Program	Competency	Improvement Action Plan (IAP)
B.S. Early Childhood	1.1	• Action Plan A: This program does not go as in-depth into child development until the 300 levels so perhaps the program needs to go in-depth about child development earlier in the program so that students have the understanding of developmentally appropriate practices in order to meet these competencies. • Action Plan B: Schedule adjunct faculty to teach the course multiple times to develop competency, resources, and support. • Action Plan C: Allow SMEs to teach the courses they develop. They then can develop resources that can be shared with all faculty that teach the course. This could also be offered to OFTF to specifically teach a course to develop solid resources/announcements/classroom assessment techniques to share with adjuncts.
	1.2	• Action Plan D: Intentional practicum activities to chart activities. Design practicum menu options to require specific instructional techniques and age groups. Can also require students to specifically observe technology. Increase student understanding that even if they aren't interested in ages 0–2, they still need the knowledge for their preferred grade band.

Do: Data-Driven Decisions and Outcomes

Once the areas of improvement were identified, the faculty and staff moved to the "Do" phase, where they developed and implemented targeted improvement strategies. From the data analysis during the 2021 Assessment Summit, it was determined that changes were necessary to improve the Early Childhood Education program. Changes were needed in introducing foundational topics into the program, how practicum and field experience hours were organized, and in the scheduling and support of adjunct faculty. The resulting program improvements were executed through program development as well as through faculty collaboration. These strategies aim to address the identified gaps and challenges in the Early Childhood Education program, such as enhancing the curriculum's focus on child development or providing intentional practicum activities to enhance understanding.

Program Revisions

Program revisions are an essential aspect of any academic program, ensuring that it remains up to date, relevant, and effective in meeting the needs of its students. In the field of ECE, program revisions are particularly crucial as the field is constantly evolving. The following program revisions were made for the purpose of continuous improvement, resulting in providing more flexible practicum options, curriculum emphasis on application-based assignments and ethical practice, and ensuring that the faculty assigned to teach these courses are well-qualified to teach all ECE content. The actions taken through program revisions addressed Improvement Action Plans A, C, and D.

The first program revision resulted in fewer courses containing practicum hours, while still maintaining the same programmatic hour requirement. Rather than dispersing hours among all courses, student practicum hours were set up in a block model. Students are given a list of suggested activities that are scaffolded to match progression through the program, from introductory to collaborative to application based. By providing students with more choices in their practicum experiences, they can select activities that align with their personal and professional interests, thus making their learning experience more meaningful, engaging, and authentic to their placements in the field (Improvement Action Plan D). This change aimed to enhance partnerships with schools and mentor teachers by providing more opportunities for ECE students to engage in hands-on experiences with children. By reducing the number of courses with practicum hours, students could also concentrate on gaining practical experience and building stronger relationships with mentors (Improvement Action Plan A). This revision allowed for better alignment between the academic curriculum and practical experience.

Another program revision aimed to address Improvement Action Plan A by emphasizing application-based assignments through scenarios and case studies. This revision also included additional emphasis on professionalism and ethical practice through assignments, resources, and discussion questions. By integrating these elements into the curriculum, students apply theoretical concepts to real-world scenarios, preparing them for the challenges they may face in their careers. Additionally, the emphasis on professionalism and ethical practice helps students to develop a strong sense of personal and professional responsibility, making them more effective educators and leaders.

The course sequence was also updated to improve the scaffolding of content. This revision aimed to ensure that students have a clear understanding of the content and can apply what they have learned in subsequent courses. This revision also helps to address Improvement Action Plan D by providing students with a clear path to progression and allowing them to build upon their knowledge and skills as they progress through the program.

Lastly, the faculty assigned to teach ECE courses were reviewed to ensure that they are highly qualified to teach all ECE content. This revision addressed Improvement Action Plan C by ensuring that only qualified faculty members are teaching ECE courses. Additionally, Subject Matter Experts who worked on the program were added to the approved faculty list due to their extensive knowledge of the program. By ensuring that only qualified faculty members are teaching ECE courses, students can be assured that they are receiving a high-quality education that will prepare them for their careers, and COE stakeholders are assured that qualified individuals are addressing the most difficult concepts for students.

The program revisions made to the ECE program were a direct result of the data analysis during the COE Assessment Summit. The changes aim to enhance partnerships with schools and mentor teachers, provide more flexible practicum options, emphasize application-based assignments and ethical practices, improve the scaffolding of content, and ensure that the faculty assigned to teach these courses are well-qualified to teach all ECE content.

Instructional Support and Collaboration

Virtual Collaborative Circles. In response to the need for greater connection between faculty teaching in similar programs located around the United States, the Early Childhood Education faculty met virtually through a Collaborative Circles platform. This virtual collaborative platform allowed the faculty to support one another, address program improvement areas, and share resources they had created, thus creating a collaborative space to bring all program faculty together. The actions taken through the collaborative circles addressed Improvement Action Plans B and C.

The Collaborative Circles were led by faculty liaisons who were selected by the college as experts in their content area and instruction. The Circles allowed the ECE group to address Improvement Action Plan B and C, which call for faculty collaboration and ongoing professional development. By bringing faculty together in a virtual space, the Collaborative Circles allowed for greater sharing of resources and communication, leading to the improvement of the ECE program.

Within the Collaborative Circles, faculty were able to ask questions about the content they were teaching, present tips for engaging students in person and online, and share resources they had created. Circle facilitators as well as faculty could answer the questions asked and share their ideas, thus creating a space for ongoing collaboration and discussion. This platform allowed faculty to share their knowledge and expertise with one another, leading to the creation of a community of practice within the ECE program.

The Circle facilitators were also able to post specific questions each month that related to the identified areas of need for the ECE program. This approach ensured that faculty were addressing program improvement areas and allowed for ongoing professional development. Appendix B is an example of how facilitators responded to ECE faculty needs, shared resources, and promoted discussion. This approach allowed for targeted collaboration and discussion, leading to the improvement of the ECE program and the ongoing professional development of faculty. ECE faculty were able to share their knowledge and expertise with one another, leading to the creation of a community of practice within the ECE program.

The implementation of virtual collaborative circles posed challenges for faculty and staff related to fostering engagement. One barrier was the difficulty of effectively engaging adjunct faculty located across the country. Their remote locations made it challenging to establish meaningful connections and encourage active participation in discussions. To overcome this barrier, various techniques were used to encourage engagement. One approach involved implementing pre-planned monthly themes and providing a structured framework that encouraged focused discussions. Monthly Zoom calls were also used to bring faculty together to build community and discuss content.

Monthly Zoom Calls. In addition to the virtual collaboration facilitated through the Collaborative Circles, faculty members were extended invitations to participate in monthly Zoom calls. These calls served as another avenue for fostering collaboration and idea sharing among both full-time and adjunct faculty. Leading these monthly meetings was the Collaborative Circle Facilitator, a professor whose role was to bring faculty members together and facilitate productive discussions. The goal was to create a space where faculty members could collaborate, exchange ideas, and learn from one another.

Each monthly meeting revolved around a specific theme, carefully selected to address strategic topics for discussion and collaboration. The themes covered a wide range of areas, including educational technology, professionalism, ethical decision-making, and age-appropriate instructional strategies. By focusing on these themes, the meetings aimed to enhance faculty members' understanding and implementation of these crucial aspects in their teaching practices.

To further enrich these meetings, the Collaborative Circles Facilitator sought out subject matter experts who could contribute their knowledge and expertise. These experts were invited to present and share their insights during the meetings, providing valuable information to the participating faculty members. These presentations served as a springboard for subsequent collaboration and allowed faculty members to work together to incorporate the presented ideas and strategies into their respective classes and instructional approaches.

By combining the virtual collaboration through the Collaborative Circles with the monthly Zoom calls, the institution fostered a dynamic and inclusive environment that encouraged faculty members to actively engage with one another, learn from experts in various fields, and collectively enhance their teaching practices. These initiatives empowered faculty members with the necessary tools and knowledge to deliver effective and engaging instruction to their students.

Study and Act:
Evaluating the Impact and Making Adjustments

In the forthcoming phases of "Study" and "Act," the College of Education will persistently engage in the collection of benchmark assessment data from recently revised assessments, establishing a foundation for future continuations of data analysis. The future Assessment Summits will facilitate an extensive examination of new student performance data, related to the new assessments within the Early Childhood Education program. This imminent analysis will encompass a broader scope, integrating end-of-program survey data that are intricately linked to the specifics of the Early Childhood Education program.

During the "Study" phase, COE stakeholders meticulously dissect new data, collected after the programmatic revisions and faculty supports were implemented. The evaluation process will diligently search for patterns, trends, and insights into student accomplishments and areas necessitating refinement. This data-centric evaluation will lay the groundwork for making informed decisions.

With the conclusion of the evaluation, the COE will seamlessly transition into the "Act" phase. Guided by the insights gleaned from the data analysis, determinations about next steps in program revisions will be made. The strategies determined during this phase will address the identified areas of continued need and optimize student learning outcomes. Consequently, the COE will further strengthen its commitment to delivering a cutting-edge educational experience by continually adapting and advancing its programs through ongoing evaluation, establishing a harmonious connection between data analysis and programmatic improvements.

In the domain of instructional support and collaboration, COE is slated to hold monthly meetings between leaders of virtual collaborative circles and college leadership. These meetings will ensure the seamless operation of virtual collaborations, aligning the focus with identified needs and college initiatives. Moreover, strategic plans will be devised for the continuation of this collaborative effort into the following academic year, fostering a culture of shared expertise and continuous improvement.

Conclusion

The case study presented in this chapter highlights the importance of communication, collaboration, and a culture of continuous improvement in higher education. The success of data analysis and program evaluation initiatives depends on the involvement and collaboration of all college departments and teams. Grand Canyon University's College of Education exemplifies this collaborative approach by involving faculty members, administrators, and staff in the process of improving student outcomes. While barriers in engagement and collaboration among faculty across the nation appeared, initiatives were employed to overcome these barriers and bring faculty together.

Through the implementation of a centralized curriculum, instructional autonomy, and the PDSA Improvement Model, the College of Education was able to identify areas for improvement in the Early Childhood Education program. The faculty and staff analyzed student performance data, collaborated on curriculum development, and created a virtual community for ongoing support and collaboration. These efforts led to program revisions that enhanced partnerships, provided more flexible practicum options, emphasized application-based assignments, improved content scaffolding, and ensured qualified faculty were teaching the courses.

The success of the College of Education's initiatives demonstrates the power of data-driven decision-making and the value of collaboration in improving student outcomes. By regularly analyzing student performance data, identifying areas of improvement, and implementing targeted action plans, colleges can ensure their programs are constantly evolving to meet the needs of students and the demands of the field of education.

The case study of Grand Canyon University's College of Education underscores the importance of communication, collaboration, and a culture of continuous improvement in higher education. By embracing these principles, colleges can strive towards excellence in program development, instructional practices, and student outcomes. Through data analysis, collaboration, and ongoing support, colleges can ensure that their programs remain relevant, effective, and prepare students for successful careers in their chosen fields of study.

Appendix

Appendix A.

Assessment Summit Table Work #1

GRAND CANYON COE Assessment Summit
U N I V E R S I T Y·

COLLEGE OF EDUCATION

Programmatic Assessment

TABLE WORK #1

Group: ___Early Childhood and Elementary___

Approximately 15 minutes in breakout group, 5 minutes to report out

1. Review Findings data for all assigned programs.

   a. Are students meeting / exceeding the expectations?

   b. Are there any programs or competencies where students are not meeting the targets?

2. How does student achievement differ across modalities (if applicable)?

3. What are the overall trends?

Appendix A. Assessment Summit Table Work #1.

Appendix B.

CIRT Collaborative Circles Facilitator Post

Home | Discussions | Files   ⚙

GCU Faculty › College Specific Material › College of Education › Course and Program Collaborati... › Early Childhood Collaborative ... › Discussions ›

Discussion

📋 Discussions 🔔

📋 Published on October 14, 2022 | 8 views | 3 followers   ⚙

▮▮▮▮▮▮   Assistant Professor   [+ Add a topic] [⌄]

Hello All,

Happy Friday!

We had a small group of our ECE/ESCS team that noted the desire to learn more about assessment from birth to age two. So, I created a video and slideshow to support our understanding. Please respond with your assessment experiences with birth to two years of age or with questions. Let's get the conversation going!

Please see the Zoom link below:

https://gcu.zoom.us/rec/share/a3BYBavm3PtokLZgZJYNuEz08stOlrZ3cs54-4s8drhZyQwF4o2Hq8JWztVgmTR8.TYDjdSYY7LMvr-qw?startTime=1665760433000

Google Slide:

https://docs.google.com/presentation/d/1zbn7pWdn18uz3_XJ3yXWM5MrGWQ7axBhzLst3xaJsXo/edit?usp=sharing

---

Also, please see the discussion titled: P.S the title below is a hyperlink. Click it.

"Arizona Department of Education ECE Updates and Opportunities." They will offer training discussing the new Kindergarten Entry Assessment.

Best Wishes,

Appendix B. CIRT Collaborative Circles Facilitator Post.

References

Chang Y. C., & Menzies, H. M. (2022). Data-informed decision-making in higher education: Lessons from a teacher education program. *Research & Practice in Assessment, 17*(1).

England, N. H. S. (2022). Quality, service improvement and redesign tools: plan, do, study, act (PDSA) cycles and the model for improvement. https://www.england. nhs.uk/wp-content/uploads/2022/01/qsir-pdsa-cycles-model-for-improvement. pdf

CHAPTER FIFTEEN

Engagement in Continuous Improvement in Service of Accreditation Leads to More Nuanced Understandings of Data

JULIET MICHELSEN WAHLEITHNER

In winter 2020, leaders within California State University, Fresno's (Fresno State) Kremen School of Education and Human Development made the decision to seek national accreditation for the university's educator preparation programs from the Association for Advancing Quality in Educator Preparation (AAQEP). Through the process of selecting and analyzing data while engaging in the continuous improvement process required for AAQEP accreditation, faculty across programs realized the need for more thoughtful and purposeful data collection in order to engage in meaningful learning about how to improve program practices.

Background

Situated in California's Central Valley, Fresno State is a large, regional institution that serves approximately 25,000 students annually; about 22,000 of these are undergraduate students while the remaining nearly 3,000 are graduate students. Nearly two-thirds of these students identify as first-generation. In fall of 2021, 56% of students identified as Latino/a, while just 13.7% identified as White. The next largest subgroup of students (5%) identified as Hmong.

Fresno State provides three teacher preparation programs: Multiple Subject (elementary), Single Subject (secondary), and Education Specialist (Special Education): Mild-to-Moderate Support Needs, and Extensive Support Needs. Additionally, Fresno State has 10 other educator preparation programs. Three of these programs are directly linked to initial teacher preparation: Bilingual Authorization, Agriculture Specialist, and Deaf Education. The remaining seven programs lead to advanced credentials: Preliminary Administrative Services, Reading and Literacy Added Authorization/Reading and Literacy Leadership Specialist, School Counseling, School Psychology, School Social Work/Child Welfare and Attendance, School Nursing, and Speech/Language Pathology. These programs are spread across 10 departments situated within six different colleges at the university. The School of Education and Human Development (SOEHD), which houses several of the programs, serves as the lead unit for educator preparation at the university.

Accreditation History

In spring 2014, Fresno State held concurrent accreditation site visits for both the California Commission on Teacher Credentialing (CCTC), which oversees all educator preparation programs in the state, and the National Council for Accreditation of Teacher Education (NCATE). All programs received full accreditation from each of the accrediting bodies.

In winter 2020, as they began to prepare for the next accreditation site visits scheduled for spring 2022, leaders within the SOEHD made the decision to shift from seeking national accreditation through the Council for Accreditation of Educator Preparation (CAEP) to accreditation through AAQEP. But the concurrent site visits for the AAQEP accreditation and the CCTC were just 2 years away. Shortly after the decision was made, the COVID-19 pandemic shifted working conditions so that we were all in our homes, communicating only through email and Zoom. At the same time, a new dean from outside the institution was in the process of being hired. It was definitely a time of transition within the school and across the university.

Shifting Perspectives from Accountability to Continuous Improvement

As faculty began the work of preparing for the accreditation site visits, the overwhelming understanding of accreditation was—as was traditionally the case—one focused on accountability: The purpose of accreditation was to demonstrate to the visiting team that we were doing everything "right" (Cochran-Smith & Reagan, 2021). Indeed, though the CCTC does have a Common Standard (California Commission on Teacher Credentialing) focused on continuous improvement, its orientation towards accreditation is still one of compliance: Each program is expected to demonstrate the ways in which it meets each of its corresponding program standards, while the education unit as a whole is expected to demonstrate how all programs, collectively, are meeting the Common Standards.

Yet AAQEP's orientation, as documented throughout this volume, is one focused on continuous improvement. Instead of focusing on how the education unit as a whole—and the programs within it—are meeting the AAQEP Standards and Aspects, institutions are expected to provide documentation of the ways in which they engage in purposeful data collection and analysis in service of learning where programs were in meeting those standards and aspects, reflecting on that learning, and determining next steps (AAQEP, 2023).

This chapter highlights Fresno State's experiences scaffolding the AAQEP accreditation process for faculty involved in nine of the educator preparation programs. (Four of the programs were not included in the AAQEP accreditation process because they had national accreditation through a program-specific accrediting body.) Included in the AAQEP accreditation were the Multiple Subject, Single Subject, Education Specialist, Bilingual Authorization, Agriculture Specialist, Preliminary Administrative Services, Reading and Literacy Leadership, School Counseling, and School Nursing programs. Through the process of engaging in the continuous improvement process, faculty began to think more critically about the data sources available to them and the ways in which they could use data to improve their program practices.

Preparing the Quality Assurance Reports (QAR) required shifting faculty perspective towards AAQEP's model of accreditation focused on continuous improvement, even though faculty were simultaneously preparing for the state accreditation site visit. When beginning the AAQEP accreditation process, some faculty already engaged in continuous improvement efforts at the program level, but little work was done across programs to strategically collect and analyze data to improve program practices. We viewed the preparation of our QARs as an opportunity to develop a baseline understanding of where each educator preparation program—and our institution as a whole—was in its strategic use of data to inform program practices, in addition to developing an understanding of where programs and the institution were in relation to each of the AAQEP Standards and Aspects. But doing so required shifting understandings about how to use data in meaningful ways.

Scaffolding the Accreditation Process

As an education unit, we chose to submit two QARs: one focused on preliminary educator preparation programs, which included the Multiple Subject, Single Subject, Education Specialist, Bilingual Authorization, and Agriculture Specialist programs; and one focused on the remaining advanced educator preparation programs. While some similarities exist among the programs clustered within each QAR, particularly with the initial teacher preparation programs, there are also distinct differences. For this reason, we chose to have each program engage in its own data collection and analysis processes in response to the standards and aspects.

Our first decision was to break down the process to focus, first, on Standards 1 and 2, the standards focused on completer performance. It is this process that is the focus here. To support programs in engaging in data collection and analysis in response to each of the aspects associated with Standards 1 and 2, we created scaffolds to guide programs in identifying existing data sources, determining what parts of the data sources aligned with specific AAQEP standard aspects, and then disaggregating the data to more critically reflect on program practices. It was through this process that faculty began to critically consider the data sources available to them.

Selecting Datasets

We began by asking program faculty to identify three datasets to examine in response to each of the six aspects for Standard 1 and Standard 2. These datasets could be end-of-program surveys, key assessments that all candidates in a program completed, or even focus group discussions with program completers or employers of program completers. Given the time constraints, however, programs opted to select existing datasets or datasets that could be easily administered, such as surveys. For larger datasets, we suggested that program faculty select specific items, such as responses to three to five items from a survey or assessment elements that were specific to a given aspect. But we also were clear that the same larger dataset—though not the same items—could be used for multiple aspects. Whenever possible, we asked that programs include three cycles of data, whether that be three semesters that a course was offered or three years that an end-of-program survey was administered. We also specified that the datasets needed to reflect multiple perspectives: faculty, candidates, mentor teachers, etc.

Rubric Scores

The types of datasets varied from program to program and also among the standards and aspects, as highlighted in Table 15.1. For example, the Multiple Subject and Single Subject programs both used rubric scores from Fresno State's Teaching Performance Assessment, the Fresno Assessment of Student Teachers 2.0 (FAST). In response to Standard 1: Aspect A, which states that, by the time of program completion, candidates exhibit knowledge, skills, and abilities of professional educators appropriate to their target credential or degree, including relevant content, pedagogical, and/ or professional knowledge, the Multiple Subject Program used the "Planning," "Implementation," and "Reflection" rubric scores from the Site Visitation Project candidates complete during their first of two semesters of student teaching.

Table 15.1. Program-identified data sources for Standard 1 Aspect A

Program	Dataset 1	Dataset 2	Dataset 3
Multiple Subject	Items from Educator Quality Center Completer Survey	Midterm & Final Fieldwork Evaluation	FAST Site Visitation Project rubric items
Single Subject	Items from Educator Quality Center Completer Survey	Midterm & Final Fieldwork Evaluation	FAST Teaching Sample Project rubric items
Education Specialist	Items from Educator Quality Center Completer Survey	SPED 246: Intervention Project final scores	ES Site Visitation Project rubric items
Bilingual Authorization	LEE 135: Spanish Lesson Plan scores	Items from program-specific completer survey	
Agriculture Specialist	Items from Occupational Experience Form	CI 161: Methods and Materials in Agricultural Education: Curriculum Project	Items from program-specific completer survey
Preliminary Administrative Services	CalAPA* Leadership Cycle 2 (Rubric 2.3) scores	CalAPA Leadership Cycle 1 (Rubric 1.1) scores	CalAPA Leadership Cycle 3 (Rubric 3.4) scores
Reading/ Literacy School	LEE 213: Theory to Practice Inquiry scores	LEE 244: Literature Review rubric scores	Items from program-specific completer survey
Counseling	Items from program comprehensive exam	COUN 241 (Seminar in Organization of Counseling Services) Assignment: "Research Paper and School Counselor Interview"	Site Supervisor Program Evaluation Survey
School Nursing	Items from Program Start and Completion Knowledge-Based Questionnaire	Candidate GPA at Completion of Course/Program	Items from Preceptor Checklist of Skills and Competencies

* California Administrator Performance Assessment

For the same aspect, the Single Subject program used scores from the Teaching Sample Project "Learning Outcomes and Standards" and "Appropriateness for Students" rubrics, which candidates complete during their final phase of student teaching.

Survey Responses

Other initial teacher education programs used survey responses from a system-wide survey administered to completers of all teacher preparation programs.

Advanced program that did not have existing data sources chose to create surveys that aligned with the AAQEP aspects that they administered to candidates and program completers.

Field Placement Evaluations

Another useful source of data for programs were field placement evaluations. In fact, many advanced programs chose to use scores from their program-specific field placement evaluations to address aspects.

Analyzing the Data and Reflecting on Findings

Once program faculty determined the datasets they would use, we created templates to guide them through the process of analyzing the data, documenting the results of the analysis, and reflecting on the results of both the individual datasets and the collection of datasets. They used the reflections to determine programmatic next steps.

Specifically, for each dataset, we asked faculty to respond to the following prompts:

Definition of Data Source
Perspective Captured from Data Source [Candidate, Completer, Coach, Mentor, etc.]
Rationale for using Data Source
Specific Elements of Data Source Using [rubric/assessment items, survey items, etc.]
Definition of Success for Each Element
Displays of Analyzed Data [tables, bar charts, graphs, etc.—for specific items using]
Link to Full Dataset
Interpretation of Data

In addition to the template to guide the faculty through the process of describing and analyzing the datasets, we also provided faculty with a model write-up to help illustrate what a developed response would look like. For this response, we used scores from four areas of the midterm and final fieldwork evaluation and responses to the systemwide exit survey.

Once program faculty had analyzed the datasets and articulated next steps based on their findings for each aspect, we asked them to look across the goals they had articulated for all six aspects to select overall next steps in response to the standard as a whole. These would become the focus of the next round of their continuous improvement efforts.

Multiple Subject Program Faculty Use QAR Preparation Process to Finetune Continuous Improvement Efforts

The Multiple Subject Program is the largest educator preparation program at Fresno State, preparing 200 to 250 elementary teachers annually. As highlighted above and in Table 1, the Multiple Subject Program faculty chose to use existing data sources to support its analysis for Standard 1, Aspect A, which focuses on candidates' learning of the content and pedagogical knowledge relevant to becoming elementary teachers.

Data Source 1: Survey Items

To begin with, the program selected eight items from the California State University (CSU) Educator Quality Center's (EdQC) program exit survey, which is aligned with the CCTC's Teaching Performance Expectations (TPE) for Multiple Subject and Single Subject Programs, and administered to completers of all CSU teacher preparation programs. The items the program selected include:

How well did your program prepare you to do each of the following as a teacher:

- To plan and adapt instruction that incorporates appropriate strategies, resources, and technologies to meet the learning needs of all students.

- To use effective instructional strategies to teach specific subject matter and skills.
- To engage students in inquiry, problem solving, and reflection to promote their critical thinking.
- To select, adapt, and develop materials, resources, and technologies to make subject matter accessible to all students.

Additionally, the program used a cluster of items related to content addressed in the Multiple Subject Classroom:

- To teach English Literacy and Language Arts.
- To teach Mathematics.
- To teach Science.
- To teach History/Social Studies.

Within their write-up, the program included bar graphs of completers' responses for the identified items from each of the past 3 academic years. For each dataset, programs were asked to define what success looked like. The CSU EdQC survey offers responders a five-point Likert scale, with options ranging from "Not at all prepared" to "Very well prepared." The Multiple Subject program faculty indicated that their goal was to have 85% of candidates respond with a Likert rating of 3 (Adequately prepared) to 5 (Very well prepared) on the identified items. The data displayed illustrated that, in all areas except history/social science, at least 85% of the responding completers rated their preparation at a level 3 or higher for the selected items.

Data Source 2: Fieldwork Evaluation

As a second data source, the program used two items from the midterm/final fieldwork evaluation used to evaluate candidates in the field placements: Item 10: Critical and Creative Thinking and Item 11: Subject Matter Knowledge. All items on the evaluation are tied to the CCTC's TPEs, and candidates are evaluated on a scale of 1 (Unobserved) to 5 (Developing: Consistently attempting, somewhat effective). Coaches, or university-based supervisors, use the fieldwork evaluation tool at both the midpoint and the end of each semester to provide formalized feedback to candidates. The programmatic goal was to see 75% of candidates scoring at a Level 4 (Emerging) or Level 5 by the end of their final semester of student teaching, so at their fourth formal observation.

The program analyzed four cohorts' data across their two semesters of field experience on each rubric item, creating tables to show the percent of candidates scoring at the mid and final evaluations each semester. The analyses demonstrated that candidates in all cohorts except those that began in spring 2020 did make positive gains for Item 10, with at least 75% of the cohort scoring at Levels 4 or 5. Only 64% of the cohort that began in spring 2020 were scored at Level 4 or 5 in their final evaluation. For Item 11, candidates in all cohorts were scored at Levels 4 or 5 in their final evaluation. In their discussion of these results, the program faculty reflected on the content of Item 10 and offered possible reasons why scores were lower, particularly because of the emphasis continually placed on direct instruction in many of our local districts.

Data Source 3: Site Visitation Project Rubric Scores

The final set of data the Multiple Subject program faculty used to evaluate how well the program was preparing candidates with the content and pedagogical knowledge relevant to becoming elementary teachers was candidates' scores on the Site Visitation Project (SVP), which is the FAST component candidates complete during their first semester of their field experience. The SVP includes three rubrics—Planning, Implementation, and Reflection, each of which is scored by coaches and program faculty on a four-point scale. Candidates must score at least a 2 to pass the SVP and advance to their final semester. Program faculty defined success as all candidates scoring at least a three on each of the rubrics.

For their analyses, the program faculty analyzed candidates' scores on each rubric for five semesters. They created tables to indicated the percentage of candidates who received each score on each rubric each semester, along with the mean score for that semester. While not all candidates scored a 3 on each rubric, looking across the semesters, the program faculty highlighted a positive trend in the number of candidates scoring a 3 each semester. The only semester where the increase was not as significant was fall 2020, when candidates were still completing their student teaching virtually.

Synthesizing the Findings

While the analysis of each of the datasets above led to new understanding about areas for program shifts and candidate growth, one of the biggest takeaways for faculty from working through this process was the need for better systems to collect and analyze data, as well as better systems for tracking different cohorts of candidates. For example, even though most candidates indicated they believed they were at least adequately prepared on the survey items related to pedagogical and content knowledge, faculty wondered why some candidates indicated they were not at all prepared. Additionally, the Multiple Subject Program contains multiple different pathways (residency options, internships, traditional, etc.), yet the survey data were only available in aggregate form.

Reading/Literacy Program Utilizes Key Assignments to Better Understand Candidate Preparation

In contrast to the Multiple Subject Program, the Reading/Literacy Program is much smaller, enrolling just 10 to 15 candidates in each cohort of the four-semester program. As highlighted in Table 1, the Reading/Literacy program faculty chose to use scores from candidates' literature reviews in two courses along with a self-assessment survey to analyze candidates' learning of the content knowledge relevant to becoming reading/literacy specialists.

Data Source 1: Theory to Practice Literature Review Rubric Scores

One of the first courses candidates take during the Reading/Literacy Advanced Credential Program is a course focused on teaching the English Language Arts in K-12. Within this course, candidates complete a theory to practice inquiry, which includes an articulation of key findings from the literature related to their inquiry focus. Program faculty chose to focus on the rubric element that aligns with this component, as it relates to the develop of candidates' content knowledge.

The rubric itself has three points, ranging from 1 (Beginning) to 3 (Proficient). The goal of program faculty was that each candidate would score at least a 2 (Developing) for this area on the rubric. Faculty created a table to analyze the scores of candidates from the past three cohorts. They included both the average score of each cohort and the percent of candidates scoring at least a 2. In doing so, they demonstrated that, indeed, all candidates did score at least a 2, demonstrating their mastery of content knowledge related to becoming a reading/literacy specialist.

Data Source 2: Understandings of Research in Key Areas

Similarly, candidates also take a course titled "Research for Reading Professionals," which focuses on developing candidates' knowledge of past and current research in reading related to instructional issues, as well as their ability to apply that knowledge to the analysis and planning of curricula. The content and pedagogical knowledge they develop within the course is necessary for the role of reading specialist.

Within the course, candidates complete a literature review, in which they are required to provide summaries and key details of a number of studies, particularly highlighting how the studies address emergent literacy, comprehension, and emergent multilinguals. Depending on the number of studies and key topics candidates discuss within the scope of their literature review, they receive from 30 points (1–4 studies and 1–2 topics) to 40 points (7–10 studies and 5 topics). Programmatically, faculty defined success as at least 75% of candidates scoring at least 34 points. The program created a table to detail the average scores of candidates in each of the three past cohorts, along with the percent of candidates scoring at least 34 points.

While the table created by the faculty highlighted that all candidates did meet the program faculty's goal, the faculty discussed that the rubric used did a poor job of teasing apart candidates' knowledge of the particular focal content areas covered within the course, suggesting an area of growth for the program as it continues on its continuous improvement journey.

Data Source 3: Candidates' Own Assessment of Their Learning

As a way to capture candidates' own assessment of their own preparation for becoming reading/literacy specialists, the program created a six-item survey in fall 2020 to be completed by candidates when they completed the program. Included within the survey is an item that asked candidates to indicate on a scale of 1 (strongly disagree) to 5 (strongly agree) with the statement: "The program prepares graduates with knowledge of varied instructional approaches in the development of oral language, reading, and writing. The program chose to use the responses to this item as its third dataset, defining success as all candidates selecting 4 or 5 on the scale."

Faculty chose to use a bar graph to illustrate the responses from the one cohort of candidates from whom data were available. Overwhelmingly, 91.7% of these candidates indicated they strongly agreed with the statement.

Considering Next Steps

Looking across the results of their analyses of the three datasets led the program faculty to the conclusion that the program does provide strong support for candidates to develop the requisite content and pedagogical knowledge to become reading specialists. Yet going through this process of selecting data to analyze and then analyzing the datasets also led the program to realize the shortcomings of the datasets to which it had access. In particular, faculty realized that the rubrics used to assess candidates were not nuanced enough to really tease apart how candidates' knowledge is developed across the program and within specific courses, as well as specific areas where candidates' knowledge might not be as developed.

Continuous Improvement Process Leads Programs to Critical Consideration of Data Sources

After completing the process of selecting and analyzing at least three sources of data from different perspectives for each of the aspects of Standards 1 and 2, programs were asked to identify specific next steps faculty would take to address their findings from the process. Included within the next steps were the actions the program intended to take, the rationale for those actions, and specific steps with a timeline. Both the Multiple Subject Program and the Reading/Literacy Program highlighted the need to improve on their data collection efforts in order to engage in more thoughtful and purposeful continuous improvement efforts.

Plans for More Strategic Collection of Data Sources

As discussed above, the Multiple Subject Program relied heavily on program-level data, such as FAST rubric scores, evaluation rubrics, and completer survey responses. Many of these data sources could not be disaggregated by program pathway. While these data are useful in providing a broad portrait of candidates' learning across the program, they do not provide nuanced information about candidate learning at specific points in the program or in specific areas. Consequently, the program created two next step goals related to data collection and analysis. First, the program hoped to work with survey administrators to create a way to disaggregate completer survey results by program pathway to better understand the areas of strength and areas for growth within each pathway. Additionally, the program hoped to select key assignments tied to the CCTC's Teaching Performance Expectations as a way to examine candidate learning at the course level. Not only could collecting and analyzing data in this way serve to better understand areas where candidates were excelling and where they could use additional support, but findings could also be used to generate conversations among faculty who teach the same sections of courses as a way to examine and potentially improve instructional practices.

The Reading/Literacy Program also identified key ways to improve upon its data collection and analysis efforts. The examples above illustrated how the program relied heavily on rubrics for key assignments. Yet these rubrics were not nuanced enough to really examine candidates' learning in key areas. As the program articulated in the QAR, "Many of the assessments currently in place are not specific to the content of the course, making it difficult to determine where candidates have challenges." And so the next steps goal became to revise these assessment tools to better align with course content. The program also relied on a survey sent to completers to evaluate their perceptions of their preparation. However, candidates did little more than select an option on a Likert scale. Moving forward, the program intended to hold focus group discussions with recent completers and year-out completers to learn, more specifically, about the ways they believed the program had and had not prepared them for becoming a reading/literacy specialist.

Similarly, other programs also articulated the need to more thoughtfully consider what data they collected, how they collected it, and from whom in order to develop better understandings of their programmatic strengths and areas for growth. For example, the School Nursing program faculty realized they needed to develop tools to collect data from multiple key stakeholder groups. By reviewing and analyzing the data they collected from the survey they sent to employers of their program completers, they came to understand that it needed to be revised to more accurately reflect the key areas emphasized within the program. The same held true for the end-of-program data collected from completers. While they had some systems in place to collect feedback, they realized they needed to formalize this process by developing an end-of-program survey that aligned with key aspects of the program. Like the Reading/Literacy program, faculty within the Education Specialist program realized that many of the rubrics for signature assignments they selected as data sources were not as aligned with specific program standards as they had hoped. Consequently, they planned to develop measurement tools that would provide them with data points that would help them to better understand where candidates were excelling and where they needed additional support.

Implementation of Unit-Wide Completer Survey

Building on their new understandings about the types of meaningful data programs needed to collect, coordinators of all programs—those involved in both the AAQEP and CCTC accreditations and those only involved in the CCTC accreditation—worked together in spring 2023 to develop a new unit-wide survey to administer to completers of all programs. Efforts were made to ensure the alignment of survey items with AAQEP Standards and Aspects, as demonstrated in Table

15.2. The final survey included 15 items that completers of all educator preparation programs were asked to respond to. Because of past challenges with being able to disaggregate data by program and pathway, background and demographic items were also included to learn, specifically, which program and program pathway responders had completed along with basic demographic information (gender, ethnicity, age). In addition to the common items, programs also had the opportunity to add specific items that pertained just to their program and that would help them to critically analyze their specific program practices. By requiring survey completion of all completers who wanted to apply for a credential from the state, nearly 90% of program completers responded.

Table 15.2. Alignment of Exit Survey Items with AAQEP Standards and Aspects (asterisk indicates an aspect aligned with more than one survey item)

Exit Survey Item	AAQEP Standard & Aspect
I am prepared to use techniques to engage and build rapport with students/clients.	2c. Create productive learning environments and use strategies to develop productive learning environments in a variety of school contexts
I have acquired the knowledge and skills to organize my professional responsibilities.	1a. Content, pedagogical, and/or professional knowledge relevant to the credential or degree sought*
I am prepared to respond effectively to students/clients in regards to matters of justice, equity, diversity, and inclusion.	2b. Engage in culturally responsive educational practices with diverse learners and do so in diverse cultural and socioeconomic community contexts
My preparation has upheld the concept that all individuals can reach their goals.	1f. Dispositions and behaviors required for successful professional practice
I have an appropriate understanding of the theories that support my practice.	1b. Learners; learning theory, including social, emotional, and academic dimensions; and application of learning theory*
I am familiar with the current research in my field.	1a. Content, pedagogical, and/or professional knowledge relevant to the credential or degree sought*

Exit Survey Item	AAQEP Standard & Aspect
I have applied my learning to actual situations in schools/professional settings.	3b. Develops and implements quality clinical experiences, where appropriate, in the context of documented and effective partnerships with P-12 schools and districts*
I can assess/evaluate the progress of students/clients.	1d. Assessment of and for student learning, assessment and data literacy, and use of data to inform practice
I know how to conduct myself in accordance with professional ethics and standards.	1f. Dispositions and behaviors required for successful professional practice*
I have skills to successfully collaborate with others in the workplace.	2f. Collaborate with colleagues to support professional learning
I feel that I received a helpful and appropriate amount of supervision to support my development as a practitioner.	3b. Develops and implements quality clinical experiences, where appropriate, in the context of documented and effective partnerships with P-12 schools and districts*
I feel that I received a helpful and appropriate amount of academic and professional advising during my credential program.	3f. Maintains capacity for quality reflected in staffing, resources, operational processes, and institutional commitment
I can think critically about theory and research in my field and apply it into practice.	1b. Learners; learning theory, including social, emotional, and academic dimensions; and application of learning theory*
I have learned to establish goals for my own professional growth and engage in self-assessment, goal setting, and reflection	2e. Establish goals for their own professional growth and engage in self-assessment, goal setting, and reflection
I feel prepared to begin a full-time position in my area of professional preparation.	1f. Dispositions and behaviors required for successful professional practice*

Conclusion

In conclusion, as a result of engaging in the scaffolded continuous improvement process in service of the AAQEP accreditation, faculty across programs came to develop their own data literacy (Jacobs et al., 2009; Popham, 2008) as it relates to program improvement. While many faculty had understandings of using data to engage in research related to their areas of expertise, fewer had thought about how to purposefully collect and analyze data from key stakeholder groups—current candidates, program completers, coaches/university supervisors, employers of completers—to critically reflect on the work they do to prepare future educators. The result was that existing tools often did not yield meaningful data: Rubrics were not nuanced enough to uncover complexities in candidates' developing understandings and surveys were not aligned with key program outcomes. It was working through the continuous improvement process that faculty began to realize the affordances of different types of data and how tools were constructed.

It is important to highlight the role that the AAQEP accreditation process had in leading faculty to these developing understandings. Rather than focus on documentation of how programs were meeting specific standards, as is the case with accreditation systems focused on accountability (Cochran-Smith et al., 2018), AAQEP asks institutions to select data sources that are contextually relevant and meaningful to analyze as part of the continuous improvement process. The expectation is not that programs will be meeting each aspect of each standard perfectly. Instead, the expectation is that programs will document their processes for where they are in their ongoing journey *towards* meeting those aspects and standards and what they will do with their learning from their investigations—what steps they will take to work towards continuous improvement. For the educator preparation program faculty at Fresno State, it was the engagement in this authentic process in service of accreditation that led not only to deeper understandings about how to improve their practices for developing new educators but also to how to collect and use data in meaningful ways to engage in continuous improvement. In this way, the accreditation process moved faculty towards collaborative, data-informed change (Davis, 2023).

References

Association for Advancing Quality in Educator Preparation (AAQEP). (2023). *Guide to AAQEP Accreditation.* https://aaqep.org/guide

California Commission on Teacher Credentialing. (2023, March 22). *Common Standards.* https://www.ctc.ca.gov/educator-prep/common-standards

Cochran-Smith, M., Carney, M. C., Keefe, E. S., Burton, S., Chang, W.-C., Fernández, M. B., Miller, A. F., Sánchez, J. G., & Baker, M. (2018). *Reclaiming accountability in teacher education.* Teachers College Press.

Cochran-Smith, M., & Reagan, E. M. (2021). *"Best Practices" for evaluating teacher preparation programs.* National Academy of Education.

Davis, S. C. (2023). Engaging faculty in data use for program improvement in teacher education: How leaders bridge individual and collective development. *Teaching and Teacher Education, 129.*

Jacobs, J., Gregory, A., Hoppey, D., & Yendol-Hoppey, D. (2009). Data literacy: Understanding teachers' data use in a context of accountability and response to intervention. *Action in Teacher Education, 31*(3), 41–55.

Popham, W. J. (2008). Assessment literacy for teachers: Faddish or fundamental? *Theory into Practice, 48*(1), 4–11.

CHAPTER SIXTEEN

Data, Data Everywhere, But Is It What You Think?

SUNNY DUERR

W e've all been there. You're on the cusp of your next accreditation review cycle and it's time to start pulling together
the evidence that will support claims about the quality of your programs. Coffee in hand and with a relatively clear calendar, you begin
to download data from every source imaginable: GPA and candidate
demographics data, local assessment data, state certification exam
data, survey data, clinical experience placement data—and that's
just the data on current candidates and recent graduates. To say that
education programs are often drowning in data is not an exaggera-
tion in many cases.

One of the problems that EPPs can encounter stems from this
abundance of data; it can be difficult to figure out where to start,
what data to report on, and how to present the data so that they
accurately represent the institution while also being understandable
to consumers of the information. One common approach I've seen
for addressing this problem is to simply include everything—something I've come to refer to as the *everything and the kitchen sink*
approach (which is related to but slightly different from the *throw it
at the wall and see what sticks* approach). This commonly manifests
as an abundance of charts, tables, and graphs, often without supporting contextual or interpretive narrative. This approach causes
more problems than it solves, however; it might effectively show that
the EPP *has* a lot of data, but it can fail to show the more important
piece of information, which is what the data *mean* to the institution.

The result is that the EPP can come across as being data rich but information poor.

This is exactly the situation that my institution was in when I was hired as Coordinator of Assessment and Accreditation in 2013. At the time, we were beginning the final round of legacy NCATE reviews, and the institution submitted 26 SPA reports on my first day on the job; that was, in fact, the very first thing I did—hit the submit button for 26 SPA reports, despite the fact that I had no idea what a SPA report was. Once that task had been accomplished, I was shown the various sources of data that were at my disposal, provided resource links for writing the self-study report, and given some well-wishes by the retiring Associate Dean, who was very happy to not be responsible for this work anymore.

For the remainder of this chapter, I will present some of the key considerations that have helped my institution build assessment data and reporting processes that facilitate continuous improvement while also supporting the accreditation and reporting landscape of educator preparation. And as a disclaimer, none of the data presented in this chapter are from any actual dataset, real or imagined; it has been fabricated to support the demonstrations contained herein.

Understanding the Data

One of the primary components to building an assessment system that supports your program's needs is how well you understand your data. Key considerations include the sources of data and the perspective(s) that the data represent; the characteristics of the data and how it should be reported; and importantly, the relationship between the assessment instrument(s) and the resulting data. Additional consideration must be given to the data that you *need* to have, according to some external organization such as an accreditation agency or state education department.

An exercise that we found helpful was to create a construct map that showed the existing data sources and mapped them onto the accreditation standards. This allowed us to identify the sources of data we had available, and to determine whether there were any constructs for which we had no previously identified data sources. Table 16.1 below shows each of the sources of data we have available for AAQEP's Standard 1 aspects, and how individual items from each assessment align with the aspects.

Table 16.1. Assessment Map between data sources and AAQEP Standard 1 aspects.

Date Source	AAQEP 1a	AAQEP 1b	AAQEP 1c	AAQEP 1d	AAQEP 1e	AAQEP 1f
GPA	X					
State Certification Exam	X		X			
Teacher Performance Assessment	1	1	1,5	4	2,3	3,5
Planning Assessment	1,3	2,5,6	6,10	8	10,11	10,11
Learning Assessment	1	1,2,3,4	2	2,3,4,5	5	
Pedagogical Practice Assessment	1	3,5,6,7	5,6,7	3	4,5,6,7	2,3,4,5, 6,7,8
Dispositions Assessment			7,8,9		7,8,9,10	1,2,3,4, 5,6,7,8, 9,10,11, 12,13,14

A similar table can be completed for the other AAQEP Standards, though for Standards 3 and 4, it would be more accurate to identify *evidence sources*, rather than *data sources*, since those two standards are less about candidate-level, performance-based data. Furthermore, such tables are easily translatable to any other accreditation agency or reporting requirement that you might have. For example, creating such a table for the institutional accreditation process (e.g., Middle States, HLC, etc.) could also prove to be useful.

After identifying the available sources of data, it is important to outline the characteristics of the data, a process that is intrinsically related to the form of the assessment instrument or measure that was used to collect the data. One of the first steps in this process is to determine what type of data you're dealing with. Is your data the result of a survey with a Likert scale, or is it a standardized test with scaled scoring (common in state certification exams)? If so, you may have continuous data that can be meaningfully analyzed using descriptive and common inferential statistics. Did you use an internally designed rubric? If so, you might have categorical or ordinal data, which would be better represented through percentages above and below performance benchmarks.

The question you are seeking to answer with your data should always include: *What does this tell us?* or *What does this mean?* To that end, understanding the difference between continuous data and ordinal data comes down to the interpretability of the data. If someone tells you that the mean score on a state certification exam for candidates in your program was 522, that doesn't necessarily mean much. If they tell you instead that 83% of your candidates passed the certification exam, that information is more useful. Naturally, you can drill down into either of these values to truly understand what is happening; if scores on the certification exam range between 400 and 600 and the passing score is 520, the mean score of 522 for this group of candidates now has more context.

On the other hand, if we're talking about a rubric with four levels—say Unacceptable, Developing, Acceptable, and Exceptional—and you find out that the mean for candidates on that rubric was 2.5, that can be somewhat confusing. Does that mean the candidates are somewhere between Developing and Acceptable? What do you do with that information? The reason the mean is more difficult to interpret in this case is that the data are ordinal in nature—although the levels grow from lowest to highest, there is no mathematical justification for the mean of 2.5 to mean anything concrete. This situation would benefit from setting an expected benchmark of performance and then looking at the percentage of candidates who met that benchmark versus those who failed to do so.

Looking at the example data in Table 16.2 provides some actionable information. For example, we can see that candidates in the Adolescence Math program for this cohort struggled with two of the five assessment indicators for Aspect 1a. The faculty for this program can then look at the raw data to identify which candidates struggled and determine if there was any systematic reason for this low performance. Additionally, conclusions could be drawn for the

Table 16.2. Percent of candidates performing at or above benchmark on items aligned with Standard 1a.

Program	N	TPA 1	Planning 1	Planning 3	Learning 1	Pedagogy 1
Undergraduate	129	90%	88%	94%	82%	97%
Elementary	64	94%	91%	92%	83%	97%
Adol English	21	90%	81%	95%	86%	95%
Adol Math	11	73%	82%	100%	64%	100%
Adol Science	10	90%	90%	90%	80%	100%
Adol S. Studies	23	87%	91%	96%	87%	96%
Graduate	48	96%	94%	92%	96%	96%
Elementary	15	93%	93%	100%	93%	100%
Adol English	9	100%	89%	89%	89%	100%
Adol Math	7	100%	100%	86%	100%	86%
Adol Science	5	80%	80%	80%	100%	100%
Adol S. Studies	12	100%	100%	92%	100%	92%

Note: Benchmark performance on internal assessments is at the Acceptable level or higher.

entire EPP around undergraduate performance on the P-12 learning assessment, which has the lowest percentage of Acceptable or higher scores out of all items identified to be in alignment with AAQEP Standard Aspect 1a.

Finally, some thought needs to be given to the number of times your candidates are evaluated using the same assessment instrument, and what the best way to represent that data would be. It is common for education preparation providers to utilize the same rubric throughout the candidates' time in the program. Candidates might be introduced to an assessment of their lesson planning skills early in the program, during the first methods-oriented course, and that same assessment might be used in each methods course in which one or more of the assignments has to do with lesson planning. Then, the same assessment might be used during the final clinical experience, student teaching, or practicum. And to add complexity to the situation, there will often be more than one rater—a mentor teacher and a university supervisor. In some states, you might be required to have two separate placements during student teaching, in which case the number of entries for a single candidate during student teaching is doubled to four; if there are three methods courses in the program prior to student teaching, one candidate would have seven entries on this assessment by the time they complete the program.

How this information is utilized by the program might seem simple enough; in an ideal situation, faculty would look at the assessment data from class to class throughout the methods sequence expecting to see signs of improvement and growth. Struggling candidates would be identified and supported, and by the time student teaching occurs, most candidates would be performing at or above the benchmark of expected performance on this assessment.

The challenge associated with this scenario comes in how the data should be reported, and who the audience consuming that information is. If we're considering the semester-to-semester operations of the program, then a graphical comparison for each student might be used during an annual meeting focused on a review of the program's assessment data.

Table 16.3 demonstrates a graphical representation of candidate performance on a single item from one assessment. Candidate performance can be quickly reviewed by program faculty, and in the case of candidates who have yet to enter student teaching (Candidates 8, 9, and 10 in this example), the faculty can see that none of these candidates are below the Developing level prior to entering student teaching. In the case of those candidates who have completed student teaching (Candidates 1 through 7 in this example), faculty can see that all candidates have met the expected benchmark performance of Acceptable by their final student teaching placement.

Reviewing the data in this way has the potential to be useful for the program's faculty, but it would be difficult to envision using this kind of data presentation for reporting purposes. For one thing, this data example includes only 10 candidates, and many programs have hundreds (or thousands) of candidates. This example also only represents one item from one assessment, and if we were to use this data reporting technique for a report, we would need to build a

Table 16.3. Candidate performance on Planning Assessment Item 1 for 2022 completers.

Candidate	M 1	M 2	M 3	ST CT1	ST SUP1	ST CT2	ST SUP2
C 1	1	2	3	4	3	4	4
C 2	2	2	2	2	2	3	3
C 3	2	2	3	3	3	3	4
C 4	2	1	2	3	2	3	3
C 5	2	3	3	4	4	4	4
C 6	2	2	3	3	3	3	3
C 7	2	2	2	2	3	3	3
C 8	1	2	2	/////	/////	/////	/////
C 9	2	1	2	/////	/////	/////	/////
C 10	2	2	3	/////	/////	/////	/////
	Unacceptable	Developing		Acceptable		Exceptional	

similar image to represent four more items from three more internal assessments (based on the data sources presented in Table 1), and that's just to cover Standard Aspect 1a.

Reporting Data Externally

When it comes to reporting data to external stakeholders, whether they are campus partners, local professional partners, or accreditation partners, it's important to be mindful of the cognitive load that is necessary to interpret the data you present. None of these partners are going to be *as* invested or *as* interested in your data as you are—nor should they be. They want to see the *most important* pieces of information, and you need to make it easy for them to understand what's being presented and why it matters to them.

This is where some important decisions need to be made. Based on your audience, what information is necessary changes dramatically. What program faculty need to know about their candidates throughout the program is quite organic; each semester builds upon the next, so faculty need to be able to see candidate performance in a real-time fashion, or semester over semester at least. In the case of something that covers a longer period of time and multiple programs, like an accreditation report, that much information is unnecessary and, in fact, burdensome.

Generally speaking, external consumers of your data do not need to see every data point that you have on your candidates. Rather, they need to see information that conveys a certain message. In the case of an accreditation report, for example, the external consumer needs to see the data that support the claims associated with a given standard aspect. In the case of candidate-level performance data, what is important for an external consumer to see is that your candidates have performed at the established benchmark for performance at the end of the program, thereby substantiating the claim that the standard aspect has been met.

Continuing with the model outlined in Table 16.3 above, assume we have three methods courses, two student teaching supervisor evaluations, and two student teaching cooperating teacher evaluations, for a total of seven data points per candidate. As was previously pointed out, candidate performance during the methods courses is not as important for this kind of data reporting as their performance during the culminating activity of student teaching. We can therefore prune out those three data points from consideration, leaving us with four data points to think about.

There are a couple of ways to approach this, and how you use the data internally can influence the decision. One approach would be to report each candidate's highest score between the two placements, representing the candidate's "best attempt"; this is the way that state certification exam results are often reported, because the goal is for candidates to demonstrate that they are capable of performing at the benchmark level at least once. Another option would be to report the data using the values from the final placement, which would be using the philosophical approach that the final placement represents the candidate's full growth right before program completion.

Tables 16.4 and 16.5 below show how these two approaches would represent the data differently for a single program. In this fabricated dataset, 25 student observations were randomly assigned using a random number generator with the simple rule that 90% of the values would be at the "acceptable" level or higher.

Table 16.4. Percent of Candidates Performing at or Above Benchmark During at Least One of the Two Placements.

Evaluator	N	TPA 1	Planning 1	Planning 3	P-12 Learning	Pedagogy 1
Supervisors	25	96%	100%	100%	96%	100%
Mentors	25	100%	100%	100%	100%	100%
Total	25	98%	100%	100%	98%	100%

Notice that the "best attempt" method shown in Table 16.4 shows that nearly all candidates have demonstrated the expected level of performance at least once during the student teaching semester, as evaluated by both the mentor teacher and the university supervisor. By comparison, the "final placement" method in Table 16.5 shows significantly more variability in the data. The decision for which way to present the data comes down to your philosophical argument for *why* you are presenting the data in this way, and then being consistent with that presentation throughout the report.

Table 16.5. Percent of Candidates Performing at or Above Benchmark During the Final Student Teaching Placement.

Evaluator	N	TPA 1	Planning 1	Planning 3	P-12 Learning	Pedagogy 1
Supervisors	25	92%	92%	94%	78%	96%
Mentors	25	88%	92%	96%	72%	92%
Total	25	96%	92%	92%	84%	100%

Obviously, there are dozens of other ways to present these data, but the key is to keep the audience of the report in mind and attempt minimize the cognitive load required for them to understand your presentation of the data, which brings me to a final point: Don't forget the narrative. I have found that some EPPs include information on their context only at the beginning of a report, talking about their location, number of students, how long they've been serving their region, etc. This is important information, but your context doesn't stop there. Continue to elaborate on your context throughout the report, and be sure to explain how the data are being reported and why you're reporting them that way. One thing we did during our last accreditation report was insert text boxes containing expository information, which we titled Background Knowledge Boxes. We included a Background Knowledge Box the first time we presented something that reviewers might have questions about, including one on interpreting the state certification exam data and another on the reliability and validity evidence for our internal assessments. Figure 16.6 shows the Background Knowledge Box we used to explain our internal assessment data.

Background Knowledge Box:
What are the Values Reported in These Tables?

For this report, the data from our internal assessments were recorded at the student level in LiveText and/or Via. Considering the large number of programs and the resulting amount of data available to show, we are presenting these tables as examples from the overall data in a way that makes sense for a reviewer to be able to interpret. In most cases, the data shown in the narrative represents one academic year of data, but multiple years of data are provided in Appendix A, demonstrating that we can and do disaggregate the data by year and by program.

The presentation of data for reporting purposes is different from the two ways in which the data are actually used throughout our programs: Monitoring and decision-making for individual students, and systematic program review for improvement represented by the annual reporting cycle.

Under normal circumstances (and represented in all tables in this report), most candidates (i.e., all initial certification candidates) complete two placements during student teaching, and therefore have two evaluations on each assessment. In the case of the Assessment of Pedagogical Practice (APP), candidates are evaluated by both the mentor teacher and the university supervisor for each placement (for a total of four evaluations). Mentor teachers and supervisors discuss the

---

candidate's performance on these assessments throughout the placement and observation process, so candidates are receiving real-time feedback during the placement.

For the purposes of this report, we included each candidate's highest rating for a given item, reflecting the common practice of someone's best attempt being the one that counts (as is the case in high-stakes testing such as the SAT or GRE). We feel that this demonstrates to our candidates that a rating of Developing simply identifies an area for opportunity, rather than immediately resulting in a punitive consequence.

In these tables, N represents the individual candidates evaluated during the student teaching semester. Percent (%) Acceptable is the percentage of those candidates who were rated at the Acceptable level (again, based on best performance per item).

Figure 16.6. Background Knowledge Box.

Focus on Improvement—Not Accreditation

The SUNY system is comprised of several universities with education preparation programs serving New York State. Nearly 10 years ago, I was a founding member of what is now known as the SUNY EPP Assessment Consortium, which is a collection of deans, directors, and data managers of assessment and accreditation for those EPPs. We meet annually for a day where we share successes, discuss challenges, and help each other navigate the ever-changing landscape of educator preparation.

One of the core tenets that the SUNY EPP Assessment Consortium has adopted is that the focus of our work as deans, directors, and data managers of assessment should always be on program improvement. For us, assessment processes and assessment data should serve students, faculty, and programs first. If we build assessment systems that serve the purpose of continuous improvement, accreditation will come as a natural consequence. If your assessment data work for you, are based on fair, reliable, and valid measures, and lead to data-informed decisions, then the only thing that remains is to use that data to effectively tell the story of your institution. I hope this chapter has provided some insight on how to approach that task.

ABOUT THE AUTHORS

Dr. Stephanie Atchley is a graduate faculty member for the Department of Educational Leadership and Technology at Tarleton State University. During her time at Tarleton, Dr. Atchley served as program coordinator for the principal certification program, and she has extensive experience as a practicum supervisor. Dr. Atchley's research interests are inspired by her time as a campus and district-level administrator. Her research interests include Principal Preparation, Educational Leadership, Leadership in Special Education, Leadership of Special Programs, and bilingual/EL Education. Dr. Atchley's work has been published in national and international journals, including the *National Association of Secondary School Principals Bulletin* and the *International Journal of Disability, Development, and Education.* She has secured over $1.5 million in grant funding and serves as an editor for the *International Journal of Modern Education Studies.* Prior to joining the faculty at Tarleton State University, Dr. Atchley served 20 years in K-12 education as a special education director, principal, and teacher.

Rebecca Bahr has held diverse professional roles in education, non-profits, and the government that have spanned several states and three countries. Her work has had a common thread of advocacy and support for those who have experienced barriers to their educational pathways during her 24 years as an educator and administrator at both the K-12 and postsecondary levels. She has a deep commitment to ensuring that all learners, including those facing unique challenges, have the opportunity to access quality education and support to overcome the barriers that may hinder their academic success and vocational success. Ms. Bahr's research interests include the effects of trauma on memory and cognition in refugee and immigrant students, the transfer of literacy skills, the role of culture in language teaching and learning, and assessment bias. She has a Bachelor of Arts in Latin American Studies, a Master of Arts in Teaching ESL, and postgraduate work in reading instruction.

Susan Boe is a secondary classroom teacher and author with a demonstrated history of working in Education. Dr. Boe is currently the Licensure Pathways Policy & Academic Program Specialist for Oregon Teacher Standards and Practices Commission.

Heather Ann Bower began her career as a middle and high school English language arts teacher. After several years as a classroom teacher, she obtained her Masters in School Administration at UNC-Chapel Hill and then worked as the College Access Programs Coordinator for a large school district. Realizing that schools needed more support on the state policy level, she returned to UNC-Chapel Hill and earned her PhD in Education with a focus on Culture, Curriculum, and Change. Bower began working at Meredith College as an adjunct in 2010. In spring of 2013, she became interim director of the Teaching Fellows Program. In summer of 2013, she accepted the full-time position of Director of the Teaching Fellows Program and Assessment Coordinator for the Department of Education. In Summer of 2019, Bower stepped into the Director of Teacher Education position, and in Summer 2020, she stepped into the role of Department Head. Throughout her years at Meredith, she has taught in the undergraduate and graduate education programs, specializing in foundations, literacy, and leadership. Her research focuses on family involvement, classroom and behavior management, and school culture, particularly as it pertains to teacher identity and school reform. She currently serves as the president elect for the North Carolina Association of Colleges for Teacher Education.

Hope G. Casto, PhD, is an Associate Professor and Department Chair of Education Studies at Skidmore College. She earned her doctorate at Cornell University in Learning, Teaching, and Social Policy and her Master's degree in Social Foundations of Education at the University of Virginia. In addition to the examination of continuous improvement in teacher education programs included in this volume, Hope's research has included theoretical and empirical contributions to the field of rural education. Her explorations of the connections between schools and communities include studies of rural high schools enrolling international students, teacher and school

leader perceptions of community and school-community partnerships, and the partnerships created between schools and community as a result of the Universal Pre-Kindergarten policy in New York
State. Her work on the connections between rural schools and communities has been published in *The Rural Educator, Educational
Policy, School Community Journal, Educational Policy Analysis
and Archives, Early Childhood Research Quarterly,* and the *Journal
of Rural Studies.*

Dr. Lina Darwich is an associate professor in teacher education at
Lewis & Clark College in Oregon. She obtained her BEd from the
American University of Beirut, Lebanon. She started her career in
education as an elementary school teacher in Dubai (UAE). Her
research focuses on teacher resilience and social and emotional
learning (SEL) through an equity lens. She teaches courses on adolescent development, creating supportive classroom communities,
and a seminar on SEL.

Dr. Travis Dimmitt is an assistant professor of education at
Northwest Missouri State University, in Maryville, Missouri, where
he teaches courses in curriculum, instruction, assessment, classroom management, and school administration. Prior to his time at
Northwest, Dimmitt was a middle and high school social science
teacher for several years in rural Missouri. While a classroom teacher,
he was selected as one of 20 teachers in the state of Missouri to train
and serve in the state's Select Teacher as Regional Resource (STARR)
Program. Through this experience, Dimmitt traveled to numerous
school districts, educating hundreds of practicing teachers on how to
better implement research-based teaching strategies in their classrooms. He was later an educational consultant, dealing specifically
with the implementation of Positive Behavior Interventions and
Supports (PBIS) in numerous K-12 school settings. After his time as a
consultant, Dimmitt became a building principal, also at the middle
and high school level in rural Missouri. After leaving public education, he spent four years as a campus minister at Northwest before
coming to his current position. Dimmitt is married with three children. He and his family make their home in Maryville.

Dr. Kristen M. Driskill is an accomplished educator and researcher, currently serving as an Associate Professor of Inclusive Education at St. John Fisher University in Rochester, NY. With a strong focus on clinical practice, culturally responsive teaching, and school–university partnerships, she has made substantial contributions to the field. Her book *The Mentor Teacher Blueprint: Building Effective Clinical Practice Through School-University Partnerships* highlights her expertise in clinical practice, offering a proven plan for identifying, training, and supporting mentor teachers. In her work, Dr. Driskill has guided school–university partnerships to maximize the clinical experience of preservice teachers and, thus, provide classrooms with highly qualified teachers. Dr. Driskill's most notable achievement is her establishment of a rigorous quality assurance system in her previous position, where she was the Dean of the School of Education and Chair of the Department of Teacher Education at Roberts Wesleyan University. Her innovative approach has not only improved educational outcomes for preservice teachers, but has also fostered a climate of data-informed decision making at the institution.

Dr. Sunny Duerr is the assistant dean for assessment and accreditation and director of compliance for the School of Education at the State University of New York (SUNY) at New Paltz. With a doctorate in behavioral science research methods and a master's degree in applied statistics and research methods, Duerr has served as an accreditation reviewer and team lead for several CAEP and AAQEP teams, and successfully led SUNY New Paltz through NCATE/CAEP accreditation in 2015 and AAQEP accreditation in 2022. Duerr was a founding member of the SUNY EPP Assessment Consortium in 2013 and served as a steering committee member for that group until 2023. In addition to his volunteer service with AAQEP as an accreditation reviewer, team lead, and commissioner, Duerr serves on the New Paltz Human Research Ethics Board. For fun, Duerr teaches graduate courses in research methods and statistics for several New Paltz programs in Education, Music Therapy, and Psychology.

Dr. Veronica L. Estrada is a Professor in the Department of Teaching and Learning at The University of Texas Rio Grande Valley (UTRGV) where she is also currently serving her college as the Associate Dean for Assessment and Accreditation and Interim Chair for the Department of Counseling. Dr. Estrada is a first-generation college graduate and a Rio Grande Valley native from San Isidro, TX, a small rural community located along the Texas/Mexico border. She is a former high school English teacher with 30 years combined teaching experience at the secondary and university levels. Dr. Estrada's research is centered on the impact of teacher quality on student success of Hispanic/Latino students. Her research interests and publications are in the areas of teacher development and preparation, teaching and leading in rural schools, practice-based teacher education, language and literacy research of postsecondary students, and most recently, in improvement science as a methodology for systemic improvement.

Joan Flora has enjoyed four decades as an educator, instructional leader, and leadership coach. She currently directs the Teacher Candidate Clinical Practice at University of Portland. Closely studying change leadership and implementation processes, "Triangulating Data through Action Research to Set Priorities, Connect to Partners, and Design Program Improvements" represents important processes in improvement science and stakeholder voice in implementation projects. Dr. Flora comes to the University of Portland with many experiences in education, from teaching to instructional coaching to leading districts through curriculum adoption processes. After a decade of high school teaching, Joan transitioned into a community college and university instructor in developmental and adult education and returned to K-12 education as an associate director of teaching and learning with North Clackamas School District. Aside from being a voracious reader, Joan is an avid kayaker, rower, and women's lacrosse fan. She recently completed her dissertation on teacher candidate reflective practice.

Criselda G. Garcia As a teacher educator for 22 years, she has been preparing prospective teachers in a university-based elementary and secondary program at a Hispanic Serving Institution in south Texas. In addition, Dr. Criselda Garcia serves as associate dean in the College of Education and P16 Integration. She is a full professor in the Teaching and Learning Department in the college. Although her teaching has included both graduate and undergraduate programs, Dr. Garcia's primary teaching areas include literacy development, literacy instructional methods, general instructional methods, and assessments along with culturally sustaining pedagogies. The context of her scholarship has been on organizational change to facilitate and manage educational improvements. Specific lines of research have focused on Latino preservice teacher preparation specifically for leveraging culturally relevant pedagogies for working with diverse K-12 students successfully. Dr. Criselda Garcia's recent research has included equity-focused coaching using mixed reality simulated learning environments and cross collaborative research in the area of developing cultural competence in teaching and other professions.

Dr. Vincent Genareo is an Associate Professor and Assistant Dean for Program Assessment in the Seidel School of Education at Salisbury University. He specializes in assessment and program evaluation of education programs in K-12 and higher education. Dr. Genareo earned his PhD from the University of North Dakota in 2010 and served a postdoctoral research associate position at Iowa State University from 2013 to 2016, where he taught in the School of Education and assisted with grant research and evaluation at the Research Institute for Studies in Education (RISE). He has served as a school-based grant program evaluator for over 10 years, assisting local school systems across the country to improve their programming to meet the needs of their students and staff. He serves multiple roles as an assessment specialist across Salisbury University, with professional organizations, and in collaborations with other universities across the country. His primary teaching duties relate to assessment and learning.

Dr. Joseph Haughey is an associate professor of English education and assistant director of teacher education at Northwest Missouri

State University, where he teaches courses in ELA methods and content. His research interests include strategies for teaching Shakespeare, the use of graphic adaptations in teaching challenging and canonical texts, issues in teacher preparation, critical literacy, antiracism in education, and rural education. Before joining Northwest, he taught middle and high school English in California and Alaska.

Dr. Deirdre Hon is an Assistant Professor in the School of Education at the University of Portland. She received an MEd in Mind, Brain and Education from Harvard Graduate School of Education and her Ph.D. in Human Development and Family Studies from Penn State University. She teaches courses in Developmental Psychology and Research Methods and began a Certificate in SEL for undergraduate and graduate students in education at her university. She is the director of UP's Specialty in SEL that is recognized as an endorsement on teaching licenses by Oregon's TSPC. Her research focuses on evaluating schoolwide approaches to SEL and exploring the process through which teachers gain skills to implement effective SEL and cultivate their own well-being. She is involved in multiple statewide projects related to building culturally sustaining SEL in Oregon including the development of SEL standards for K-12 and teacher preparation programs as well as leads the Oregon Collaborative for SEL in Educator Prep (OCSEP). Her background as a middle and high school teacher makes her especially passionate about how schools can support the social and emotional development of adolescents.

Dr. Amanda Howerton-Fox is an associate professor, department chair, and accreditation coordinator for the Education department at Iona University. She teaches courses in literacy development, social justice, and methods of educational research. Her own research and advocacy address the critical importance of early language access for deaf children and high-quality bilingual bimodal instruction based on research findings in comparative linguistics, bilingual language acquisition, literacy development, and deaf epistemologies.

Julie Kalnin is an Assistant Professor at the University of Portland's School of Education. She completed her PhD (2000) in Literacy,

Language, and Culture at University of California at Berkeley. While at the University of Minnesota, in addition to supporting a district-wide teacher residency program, she developed partnerships between schools and universities to support professional learning teams and strengthen teachers' abilities to carry out research in their own classrooms. At the University of Portland (UP), she focuses on clinical practices; her research as a teacher educator focuses on assessment practices, particularly proficiency-based grading, formative assessment, and teacher performance evaluation. She served in a statewide initiative in Oregon to develop a teacher performance framework that allows educator-preparation programs to develop contextualized and rigorous alternatives to edTPA. With a strong team of colleagues, she helped to design and implement a unique teacher performance assessment at UP. More broadly, her research examines teacher change and effective professional development across the career span; as a result, she has carried out applied research and program evaluation projects in partnership with schools, districts, a department of education, and a national environmental education organization.

Mark A. Kessler is a geophysicist with a PhD from UCSD. In his scientific work, he developed and published on numerical simulation models of Earth surface landforms, including glaciers, patterned ground, and thermokarst terrains. Recently, he is a data analyst at Iona University and manages the United Interfaith Food Bank.

Dr. Alicia Kozimor is the Faculty Chair of the College of Education at Grand Canyon University. With a strong foundation in education, she holds a Bachelor of Science in Elementary Education from Northern Arizona University, a Master of Education in Educational Administration, and an EdD in Teaching and Learning with an emphasis in Adult Learning, both from Grand Canyon University. Hailing from Phoenix, AZ, Alicia's commitment to education stems from her personal connection to her hometown. Born and raised in Glendale, she had the privilege of teaching at the very Title I elementary and middle school that she attended as a student. This unique experience fostered a deep understanding of the importance of providing quality education to students from diverse backgrounds and life experiences. Alicia's true passion lies in preparing future educators to become passionate, effective, and transformative agents in the field. Her expertise and dedication have led her to deliver notable presentations on various educational topics, including "Restoring Classroom Communities Through Restorative Practices," "Science and Literacy: A Winning Combination," and "Meeting Community Needs: Emergency Substitute Cohorts." Additionally, she has contributed to the field through her published works, which include titles such as Literacy in Content Area Instruction (2021), Barriers to Implementation of Problem-Based Learning in Online Undergraduate Instruction (2021), and Cooperative Learning to Increase Engagement (2022).

Virginia R. Lee is a Teaching Professor and Accreditation Officer in the Education Studies Department at Skidmore College. Beginning her career as a middle school mathematics teacher, she later completed her doctorate with a federal leadership fellowship in educational psychology with a concentration in special education and an emphasis on mathematics education. Her commitment to advancing the field of education has driven her work in teacher preparation programs at the graduate and undergraduate levels, in addition to consultant work for local and national teacher education networks. Primarily teaching courses in mathematics and science methodology, she has also taught courses centered on human exceptionality, child development, and international perspectives on education. Her dedication to advancing educational practices and assessments includes trainings, webinars, and workshops focused on empowering other professionals to implement and enhance quality teacher education. This work has included designing Next Generation assessments and scoring rubrics for national databases, compiling resource systems for students and alumni of teacher preparation programs, and providing professional development for college accreditation personnel.

Mike McBride is the Associate Director of Accreditation and Assessment at Northwest Missouri State University in Maryville,

MO. Mike works collaboratively with students, faculty, program
coordinators, and unit leaders to properly assess the teacher, administrator, and counselor preparation programs at Northwest Missouri
State University. In 2016 he completed the MU–NW Collaborative
EdD in Educational Leadership and Policy Analysis program. His
interests include teacher candidate efficacy, student–teacher evaluation, educator quality, and meta-analysis of program and school
effectiveness data. Mike is an adjunct instructor in the use of statistics in educational research, collaborates on various educator preparation grant projects, and partners with other stakeholders on statewide educator preparation data analyses. In addition, he participates
in compliance reporting duties, qualitative analyses, and accreditation requirements on the Northwest Missouri State campus. He has
worked in preparation program research and assessment since 2011.
While not working he enjoys spending time with his wife, son, and
their dogs, coaching youth sports, and watching old movies.

Linda McKee serves as the Chief Operations Officer and is a
founding team member for the Association for Advancing Quality
in Educator Preparation (AAQEP). Linda's relevant work experience
includes strategic planning and administration to promote continuous improvement and performance measures, documentation of
the outcomes in a variety of contexts, and research into optimal use
of evidence for program improvement. Prior to AAQEP, McKee was
the senior director for the Quality Support Center at AACTE. She
has served as director for member and state relations with a national
accreditor for education programs and spent over 10 years as director of the Tulane University's Teacher Preparation and Certification
Program. McKee has served education as a classroom teacher, district and state administrator, educator preparation administrator,
leader for national organizations and a national consultant. Her
teaching experience includes teacher preparation, leadership preparation for educators, continuous improvement for PK-16, secondary
language arts, and gifted education.

Emma L. Mecham is a Professional Practice Assistant Professor
in the School of Teacher Education and Leadership in the Emma

Eccles Jones College of Education and Human Services at Utah State University. She holds a PhD from the University of Utah where she studied the experiences of Native preservice teachers as they pursued teacher certification and rhetorical sovereignty in conflicting epistemological spaces. She has taught students from preschool to graduate school on three continents, and currently spends most of her time with elementary education undergraduate students. Emma takes great delight in working with and learning from preservice teachers as they develop the skills and understanding necessary to be successful teachers in the classroom. There are three main interests that guide her research. She studies how both pre-service and practicing teachers learn and develop their identities, understandings, and skill sets, the ways in which educational policy and practice impact equity in education, and the impacts of place-based pedagogy on students, schools, and communities.

Dr. Hillary Merk is an Associate Professor and the Director of Teacher Licensure Programs and Accreditation at the School of Education at the University of Portland, in Portland, OR. Hillary received her PhD in Education with an emphasis in classroom management and diversity, and a specialization in Cultural Studies and Social Thought in Education from Washington State University in Pullman, WA. Dr. Merk's title of her dissertation was "Community Building "Makes it Nice for Everybody"?: Elementary Teachers' Understandings and Practices of Classroom Management." She taught elementary-aged students for several years in Los Angeles County, CA and continues to find opportunities to stay engaged with K-8 schools by supervising student teachers as well as substitute teaching. Dr. Merk co-coordinates the accreditation efforts in the School of Education at both the state and national level. She researches in the area of classroom management, cyberbullying, diversity, new teacher development, co-teaching, and teacher education.

Dr. Shara MonDragon, a senior education policy analyst at the Oregon Teacher Standards and Practices Commission, has 20 years of experience as an educator, school leader, and researcher. She's passionate about promoting diversity and sustainable practices in the educator workforce. Dr. MonDragon's research interests include learning and assessment practices, equity in educational opportunity, and teaching preparation and sustainability.

Kirsten Plumeau serves as the Administrator Pathway, Policy, and Academic Program Specialist at the Oregon Teacher Standards and Practices Commission. Her work includes coordinating the Administrator Scholars Program, which supports diverse educators who are aspiring leaders in the state and supporting school administrators. Kirsten has served in education for over 27 years as a teacher, principal, district level administrator, and professional consultant. She holds a Bachelor's degree in Psychology and an MAT from the University of Portland.

Dr. Nicole Ralston is an Associate Professor in the School of Education at the University of Portland in Portland, Oregon. She received her MEd in Curriculum and Instruction from the University of Nevada Las Vegas (UNLV) and then received her PhD in Educational Psychology, specifically Measurement, Statistics, and Research Design, from the University of Washington. Her dissertation focused on developing a diagnostic assessment of algebraic thinking for elementary school students, and focused on understanding specifically the development of equivalence knowledge across the elementary grades. She now teaches primarily math methods and educational research courses to preservice teachers and practitioner-scholars. An elementary school teacher at heart, she loves supervising elementary student teachers and supporting local school districts by being the co-director of the Multnomah County Partnership for Education Research (MCPER), a research-practice partnership that provides district-driven research to the six local school districts in Multnomah County. In her spare time, she loves spending time with her two elementary-aged children exploring the gorgeous nature of the Pacific Northwest.

Sylvia Read is Associate Dean for accreditation and undergraduate studies for the College of Education and Human Services and Professor in the School of Teacher Education and Leadership at Utah State University. She has been on faculty at USU since 2003 after teaching for 13 years in public schools. As associate dean, she focuses on accreditation and program approval for all programs in the college, educator licensure, student success, and recruitment. She also engages at state and national levels in accreditation and assessment of educator preparation programs at other institutions of higher education, including service on AAQEP working groups and Quality Review Teams. Read led USU to become the very first educator preparation provider to receive AAQEP accreditation, in spring 2019.

Debbie Rickey is currently serving as a Quality Assurance consultant for AAQEP since fall 2020 and has been involved with AAQEP and accreditation in various ways. Prior to fall 2020, Dr. Rickey served as the associate dean in the College of Education at Grand Canyon University and led her college to be one of the first accredited by AAQEP in spring, 2019. She also served as Director of Graduate Programs in Education at Earlham College and prior to that, spent almost 18 years in K-12 education serving a number of roles from classroom teacher to high school principal. Her educational pursuits have included continuous improvement, action research, strategic planning, and leadership development and has co-authored a number of articles with Dr. Randall Wisehart and a book with Dr. Richard Sagor, *The Relentless Pursuit of Excellence.*

Dr. Sharon Ross is an assistant professor in the Department of Educational Leadership at Texas A&M University Commerce, in Commerce, TX. Prior to joining academia in higher education, Dr. Ross led a successful K-12 education career as an elementary teacher, principal of elementary and secondary (middle school), assistant superintendent of curriculum and instruction, and superintendent of schools. Her experience ranged from small rural to mid-size suburban. Currently, Dr. Ross passionately inspires students in the educational leadership programs who desire to become campus principals and superintendents. In addition, she works with the doctoral program and loves to serve hope to those completing the dissertation journey. In the area of research, Dr. Ross embarks upon primarily qualitative studies with an emphasis on issues pertaining to women superintendents and women of color in leadership, resilience, self-care, and current issues relevant to campus and district leadership. Dr. Ross has successfully served 33 years in the state of Texas as a teacher, leader, administrator, professor, and inspiring mentor.

Kristin Rush works with the Oregon Teacher Standards and Practices Commission on embedding social, emotional, and cultural competencies into teacher preparation. Her passion for school safety through culture and climate development has been at the forefront of her work on educator wellness. She is a member of the National Association of School Psychologists working on state and federal advocacy. For 10 years prior to this role, she served as a school psychologist and district-level support specialist working on mental health initiatives.

Julie Sauve is a doctoral candidate in the Human Development, Learning, and Culture Program at the University of British Columbia. As a former teacher and instructional coach, Julie is passionate about research that advances knowledge about teaching practices, social-emotional learning (SEL), and teacher well-being. Julie is passionate about strengthening our understanding of educator SEL and exploring how systemic approaches can be leveraged across the broader educational system (eg, preservice teacher preparation, in-service professional development, educational policy) to support these efforts. Her most recent research involved interviewing early-career teachers in Oregon about the experiences they had with SEL as they completed their teacher preparation programs. This research has highlighted the importance of providing preservice teachers with a comprehensive education related to various dimensions of SEL as part of the teacher preparation process. She currently works as a Professional Learning Specialist for Sanford Harmony Academies. In the role, she is grateful to be given the opportunity to provide ongoing SEL-based professional development to educators across the nation.

Everett Singleton is an Associate Professor in the Womack Educational Leadership Department at Middle Tennessee State

University. Before joining MTSU, Dr. Singleton served as Educational Leadership faculty in the School of Education at Northwest Missouri State University; he spent nearly two decades as a Juvenile Correctional educator and counselor. Dr. Singleton's research focuses on the educational experiences of underserved student populations and youth affected by the school-to-prison pipeline, youth trauma, and low literacy.

Dr. Ashley Strickland was born in south Louisiana and is a two-time graduate from Louisiana State University. She completed her Bachelor of Science in Education degree in 2007 and a Master's degree in Library and Information Science in 2012. Prior to beginning her Master's degree program, Dr. Strickland taught high school English and History in a suburb of Baton Rouge, LA. Following her Master's degree completion, she worked as a Learning Specialist for the Cox Communications Academic Center for Student Athletes at Louisiana State University. In May of 2019, Dr. Strickland finished her doctorate at the University of Missouri. Currently, she is an Assistant Professor in the School of Education at Northwest Missouri State University where she teaches courses in curriculum and instruction and multicultural education. Her research interests include social justice in education, supporting lgbtq+ students and teachers, teacher retention, and power education as a tool in educator preparation.

Andrea Tochelli-Ward, PhD, is an Associate Professor and Accreditation Coordinator at Le Moyne College in Syracuse, NY. She has worked as the Accreditation Coordinator at Le Moyne College since 2020. Andrea is a former elementary and middle school teacher with a degree from the University at Buffalo, SUNY in Curriculum, Instruction, and the Science of Learning, concentration in Reading Education. She teaches courses focused on elementary and adolescent/content area literacy methods for preservice teachers. Additionally, she teaches courses for in-service teachers on emergent literacy, literacy assessment and instruction, and teaching children's literature in elementary classrooms. Her research interests include using children's and young adult literature in K-12 classrooms, teacher reflective practices, multimodal compositions created by K-12 students and teachers, as well as the use of video reflection in professional development. Since the fall of 2022, Andrea began working with the Diverse Book Finder as a coder for books displayed on their website.

Juliet Michelsen Wahleithner, PhD, is an Associate Professor of Literacy Education and the Director of Educator Preparation and Accreditation at the California State University, Fresno. In this role, she supports the coordinators of 14 initial and advanced educator preparation programs, which includes strengthening collaborations among faculty, university coaches, and field-based mentors; facilitating data-driven continuous improvement through cycles of collaborative inquiry; and interrogating current practices to ensure a strong commitment to equity and social justice. Additionally, Dr. Wahleithner helps oversee the administration and implementation of the Fresno Assessment of Student Teachers (FAST), Fresno State's in-house teacher performance assessment. Dr. Wahleithner also collaborates with in-service teachers through her role as director of the San Joaquin Valley Writing Project and as part of the executive team supporting the network of California Writing Project sites. In all she does, Dr. Wahleithner draws on her 8 years working in K-12 education as a high school English and journalism teacher and instructional coach.

Dr. Jennifer Wall is an associate professor of mathematics education at Northwest Missouri State University, where she teaches mathematics methods and content courses for elementary, middle, and high school pre-service and in-service teachers. Her favorite is "Effective Mathematics Teaching Practice is Building Procedural Fluency from Conceptual Understanding," and she enjoys helping others find an appreciation for mathematics. Her research interests involve using technology and manipulatives to achieve these goals.

Dr. Tim Wall is the Dean and School Director of the Northwest Missouri State University School of Education and a Professor. His research interests include teacher preparation; assessment; diversity, equity, and inclusion; standardized testing; accreditation; policy analysis; and quantitative and qualitative research. Dr. Wall serves as Accreditation Commissioner and experienced site visitor for the Association for Advancing Quality in Educator Preparation (AAQEP). He serves as a dissertation advisor and faculty member in the Missouri-Columbia/Northwest EdD in Educational Leadership and Policy Analysis. Dr. Wall is the former President of TECSCU, the Teacher Education Council of Schools, Colleges and Universities; a former President of MACTE, the Missouri Association of Colleges for Teacher Education; former member of the inaugural Research Committee for CAEP, the Council for the Accreditation of Education Preparation; member of the Executive Committee of the Board of Directors of AACTE, the American Association of Colleges for Teacher Education; and President of the AACTE Advisory Council of State Representatives; Dr. Wall was a high school Social Studies educator.

Nicole Wise is the Associate Dean for Assessment and Accreditation at the State University of New York at Oswego. Serving in this role since 2017, she is responsible for all unit accreditation activities, including coordinating and developing self-studies and program review reports. She guides the development and implementation of assessments, oversees the collection and dissemination of unit data, and engages with stakeholders to gain insights from the data. Her previous related experience in higher education includes Data Manager for Assessment for a teacher preparation program and the Administrative Director of Clinical Education for a medical program. Nicole holds a Bachelor of Science in Business from Capella University and a Master of Science in Education (Organizational Performance, Leadership, and Technology) from the State University of New York at Potsdam. She is pursuing a doctorate in Education (Learning and Teaching in Social Contexts) from the University of Buffalo. Beyond current assessment trends, her research interest includes alumni engagement to inform program practices.

INDEX